PARLIAMENT & COMMUNITY

PARLIAMENT & COMMUNITY

Edited by
ART COSGROVE &
J.I.McGUIRE

HISTORICAL STUDIES XIV

Papers read before the Irish
Conference of Historians

DUBLIN
27–30 May 1981

MICHAEL PRESTWICH   J. I. McGUIRE
ART COSGROVE   R. F. FOSTER
S. G. ELLIS   KARL HOLL
G. R. ELTON   RONAN FANNING
BRIAN MANNING   JOHN HORNE
PAUL BEW

APPLETREE PRESS

First published and printed in 1983 by
The Appletree Press Ltd
7 James Street South
Belfast BT2 8DL

Michael Prestwich   J. I McGuire
Art Cosgrove   R. F. Foster
S. G. Ellis   Karl Holl
G. R. Elton   Ronan Fanning
Brian Manning   John Horne
         Paul Bew

©1983

British Library Cataloguing in Publication Data
Irish Conference of Historians: *(1981: Dublin)*
    Parliament and community.—(Historical studies;
    ISSN 0075–0743; 14)
    1. Legislative bodies—Social aspects—Europe
    —Congresses
    2. Legislative bodies—Europe—History—
    Congresses
    I. McGuire, J. I.   II. Cosgrove, Art   III. Series
    306'.23   HM33

ISBN 0–904651–93–2

Contents

Preface

The Irish Committee of Historical Sciences inaugurated a series of biennial conferences of historians in July 1953. Since then the 'Irish Conference of Historians' has circulated among the Irish universities and university colleges, and the papers read since 1955 have been published as *Historical Studies*. Since 1975 the conferences have been devoted to a single theme, the full list being as follows:

volume	conference	editor	date of publication
I	Trinity College and University College, Dublin, 11–13 July 1955	T. D. Williams	1958
II	The Queen's University of Belfast, 22–23 May 1957	Michael Roberts	1959
III	University College, Cork, 27–29 May 1959	James Hogan	1961
IV	University College, Galway, 25–27 May 1961	G. A. Hayes-McCoy	1963
V	Magee University College, Londonderry, 30 May–1 June 1963	J. L. McCracken	1965
VI	Trinity College, Dublin, 2–5 June 1965	T. W. Moody	1968
VII	The Queen's University of Belfast, 24–27 May 1967	J. C. Beckett	1969
VIII Λ	University College, Dublin, 27–30 May 1969	T. D. Williams	1971
IX	University College, Cork, 29–31 May 1971	J. G. Barry	1974
X	University College, Galway, 23–26 May 1973	G. A. Hayes-McCoy	1977

The fifteenth Irish Conference of Historians, the bulk of the proceedings of which constitute this volume, attracted a large number of participants to hear papers on the main theme, as well as papers on individual topics outside that theme. The Irish Committee of Historical Sciences wishes to pay tribute to the hospitality of University College, Dublin, not only for the provision of facilities and services for the Conference itself, but also for a generous grant towards the publication of this volume.

The editors wish to record their special appreciation and gratitude for the executive and secretarial burdens carried by Miss Maeve Bradley.

Note: Abbreviations and citation of sources used in this volume generally conform to those recommended in 'Rules for contributors to *Irish Historical Studies*' (1st revised ed., *I.H.S.*, Supplement I, January 1968; 2nd revised ed., *I.H.S.*, xix, no. 76, 1975, pp 467–79).

Foreword

The papers published in this collection were read to the biennial Irish Conference of Historians which was held in University College, Dublin, between 27 and 30 May 1981.

In choosing the theme 'Parliament and community' the conference organisers aimed to reflect a revived and growing interest among contemporary historians in legislative and representative assemblies. The study of the history of parliament is no longer seen solely in terms of legal theory, constitutional controversy, or political division, important though these themes may be; the tendency now is to see parliament in its wider setting, in its relationship with society, with the community or communities it represented, served or dominated.

The essays in this volume reflect this wider view. Some deal directly with a particular parliament, others with the institution of parliament over an extended period, others again see parliament as a useful starting point for examining social tensions or popular movements. In all cases parliament is seen as providing a useful key to an understanding of the past.

It is hoped that this collection of papers will be found useful and informative not only by scholars whose particular interests are reflected in individual contributions, but by all those who are interested in the way societies have set out to govern themselves since the middle ages. In this respect the papers cover a wide range in terms of time, from fourteenth century England to twentieth century France and Germany, from the Irish parliament of 1460 to the Northern Ireland parliaments of the 1920s and 1930s.

The editors.

Parliament and the community of the realm in fourteenth century England

Michael Prestwich

In England in the thirteenth century the term 'community of the realm' expressed a concept of great political force. The opposition to the crown, under both Henry III and Edward I, sought to identify itself with the community with considerable success. In 1258 the baronial cause was synonymous with that of the community, and the well-known case of the villagers of Peatling Magna, who in 1265 opposed royalist troops because they were 'acting against the community of the realm and against the barons' shows how successfully this idea was propagated.[1] In 1297 the earl of Hereford put forward the Remonstrances on behalf of the 'prelates, earls, barons and the whole community of the land', and the earls' protest at the exchequer in the same year was made on behalf of 'the whole community of the realm'.[2]

It is striking that by Edward II's reign the crown's opponents rarely made such grandiose claims to be acting on behalf of the whole community as their thirteenth-century predecessors. In 1310 the magnates demanded that their grievances be redressed 'by ordinance of the baronage', and in the Ordinances of 1311 the most favoured formula for consent was 'common assent of the baronage and that in parliament'.[3] Thomas of Lancaster made no play with the concept of the community, preferring instead the newly fashionable phraseology of the 'peers of the land'. The articles put on his behalf to an assembly at Sherburn in 1321 did not mention the community, while the indenture sealed there, probably by some sixty magnates and knights, made it clear that they were acting for the salvation of the crown and people, but did not claim that they

5

stood for the community of the realm.[4] There were some dying echoes of the old tradition: in 1312 Pembroke, Warenne and Percy negotiated Piers Gaveston's surrender 'on behalf of the community of the realm', and in negotiations with the king later in the same year the earls claimed to be acting 'for the whole community',[5] but it is evident that by Edward II's reign the terminology lacked the magical appeal that it had possessed for the followers of Simon de Montfort.

Why was it that a term which had proved so effective a political catchphrase in the thirteenth century was not used in the same way in the fourteenth? Although powerful, the concept had been ill-defined, as perhaps the best political slogans are. With the development of the representative element in parliament, however, an institutional framework evolved through which the community could express itself. In 1301 and again in 1309 letters of protest directed to the papacy were simply sealed by barons, 'as much for ourselves as for the whole community of England', but by 1343 a similar letter was sent by 'the prince, dukes, earls, barons, knights, citizens, burgesses and the whole *commune* of the realm of England assembled at parliament'.[6] This was a far cry from the situation envisaged in 1258, when it was laid down that a dozen barons could negotiate on behalf of the community in parliament.[7] There has been much debate and controversy over the way in which a term, which in the thirteenth century largely embodied baronial aspirations, came in the fourteenth to be effectively identified with the representative element in parliament. Discussion has centred above all on statements which apparently attribute a legislative role to the community, notably the Statute of York of 1322, which speaks in the final clause of the 'assent of the prelates, earls and barons and the community of the realm'.[8] It might be thought that developments which both widened and defined the community would have added to the political force of the concept: how was it that this did not happen?

It was not that the terminology of community simply went out of use. It was employed in the coronation oath sworn by Edward II, and in the Statute of York. Various types of petition were attributed to the community by the clerks who drew up the parliament rolls, and by the beginning of Edward III's reign 'the community of the land' presented a wide-ranging bill which gave rise to important legislation. The problem was, in part, that the essentially aristocratic opposition to Edward II could no longer claim with justice to be acting on behalf of the community of the realm, when others were beginning to make the same claim in parliament. At the same time, a growing awareness of the way that they themselves formed a distinct group led the magnates to prefer the terminology of baronage and peerage.

An early indication of the magnates' hesitancy to speak on behalf of the community came in 1290, when they granted an aid on the occasion of the marriage of Edward I's eldest daughter on their own part and 'in so far as in them lies' on behalf of the community.[9] In 1312 in the document known as the *Prima Tractatio*, produced in the course of lengthy and tedious negotiations between the king and his opponents, it was stated that the magnates would do all they could to ensure the grant of a tax 'when they will have their peers more fully with them, and the community'. The magnates were beginning to sense that they formed a distinct group, apart from the community as a whole. Lancaster argued in 1317 that questions of importance should be discussed in parliament in the presence of 'the peers of the land',[11] and in 1321 it was the same 'peers of the land' who exiled the Despensers. By the fourteenth century the terminology of community was no longer linked with opposition to the crown as it had been so often in the thirteenth, and in the 1320s it was the king, more than the magnates, who used it. The process against the Despensers was repealed by Edward II in 1322 'by our royal power in full parliament at York with counsel and assent of prelates, earls, barons, knights of the shire, the community of the realm and others'.[12]

The important key to the changing implications of the term community is the way in which it began to be applied to the elected representatives in parliament. It seems likely that the increasing reluctance of the magnates to identify themselves with the community was the result of the way in which the term became specifically associated with the commons in parliament. Historians, however, have differed widely as to when this was. W. A. Morris went so far as to suggest that as early as 1264 'community' implied the participation of knights of the shire in parliamentary business, an unacceptable argument.[13] For Stubbs, by 1308 the term could mean nothing less than 'the community of the nation, the whole three estates', but for Strayer it still, under Edward II, meant primarily the magnates, although the word was 'of little constitutional significance. It was a redundant expression, which could be inserted or left out at the pleasure of a clerk'.[14]

At least one knight of the shire was closely involved when in 1301 a 'bill of the prelates and nobles . . . on behalf of the whole community', highly critical of the crown, was presented to Edward I, for the king later discovered that Henry of Keighley, who sat for Lancashire, was responsible for it.[15] In the Carlisle parliament of 1307 the petitions directed against the papal tax collector William Testa were from 'the earls, barons and the community of the land'. The document distinguished between the grievances of the earls and barons, who had, like the king, founded churches and endowed monasteries, and the more general complaints of the earls, barons and the community who suffered from papal exactions. The wording was careful, and implies that the representatives of shires and boroughs participated in the protests. One anti-papal document read out at the parliament had, however, more mysterious origins: the letter claiming to be written by one Peter, son of Cassiodorus, 'descended suddenly as if sent from heaven'.[16]

There are no instances in the reign of Edward I where the representatives of shire and borough alone claimed to stand for the whole community of the realm, but by Edward II's time it certainly became possible for groups which did not include magnates to present petitions on behalf of the community. In 1315 a petition from 'the community of the people of the realm' protested at the abuses of the law in which magnates were engaged: it seems unlikely that any of the latter joined in the petition. In 1320 a petition from the knights, citizens and burgesses was described in the parliament roll as being from the whole community of the realm.[17] It would, however, be very rash to assume that such petitions were put forward by the whole body of representative knights and burgesses in parliament; some other petitions make it clear that groups of very limited composition could claim to be acting on behalf of the community. In 1315 the men of east London complained in the name of the community about the condition of the roads in Stratford. It was presumably a similarly narrow group who protested in the same year about the cost of the Humber ferries, yet the petition purported to be from 'the community of the land'.[18] The rolls of parliament for this period, however, contain a mere handful of petitions of this nature, and it is unwise to try to read too much into them. Even royal clerks were not always consistent in their use of words, as when a petition about high prices in 1315 from the archbishops, bishops, earls and barons was implemented by a writ referring to the complaint of them and 'others of the community of the realm'.[19] It seems that when the clerks wrote of the community, they normally intended to imply a wider body than simply that of the magnates, but that they did not as a rule intend to exclude them.[20] Community of the realm was not yet synonymous with the commons, but equally was not the same thing as 'the baronage in parliament'. It would be wrong to place too much emphasis upon parliamentary petitions at this stage, however; it was not this activity which brought the representatives to a position of prominence.

The most important function of the representatives under Edward I and his son was their role in the granting of taxes. J. G. Edwards's powerful argument that it was in order to enable them to make effective grants that the crown insisted that representatives should be armed with full powers to act on behalf of their local community has not, however, gone without challenge.[21] It has been suggested that the crown was merely obeying the imperatives of Roman law in summoning representatives in this way, and that they were bound under the terms of the same law to make a grant if it was shown that a necessity existed.[22] If this view is accepted, then the significance of the representatives is considerably lessened. The evidence of the negotiations between the king and the opposition in 1312, however, shows that the matter of a grant was by no means a foregone conclusion, but was a question of bargaining in which both magnates and representatives would be involved. The events of 1316 show more clearly the vital role of representatives in the grant of supplies. Together with the magnates, they agreed in February that every village should provide one footsoldier for the war; the towns and ancient demesne were to contribute a fifteenth instead. This fifteenth was granted solely by the knights of the shire and the burgesses. Then the levy of footsoldiers was abandoned, and in July a tax of a sixteenth was negotiated as an alternative. No magnates were specially summoned to this meeting, though two knights were called from each shire.[23] On the basis of this evidence, it could certainly be argued that the representatives were acting on behalf of the whole community of the realm.

The problem which has perhaps provoked most argument is that of the part played by the representatives in the legislative process. The coronation oath sworn by Edward II in 1308 included a new fourth clause, in which the king promised to maintain the rightful laws and customs 'which the community of your realm will have chosen (*aura eslu*)'.[24] Much ink has been used up in attempts to show that this is not, as might seem at first sight, a virtual recognition of popular sovereignty. Contemporaries did not treat the wording of the clause with the close precision that historians have applied to it, however, and there is nothing to suggest that they considered that only some limited form of consent was implied. Although it is possible to argue over the meaning of 'community', it was clearly not intended in a narrow sense. The latin translation of the word was *vulgus*, or people, and in the articles put forward by the earl of Lincoln in April 1308 the clause was misquoted as stating that the king was bound to keep the laws 'which the people shall choose (*que le pople eslira*)'. Very similar phraseology was used in the version of the oath preserved at Bury St Edmunds, and indeed in the coronation office which was almost certainly drawn up in 1327.[25] There is no way of discovering what was in the minds of those who drafted the new clause—it may have been directed at the new king's favourite Piers Gaveston, or at the way in which Edward I had disregarded his undertakings of 1297— but it now seems likely that it was the product of considerable political debate.[26] The agreement made by a group of magnates, all former close associates of Edward I, at Boulogne in January 1308, shortly before the coronation, is indicative of considerable tension.[27] The clause can be seen as providing the community, defined in very general terms, with a significant role in the legislative process.

A clearer view of the legislative process was produced, according to the London Annals, by the magnates in 1312 when they replied to objections to the Ordinances put forward by French lawyers. They argued that there was no written law in England, but that the country was governed by ancient laws and customs. If these proved inadequate, then the king, with the prelates, earls and barons, was bound to amend them on the complaint of the people, and to establish them with certainty by common assent. This statement has not received the attention it deserves. There is no narrow aristocratic definition of community here, no limitation to the baronage in parliament as in the Ordinances of 1311. The magnates are certainly given a leading role, but they do not initiate legislation. It is not clear what form the popular complaint should take, but it is tempting to think in terms of the type of petition from the community which led to the issue of the Statute of Stamford of 1309, which even included a clause specifically dealing with the petitioning activity of knights and burgesses in parliament.[28] It seems likely that, in addition to petitioning, the representatives were expected to participate in common assent to legislation, for it was at this very period that the writs of summons were modified to include the words 'to do and to consent to what shall be ordered by common counsel'.[29]

Another piece of evidence from 1312 is suggestive, for it implies that a wide measure of consent was required for a statute, whereas the agreement of the magnates alone resulted in an ordinance. In the proposed peace treaty between the king and the barons in December 1312 a form of pardon was proposed for those who had been involved in Gaveston's death. This was to be granted in parliament by the king, and by the 'archbishops, bishops, abbots, priors, earls and barons, and the community of the realm'. It might be thought that the addition of 'community' was a piece of superfluous verbiage, for another clause provided that no one should come armed to parliament, as was agreed by the prelates, earls and barons. But in their reply to these proposals, the earls described the pardon as a statute, and the other clause as an 'ordinance (obeisaunce) made in full parliament, by common assent of peers'.[30]

It would be wrong, however, to assume from this evidence that these ideas regarding legislation commanded universal agreement. Although a general consent formula was employed for statutes in 1318 and 1321, the statute concerning sheriffs of 1316 referred solely to magnate consent.[31] According to a Rochester chronicle, in 1321 the magnates declared roundly that 'they had the power, since they were peers of the realm, to promulgate and establish a new law in parliament in accordance with the custom of the realm'. The peers did, of course, exile the Despensers in that parliament, and the community was only mentioned as participating in the initial indictment.[32] The fact that the opponents of the king and the Despensers took such an apparently oligarchic view is perhaps relevant to the celebrated Statute of York of 1322.

The Statute of York was intended to annul the Ordinances of 1311 and to ensure that no similar legislation intended to confine the king's freedom of action could be enacted in future.[33] Perhaps the most significant element of the final clause was not the definition of the way in which consent should be obtained, but the fact that this was to be done 'as has been the custom heretofore'. The statute was thoroughly conservative in intent. However, in specifying that 'things' were to be 'treated, agreed and established in parliaments by our lord the king and by the assent of prelates, earls, and barons, and the community of the realm',[34] the statute could be read as giving the representatives in parliament a voice in legislation. Although Strayer argued that the phrase 'community of the realm' as employed in the statute had little constitutional significance,[35] it could not, by 1322, have been intended as a mere superfluous synonym for the magnates. It made obvious sense for the statute annulling the Ordinances to use a different consent formula from that document, with its emphasis on 'the baronage in parliament',

11

and there may also have been a reaction to the claims of the magnates to legislative authority expressed in 1321. It should not be a matter of surprise that the crown preferred to adopt a wider formula, particularly since the phraseology was nothing new. As long ago as 1275 the Statute of Westminster I had been made 'by the assent of the archbishops, bishops, abbots, priors, earls, barons and the community of the land'.[36] Of course, the implications of the term 'community' had not been the same then as in 1322, but the Statute of York could nonetheless be seen as representing a return to the practices of the past.

Did the use of the term 'community of the realm' in the Statute of York imply the representatives of shires, boroughs and lower clergy in parliament? For Sayles, such an assumption is unwarrantable. His suggestion is that the community consisted rather of 'the persons of those whom the king has sought fit to summon for consultation', which might, but need not, include representatives. He also argued, along with Richardson, that in 1325 the community petitions 'embody the requests of the general body of suitors attending parliament', and not of the knights and burgesses.[37] One contemporary at least held otherwise. The author of that most controversial of documents dealing with the medieval parliament, the *Modus tenendi parliamentum*, considered that the knights of the shire and representatives of boroughs and lower clergy 'represent the whole community of England'. For this writer, community meant commons, and 'two knights who come to parliament for the shire, have a greater voice in granting and denying than the greatest earl of England'.[38] Thanks to the work of Pronay and Taylor on this difficult text, it can no longer be dismissed as a late-fourteenth-century fabrication based on an Irish original. In all probability it was written in 1321, and was more legal treatise than political tract. Its author seems to have been a well-informed royal clerk, possibly William Airmyn or William Maldon.[39] If that is so, then it is surely probable that those who drafted the Statute of York would have been aware that their terminology could be interpreted as giving the representative element in parliament a say in the legislative process. It is far more likely that the community of the realm was represented by elected members, than by a wholly amorphous body of suitors present in parliament. Official phraseology is rarely as unambiguous as constitutional historians would like, but it is interesting that in the record of the proceedings of 1322 in favour of the Despensers, it is stated that in the previous year, when the opposition magnates refused to attend parliament at Westminster, the king 'caused to come before him prelates and other earls and barons, knights of the shires, and others who came for the commune of the realm'.[40] The wording is consistent with the view of the *Modus*, that the magnates came on their own behalf, and the representatives for the community.

The position of the commons was not, however, firmly established as a result of the Statute of York, a text which, as several commentators have pointed out, aroused no contemporary comment.[41] Although their role was stressed in the repeal of the judgements against the Despensers, their consent was not mentioned in the statute of 1324 relating to the Templar lands.[42] Even though the Statute of York stated that matters concerning 'the estate of the king' were to be dealt with in parliament, such business was on the agenda of an assembly in March 1325 to which 'the magnates were to be summoned to be there to give counsel etc., and not for parliament'.[43] Nor were representatives summoned to parliament in June 1325. It was the events of 1327, not the statute of 1322, which made a major difference to the position of the representative element in the English parliament.

The deposition of Edward II was a revolutionary act, and those behind it naturally tried to spread responsibility for it as widely as possible, in a way which brought the community of the realm and those who represented it into prominence. Knights and burgesses were of obvious importance in the proceedings, as is demonstrated by the length of time that they were present at Westminster. Some received expenses for no less than sixty-nine days, rather than the usual fortnight or so.[44] Henry Eastry, prior of Christ Church, Canterbury, advised Archbishop Reynolds that Edward II should be invited to attend parliament by a commission consisting of two earls, two barons, four knights of the shire and four burgesses.[45] Although it was the magnates who made the initial decision to depose the king, the commission that was sent to see Edward II at Kenilworth included knights, burgesses, and barons of the Cinque Ports. The Londoners made knights as well as magnates swear to uphold Queen Isabella's cause. The recently published account from a Canterbury chronicle tells of the way in which Thomas Wake, holding out his arms, obtained popular consent for the decision to depose the king.[46] The official announcement of Edward II's abdication used the most comprehensive formula possible, stressing the 'common counsel and assent of prelates, earls, barons, and other nobles, and all the community of the realm'.[47]

More significant, perhaps, in terms of the present argument than the unruly deposition proceedings was the bill presented in parliament by 'the community of the land' in 1327. The term used is *commune*: there is relative uniformity from the start of Edward III's reign in this usage for the commons in the parliamentary sense, as against the more general *communalte*, though the terms are often virtually synonymous. As Plucknett warned, contemporary usage 'is varied and obscure'.[48] This bill contained forty-one clauses, and it led to the production of a statute of seventeen articles.[49] The pattern was set for legislation to be enacted by common assent in response to common petitions. The real importance of the representatives was to lie not so much in their contribution to the process of consent, as in the way in which they were able to initiate the process of lawmaking through their petitions.

Caution is still necessary, however. A common petition might not necessarily be put forward by the whole body of representatives in parliament acting in a corporate sense as the community of the realm. In the 1327 petition one clause disavowed any other bills which might be presented in the name of the community.[50] In 1348 the commons envisaged the possibility that bills might be brought forward in their name, which they did not in practice support, and in 1372 an ordinance forbidding the election of lawyers to parliament used as one justification the fact that they presented petitions on behalf of their clients in the name of the commons.[51] Even late in Edward III's reign, therefore, it was still possible for small groups, or even individuals, to present petitions in the name of the community, provided that they related to matters of some general concern.

Although by Edward III's reign the knights of the shire might still on rare occasions meet separately from the citizens and burgesses, it was normal for all the representatives to form one body, the commons.[52] It was primarily through them that it was felt that the views of the community were expressed. The magnates, with their solid commitment to the war, at least until 1360, had little interest in supporting popular complaints that frequently related to the inevitable burdens that war placed on the populace as a whole. The advice of the commons was consciously sought on a wide range of business. It is striking that whereas Edward II apparently consulted only the magnates over the war of Saint-Sardos with the French, Edward III made every effort to associate the commons with his great enterprise in France.[53] The commons' role on behalf of the whole community is well illustrated by the 1352 parliament roll. They were told that if they had any petitions concerning popular grievances or legal matters, they should bring them forward. The record then states that they had long deliberations with the community (*communalte*), which presumably means that they obtained expert advice from lawyers, merchants and others. They also consulted some magnates, and then presented the king with on the one hand a grant of aid, and on the other a long set of petitions.[54] It was of course primarily because of the war that the commons came to occupy such an important position under Edward III, for it was chiefly by means of taxes conceded in parliament that the war could be financed. When other methods of obtaining supplies were attempted, they had limited success at best. As J. G. Edwards pointed out, whereas only five out of twenty-one parliaments in the first decade of the reign saw taxes granted, only about eighteen in the succeeding hundred years did not vote supplies.[55] In their petitions for redress of grievances they were able to take the initiative in many matters, though often seeking the lords' advice and assistance. It has been argued that in 1340 'for the first time the commons were seeking political remedies for the correction of misgovernment',[56] and by 1376 the commons were in a position to launch a full-scale attack in parliament on the king's ministers, with little apparent support from the magnates.[57] By Edward III's reign it could be argued that the commons held a similar position in many ways to that of the barons who in the thirteenth century had claimed to be acting on behalf of the community of the realm.

In theory the position achieved in the fourteenth century whereby the community of the realm was represented by the commons in parliament was a more satisfactory one than the imprecise thirteenth-century situation. England contained many communities at different levels, from those of the village to those of the shire. As Helen Cam demonstrated, the practice of representation was known in local communities long before the theories of Roman law provided justification for it in the thirteenth century.[58] The concept of common assent for legal measures can be seen at work in the village by-laws of the thirteenth and fourteenth century.[59] It was only logical that the summit of the pyramid of local communities, rising from the village through the shire, should be the representative commons. They were surely in a better position to speak on behalf of the community of the realm than the magnates of the thirteenth century had been.

Yet did contemporaries see the situation in such a way? It seems rather that the idealism incorporated in the mid-thirteenth century concept of the community of the realm disintegrated. The institutionalization of the community in the form of the commons was accompanied by a perceptibly cynical attitude, while several chroniclers showed little awareness of the changes under discussion. In a classic article Tout examined the relationship of parliament to public opinion in the late fourteenth century. He pointed to the great interest aroused by the Good Parliament of 1376 and the Merciless Parliament of 1388, and argued that for all the undoubted faults of English parliaments, 'they seemed to make a clear appeal to English public opinion'. From the absence of similar evidence for earlier periods, however, Tout suggested that previously 'public opinion was not interested in parliaments', and he saw the events of 1340 as the earliest occasion when parliament 'was beginning to interest the man in the street'.[60]

Although it might be argued that at least the clerk in the cloister took a great interest in the Carlisle parliament of 1306,[61] Tout's case might be put more strongly: that parliament in the early fourteenth century was widely regarded with positive disfavour. The fact that those attending at Westminster were liable to have their hats and hoods unceremoniously removed by rowdy children is not, perhaps, a true measure of public opinion. The *Flores historiarum*, however, commented on the 'ridiculous and deceitful' parliaments of Edward II's early years, in which fraudulent and heavy taxes were authorized, and from which wise men departed, having failed to find the justice they sought.[62] Similar views had been expressed a generation earlier in that curious tract, the *Mirror of justices*, in which the complaint was made that parliaments were 'held but rarely and at the king's will for the purpose of obtaining aids and collection of treasure'. Geoffrey le Baker in his admittedly biassed chronicle expressed a low opinion of the community of the realm in parliament, 'disdainful of the old, always eager for the new'.[63] Events and discussions in parliament were often not recorded: the annalist of St Paul's thought that the only matter worth noting from the Hilary parliament of 1332 was a fight between two magnates. Adam Murimuth preferred to describe tournaments rather than parliaments: he commented that nothing worthwhile was achieved in the September parliament of the same year. Although he did note the grants of taxation, he ignored the king's agreement to cancel the planned levy of a tallage, and the discussions on Scotland, Ireland and the interminable problem of law and order.[64] The author of a political poem dating from 1339 was unimpressed by the representative character of parliament, and pointed out with pardonable exaggeration that those who made grants of taxation paid nothing themselves: only the needy were charged.[65]

In contrast to the views of the author of the *Modus tenendi parliamentum* the chroniclers displayed little if any awareness of the constitutional position of the commons. The *Vita Edwardi Secundi*, probably the work of an important royal clerk, John Walwyn, does, it is true, cite the Roman law tag *quod omnes tangit ab omnibus approbetur*, which is often seen as expressing an important principle of representation. In this instance, however, the context was the approval by king and magnates of the Ordinances of 1311, and there is no suggestion of the involvement of representatives. Indeed, at no point does the *Vita* mention knights of the shire or burgesses in parliament; a typical statement is that in 1312 the king 'calls the earls and barons to his parliament by public writ'.[66] Even as late as 1341 two chroniclers defined the community of the realm in terms which, though confused, appear to imply an essentially aristocratic rather than representative assembly. Baker described the parliamentary activity of 'the earls and great men (*maiores*), namely the peers and the community', and Murimuth used almost identical terms. The latter did, however, describe protests in parliament in 1343 against papal provisors as coming from 'earls, barons, knights, burgesses and the rest of the people (*populares*)', a long-delayed recognition of the realities of the composition of parliament.[67]

Part of the answer to the question of why the concept of the community represented through elected members in parliament lacked the same sort of popular appeal as that possessed by the essentially baronial community of the thirteenth century must lie in the way in which representatives were actually selected. Here attention has to be focussed on the knights of the shire, for the burgesses do not appear to have played an important role, and there is little evidence of the way in which they were elected. In all probability their election was increasingly 'the exclusive privilege of a few of the wealthier citizens'.[68]

The knights of the shire were elected by the shire communities, which normally assembled in the county courts. J. R. Maddicott has demonstrated that these were generally large assemblies in the fourteenth century, dominated by the local magnates and their bailiffs, but also attended by village reeves and a surprising number of ordinary villagers. 'The county community was not merely a community of the governors'.[69] It was the shire assembly in the county court which lay at the heart of the representative process. Detailed analysis of the returns from 1290 to 1327 has shown that whereas the magnates had a poor attendance record, it was very rare for counties to fail to make elections and send members to parliament.[70] Re-election was not unusual: a man such as Gerard de Braybroke, sixteen times elected for Bedfordshire in twenty-six years, clearly found it worthwhile to attend parliament.[71] Another indication of the fact that to serve in parliament was a valued privilege, not a chore to be avoided, is the decline in the importance of the process of obtaining guarantors to ensure that the elected members actually attended, which is noticeable by the end of Edward II's reign.[72] An example of the eagerness that might be displayed in electing representatives comes from Wiltshire in 1315. Although the royal writ had been issued on 24 October 1314, it only reached the sheriff on 19 January 1315, the day before parliament was due to meet. Nevertheless, an election was promptly held on 20 January, and the members duly despatched to Westminster.[73]

There are, however, darker patches in this sunny picture. Evidence suggests that local communities were more concerned with the cost of sending knights to parliament than with ensuring that they were properly represented. On three occasions in 1311 the men of Kent declared that they were not obliged to pay the expenses of knights of the shire, and in many counties there was frequent difficulty in obtaining contributions from liberties. Sheriffs embezzled funds, and members complained that they were not properly reimbursed. In a notable protest the men of Lancashire complained that their sheriff had simply nominated members of parliament rather than held elections. Their objection was not to the loss of political influence, but to the charge of £20 for expenses when they could have found men willing to take half that sum.[74]

Another example of the manipulation of an election by the sheriff comes from Devon, again in Edward II's reign. Matthew de Crauthorn claimed to have been duly elected, but another was returned in his place. Interestingly, Matthew argued that he had been selected by the bishop of Exeter, Sir William Martin, 'and by the assent of other good men of the county', which suggests magnate dominance of the electoral process.[75] There is no evidence, however, that magnates found it worth their while until much later to have members of their own retinues returned as members of parliament. Great men could exercise sufficient clout in parliament on their own behalf without needing to pack the commons.[76] It was evidently common for magnates to attend with an ample following accompanying them, which could be used to overawe opponents. The quality of representatives was nevertheless a matter of some concern. In 1330 it was argued that in the past they had been members of gangs and maintainers of false disputes at law, and that they had prevented the grievances of the common people from being brought forward. The sheriffs were accordingly asked to see that men who were above suspicion were elected, but it must be doubted whether they were successful in this task.[77]

Although the men of Cumberland sent their representatives to parliament in 1339 so that they could inform the king of the dangerous state of the marches,[78] those of Northumberland, hard-pressed as they were by the Scots in Edward II's reign, showed little enthusiasm to send men to parliament to plead their cause. Rather, in 1315, the county community refused to send any representatives, on the grounds that all were needed for the defence of the border. In 1324 the excuse was that the writ had not been received in time. The men of Newcastle-upon-Tyne followed the lead of the county: in 1327 they pleaded that they could not afford to pay the expenses of parliamentary representatives, and in 1332 used the dangers of war as the explanation for their refusal to make an election.[79]

It is not possible to attempt an analysis of the returns of members of parliament in political terms until the late fourteenth century, and even then a strong case cannot be established.[80] The complex political vicissitudes of the reign of Edward II are not visibly reflected in a changing membership of the commons: the royalist reaction, for example, at the first parliament of 1322 cannot be shown to have been carried through with the help of representatives of markedly royalist interests.[81] The composition of the commons did change noticeably in 1324, but only because a number of counties returned squires, rather than knights, no doubt because their expenses were lower.[82] In theory the representatives stood for the community of the realm, and they were certainly considered by 1330 to be responsible for presenting popular petitions at parliament.[83] A community primarily represented by knights and burgesses, however, could hardly be expected to play the same part in politics as that performed by the magnates in the thirteenth century, particularly when local communities appear to have been more concerned with the costs rather than the effectiveness of the representative system, and the magnates did not see manipulation of the commons as a valuable political technique.

In many ways the concept of the community of the realm lost much of its force in the early fourteenth century. The development of the peerage had, perhaps, a divisive effect on the old sense of a united community. There is a noticeable train of thought in some of the literature of Edward II's reign to the effect that the magnates, the original leaders of the community, had failed in their function.

The author of the *Poem on the times of Edward II* condemned knights and magnates who 'brew strife and debate where there should be peace'. In the *Vita Edwardi Secundi* the magnates were criticized in a tone of considerable disillusion for their avarice and falseness. The *Brut* even attacked the nobles on the grounds of their mixed racial origins, 'which did not accord well with the kind blood of England'.[84] Such discontentment formed part of the background to the way in which the crown came to recognize the right of the representatives to speak for the community of the realm, but at the same time it has to be recognized that the position of those who were elected aroused little interest or enthusiasm in the hearts of the populace at large.

Under Edward III, however, the commons came to act with increasing effect on behalf of the community. The power they gained as a result of their right to grant taxes meant that they won many successes. They compelled, for example, the establishment of gentry keepers, and eventually justices, of the peace. They extracted important concessions from the king over such matters as military service and purveyance; their petitions inspired a wide range of legislation. Their interests came gradually to coincide more with those of the magnates, over such questions as the labour legislation in the aftermath of the Black Death, and after 1369 with the general dissatisfaction with the war.[85] Nevertheless, the term 'community of the realm' never recaptured in the fourteenth century the potent force which it had embodied in the thirteenth. The community of Simon de Montfort's day could not be institutionalized in the commons of the fourteenth century.[86]

Notes

1. F. M. Powicke, *Henry III and the Lord Edward* (Oxford, 1947), ii, 509.
2. *Documents illustrating the crisis of 1297–8 in England*, ed. M. C. Prestwich (Camden Soc., 4th ser., 24, 1980), pp 26, 115, 137. In 1297 it is possible to detect a baronial preference for the term 'community of the land', and a royal one for 'community of the realm'. In general, however, such variations have relatively little significance, although it is striking that in referring to Scotland after 1296 the English preferred to speak of the 'community of the land': see for example *Anglo-Scottish relations, 1174–1328*, ed. E. L. G. Stones (London, 1965), pp 120, 126.
3. *Chronicles of the reigns of Edward I and Edward II*, ed. W. Stubbs (Rolls ser., 1882), i, 169; *Rotuli parliamentorum* (London, 1783), i, 282.
4. B. Wilkinson, 'The Sherburn Indenture and the attack on the Despensers, 1321' in *E.H.R.*, lxii (1948), pp 23–7. The problem of who sealed the indenture is discussed by J. R. Maddicott, *Thomas of Lancaster, 1307–1322* (Oxford, 1970), pp 273–6. It is known that Lancaster kept in his archive a copy of the indenture sealed by twenty-five men, but it is unlikely that these were, as Maddicott

Michael Prestwich

suggests, his own retainers. It is more likely that Lancaster's copy was sealed by the Welsh marchers present at the meeting, and that they retained the other half of the indenture, sealed by Lancaster's men.

5. *Chronicles, Edward I and Edward II,* i, 205, 208.
6. Ibid., i, 125, 165; *Adae Murimuth continuatio chronicarum. Robertus de Avesbury de gestis mirabilibus Regis Edwardii Tertii,* ed. E. M. Thompson (Rolls ser., 1889), p. 138 (hereafter cited as *Avesbury*).
7. *Documents of the baronial movement of reform and rebellion, 1258–1267,* ed. R. F. Treharne and I. J. Sanders (Oxford, 1973), p. 105.
8. *Stat. of realm,* i, 189–90.
9. *Rot. parl.* i, 125.
10. *Chronicles, Edward I and Edward II,* i, 211.
11. *Avesbury,* p. 273.
12. L. W. Vernon Harcourt, *His Grace the Steward and trial of peers* (London, 1907), p. 326.
13. W. A. Morris, 'Magnates and community of the realm in parliament, 1264–1327' in *Medievalia et Humanistica,* i (1943), p. 70.
14. W. Stubbs, *Constitutional history of England* (4th ed., Oxford, 1906), ii, 175; J. R. Strayer, *Medieval statecraft and the perspectives of history* (Princeton, 1971), p. 289.
15. *Parliamentary writs,* ed. F. Palgrave (Record Commission, 1827–34), i, 104; Stubbs, *Constitutional history,* ii, 158.
16. *Rot. parl.,* i, 219–20; *The chronicle of Walter of Guisborough,* ed. H. Rothwell (Camden Soc., lxxxix, 1957), p. 371.
17. *Rot. parl.,* i, 371.
18. Ibid., i, 291, 308.
19. Ibid., i, 295. A similar formula was used in 1316: *Rotuli Scotiae* (Record Commission, 1814), i, 160.
20. The fullest discussion of community petitions in this period is D. Rayner, 'The forms and machinery of the "Commune Petition" in the fourteenth century', in *E.H.R.,* lvi (1941), pp 549–70. See also G. L. Harriss, *King, parliament and public finance in medieval England to 1369* (Oxford, 1975), pp 118–22.
21. J. G. Edwards, 'The *plena potestas* of English parliamentary representatives', *Oxford essays in medieval history presented to H. E. Salter* (Oxford, 1934), pp 141–54, and in *Historical studies of the English parliament,* ed. E. B. Fryde and E. Miller (Cambridge, 1970), i, 136–49.
22. Harriss, *King, parliament and public finance,* pp 23–4, 52–3; G. Post, *Studies in medieval legal thought* (Princeton, 1964), pp 91–164. For a criticism of this view, see *Documents illustrating the crisis of 1297–8,* ed. Prestwich, pp 27–30.
23. *Chronicles, Edward I and Edward II,* i, 211, 224, 227; *Rot. parl.,* i, 351, 450–2; *Parl. writs,* II, ii, 104.
24. *Select documents of English constitutional history, 1307–1485,* ed. S. B. Chrimes and A. L. Brown (London, 1961), p. 4.
25. H. G. Richardson and G. O. Sayles, *The governance of medieval England* (Edinburgh, 1964), pp 467–8; Richardson and Sayles, 'Early coronation records', in *I.H.R. Bull.,* xiv (1937), p. 9; *Three coronation orders,* ed. J. Wickham Legg (Henry Bradshaw Soc., xix, 1900), p. 122.
26. The most recent comment on this is by N. M. Fryde, *The tyranny and fall of Edward II* (Cambridge, 1979), p. 238. For a contrary opinion, H. G. Richardson, 'The English coronation oath', in *R. Hist. Soc. Trans.,* 4th ser, xiii (1941) pp 129–58. See also B. Wilkinson, 'The coronation oath of Edward II', in *Speculum,* xix (1944), pp 445–56.

27. Printed by J. R. S. Phillips, *Aymer de Valence, earl of Pembroke* (Oxford, 1972), pp 306-7.
28. *Chronicles, Edward I and Edward II*, i, 215; *Rot. parl.*, i, 443-5; Harriss, *King, parliament and public finance*, p. 120, plausibly suggests that the grievances of 1309 'did in the main emanate from the commons but were presented by the magnates'.
29. The new formula was first adopted in January 1313; *Parl. writs* II, ii, 81.
30. *Chronicles, Edward I and Edward II*, i, 222-9.
31. *Stat. of realm*, i, 174, 177, 180.
32. Ibid., i. 180-4; *Parliamentary texts of the later middle ages*, ed. N. Pronay and J. Taylor (Oxford, 1980), pp 164, 168.
33. The most recent contribution to a lengthy debate on this statute is D. Clementi, 'That the Statute of York is no longer ambiguous', *Album Helen Maud Cam* (Louvain, 1962), ii, 95-100.
34. *Stat. of realm*, i, 189.
35. Strayer, *Medieval statecraft*, p. 289.
36. *Select charters*, ed. W. Stubbs (9th ed., Oxford, 1921), p. 442.
37. G. O. Sayles, *The king's parliament of England* (London, 1975), pp 105-6; G. O. Sayles and H. G. Richardson, 'The parliaments of Edward II' in *I.H.R. Bull.*, vi (1929-30), p. 77.
38. *Parliamentary texts of the later middle ages*, ed. Pronay and Taylor, pp 77, 89.
39. Ibid., pp 25-31.
40. *Cal. Close Rolls, 1318-23*, p. 545.
41. Most recently Sayles, *The king's parliament of England*, p. 104.
42. *Stat. of realm*, i, 195.
43. *The war of Saint-Sardos*, ed. P. Chaplais (Camden Soc., 3rd ser., lxxxvii, 1954), p. 134. See Strayer, *Medieval statecraft*, p. 290, n. 80, for a similar incident also in 1324, when matters relating to the estate of the crown were put by the magnates, with no representatives present.
44. *Parl. writs*, II, ii, 365.
45. J. E. Powell and K. Wallis, *The house of lords in the middle ages* (London, 1968), p. 298.
46. Fryde, *The tyranny and fall of Edward II*, p. 234.
47. *Select documents of English constitutional history, 1307-1485*, ed. Chrimes and Brown, p. 38.
48. *Historical studies of the English parliament*, ed. Fryde and Miller, i, 223 n. 4.
49. *Rot. parl.*, ii. 7-11; *Rotuli parliamentorum hactenus inediti*, ed. H. G. Richardson and G. O. Sayles (Camden Soc., 3rd ser., li, 1935), pp 116-26 (this version of the petition has thirty-six clauses); *Stat. of realm*, i, 255-7; H. L. Gray, *The influence of the commons on early legislation* (Cambridge, Mass., 1932), pp 215-33.
50. *Rot. parl.*, ii, 11.
51. J. G. Edwards, *The second century of the English parliament* (Oxford, 1979), pp 51, 54; *Rot. parl.*, ii, 310; K. M. Wood-Legh, 'Sheriffs, lawyers and belted knights in the parliaments of Edward III' in *E.H.R.*, xlvi (1931), p. 381.
52. As in 1340, when the knights agreed a subsidy along with the magnates, while the citizens and burgesses made a separate and similar grant: *Rot. parl.*, ii, 112.
53. E. B. Fryde, 'Parliament and the French war, 1336-40' in *Historical studies of the English parliament*, ed. Fryde and Miller, i, 242-61.
54. *Rot. parl.*, ii, 237, translated by Edwards, op. cit., pp 81-2.
55. Edwards, *Second century of the English parliament*, p. 16.

56. Harriss, *King, parliament and public finance*, p. 260.
57. G. A. Holmes, *The Good Parliament* (Oxford, 1975), pp 134–9. J. A. Tuck, *Richard II and the nobility* (London, 1973), pp 23–30, lays more stress on the role of the magnates in 1376.
58. H. M. Cam, 'The theory and practice of representation in medieval England', in *Law-finders and law-makers* (London, 1962), pp 159–75.
59. W. O. Ault, 'Village by-laws by common consent' in *Speculum* xxix (1954), pp 378–94.
60. T. F. Tout, 'The English parliament and public opinion, 1376–88', in *Historical studies of the English parliament*, ed. Fryde and Miller, i, 299–301, 315.
61. A newsletter from this parliament was printed by H. G. Richardson and G. O. Sayles, 'The parliament of Carlisle, 1307: some new documents' in *E.H.R.*, liii (1938), pp 425–37.
62. *Rot. parl.*, ii, 64; *Flores historiarum*, ed. H. R. Luard (Rolls ser., 1890), iii, 143.
63. *The mirror of Justices*, ed. W. J. Whittaker and F. W. Maitland (Selden Soc., 1893), p. 155; *Chronicon Galfridi le Baker de Swynebroke*, ed. E. M. Thompson (Oxford, 1889), p. 28.
64. *Chronicles, Edward I and Edward II*, i, 355; *Murimuth*, p. 66; *Rot. parl.*, ii, 66–7.
65. I. S. T. Aspin, *Anglo-Norman political songs* (Anglo-Norman Text Soc., xi, 1953), pp 105–15. It is worth noting that this poem also argues that the king should not make war without the consent of the community of the realm, a view reminiscent of clause 9 of the Ordinances of 1311, although expressed in language more to be expected in the late thirteenth century.
66. *Vita Edwardi Secundi*, ed. N. Denholm-Young (1967), pp 16, 32, and for other references to parliament, none of which mention representatives, see pp 59, 69, 93, 112–4, 136–8. The citation of *quod omnes tangit* was an allusion to a mandate issued by Archbishop Winchelsey: see M. V. Clarke, *Medieval representation and consent* (London, 1936), pp 160–1.
67. *Galfridi le Baker*, p. 73; *Murimuth*, pp 119, 138.
68. M. McKisack, *The parliamentary representation of the English boroughs* (Oxford, 1932), p. 38.
69. J. R. Maddicott, 'The county community in fourteenth-century England' in *R. Hist. Soc. Trans.*, 5th ser., xxviii (1978), pp 28–33.
70. J. G. Edwards, 'The personnel of the commons in parliament under Edward I and Edward II', *Historical studies of the English parliament*, i, 150–67. The problem of magnate attendance is examined by J. S. Roskell, 'The problem of attendance of lords in medieval parliaments' in *I.H.R. Bull.*, xxix (1956), pp 153–204.
71. T. F. T. Plucknett, 'Parliament', *Historical studies of the English parliament*, i, 215.
72. Maddicott, op. cit., p. 33.
73. *Parl. writs*, II, ii, 149.
74. Ibid., II, ii, 56, 91, 217, 230, 232–3, 315; the problem of expenses is discussed by H. M. Cam, 'The community of the shire and the payment of its representatives in parliament', *Liberties and communities in medieval England* (1963), pp 236–47.
75. *Parl. writs*, II, ii, appendix, 138; *Documents illustrative of English history in the 13th and 14th centuries*, ed. H. Cole (London, 1844), p. 16.
76. Maddicott, *Thomas of Lancaster*, pp 52–3.
77. *Rot. parl.*, ii, 443.
78. Maddicott, 'The county community in fourteenth century England', p. 41.

79. *Parl. writs*, II, ii, 145; McKisack, *Parliamentary representation of English boroughs*, pp 26–9.
80. For a recent comment, see Tuck, *Richard II and the nobility*, p. 23.
81. G. T. Lapsley, 'Knights of the shire in the parliaments of Edward II' in *E.H.R.*, xxxiv (1919), pp 25–42, 152–71. Lapsley's conclusions need some modification as he wrongly assumed that if a knight received no writ *de expensis*, he did not attend parliament.
82. *Parl. writs*, II, ii, 336–45.
83. *Rot. parl.*, ii, 443.
84. *The political songs of England*, ed. T. Wright (Camden Soc., 1839), p. 334; *Vita Edwardi Secundi*, p. 99; *The Brut*, ed. F. W. D. Brie (Early English Text Soc., 1906, 1908), ii, 220.
85. G. L. Harriss, 'War and the emergence of the English parliament' in *Journal of Medieval History*, 2 (1976), p. 55, lays stress on the importance of the Black Death in the rapprochement of magnates and commons.
86. Since this article was written, an important contribution to the topic by J. R. Maddicott, 'Parliament and the constituencies, 1272–1377', has appeared in *The English parliament in the middle ages*, ed. R. G. Davies and J. H. Denton (Manchester, 1981), pp 61–87. G. O. Sayles has elaborated his case for an Irish origin for the *Modus* in '*Modus tenendi parliamentum:* Irish or English', *England and Ireland in the later middle ages*, ed. J. F. Lydon (Dublin, 1981). Some of my reasons for rejecting his case are set out in my review article, 'The *Modus tenendi parliamentum*', in *Parliamentary History. A Yearbook*, i (1982) pp 221–5.

Parliament and the Anglo-Irish community: the Declaration of 1460

Art Cosgrove

On 8 February 1460 the Irish parliament met at Drogheda before Richard, duke of York, styling himself lieutenant of Ireland.[1] The meeting took place in unusual, if not revolutionary, circumstances. The lieutenant was himself a refugee from English justice, his flight to Ireland a consequence of his decision not to confront superior Lancastrian forces at Ludford Bridge in October 1459. That military superiority ensured continuing control of England by the administration of Henry VI, and York and his chief adherents were forced to seek refuge abroad, York himself in Ireland, his eldest son Edward, earl of March, and the earl of Warwick in Calais.[2] Both Yorkist factions found secure havens. By the opening of 1460 it had become clear that, while Henry VI ruled in England, his authority was no longer effective in the two English 'Pales'—in France and in Ireland.[3]

Unsurprisingly, the record of the Irish parliament's proceedings makes no reference to these events—or their consequences. York's flight was followed by the passage of an act of attainder against him by the English parliament which met at Coventry during November and December of 1459. Conviction of treason meant that all York's offices, including the lieutenancy of Ireland, were stripped from him.[4] On 4 December 1459 the earl of Ormond and Wiltshire was appointed to replace him as lieutenant and he nominated John Mey, archbishop of Armagh and Thomas Bath, baron of Louth to act as his deputies within Ireland. In January 1460 the treasurer of Ireland was ordered to seize all York's Irish possessions, forfeited to the king as a result of the attainder by the Coventry parliament.[5] None of these measures could be made effective within Ireland. Nevertheless, they reflect the view of Henry VI's government that York as a convicted traitor was an illegal occupant of the lieutenancy.

How differently York was regarded in Ireland was made clear in the opening session of parliament. Despite the recent appointment of the earl of Ormond and Wiltshire, York was confirmed as lieutenant and it was made a treasonable offence to challenge his authority.[6] Parliament then proceeded to a definition of its own powers. It was claimed that Ireland was and always had been a distinct entity (*corporate de luy mesme*) and that it was not bound by laws made in England unless they were accepted by parliament in Ireland. Further it was asserted as a consequence of the fact that Ireland was 'corporate of itself' that no one could be summoned to answer charges outside Ireland unless such a summons was made in proper form, namely under the great seal of Ireland. More specifically it was laid down that any appeal of treason should be determined before the constable and marshal of Ireland, not, as had previously happened, before their counterparts in England.[7]

These enactments have generated differences of opinion and have raised a few welcome squalls in the over-tranquil backwater of fifteenth-century Irish history. In reviewing interpretations of them, it is appropriate to begin with the views of that great pioneer of Irish medieval studies, Edmund Curtis. In 1923 Curtis regarded the events of 1460 as a declaration of 'the full internal autonomy of the lordship of Ireland'. The 'legislative and legal independence of Ireland' was established and 'Richard (duke of York) had to accept it, though probably with little satisfaction, for after all he was an Englishman. But his party was scattered and Ireland was his greatest asset'.[8]

Fifteen years later, Curtis revised the expression but not the substance of his opinions in the second edition of his work:

> Thus did Ireland assert a complete separateness from England except for the personal link of the Crown.

In a footnote he did warn, however, that 'Irish nationalism in the modern sense cannot be looked for in the acts or words of this parliament'.[9]

Curtis's view on this, as on many other aspects of Irish medieval history, became the standard one. Fourteen years were to pass before it was challenged by two noted iconoclasts in the field of English parliamentary history. When they turned their attention to the medieval Irish parliament, H. G. Richardson and G. O. Sayles reached a quite different conclusion on the significance of the legislation of 1460.

> We must not be misled by the declaration of the parliament of Drogheda in 1460 . . . for this declaration, as the context shows, was a mere measure of protection devised by the duke of York, the lieutenant, who was then a refugee in Ireland from the Lancastrians . . . This assertion had no basis in history, and we shall see that after 1460 English legislation was enforced in Ireland, although it was deemed necessary in Poynings' parliament to enact a statute that reasserted the principle and removed any doubts there may have been on the subject.[10]

In the same year Dr A. G. Donaldson completed his thesis on the application of English law to Ireland prior to 1801. His judgement on the declaration of 1460 reflected, at that stage, the new orthodoxy of Richardson and Sayles:

> It was in fact a political move, a gesture by Richard of York to secure the allegiance of the English in Ireland to the Yorkist cause.

Five years later, however, Dr Donaldson had qualified this opinion and more cautiously stated that the

> current interpretation of this incident is that it was an attempt by Richard, duke of York, to enlist the Irish against the Lancastrians.

But he did allow that an

> independent sentiment . . . was expressed by the Irish parliament in this fifteenth-century meeting at Drogheda.[11]

Professor Otway-Ruthven was more forthright in dismissing the claim made by the 1460 parliament as 'totally unhistorical'. In her view it 'had no validity in law or custom' and 'must be regarded as a mere aberration, not corresponding to any constitutional fact'.[12] But Professor J. F. Lydon was unable to accept this assessment. Instead he argued that 'there was some historical justification for the 1460 claim' and that even if it was prompted by selfish motives, these 'had at least the effect if not the intent of urging forward political separation'. Subsequently he termed the 1460 claim 'the supreme example of Anglo-Irish separatism' when an 'Irish parliament proclaimed its independence in the most solemn way possible'.[13] Thus the passage of half a century had brought us almost full circle—almost if not quite back to the view expressed by Edmund Curtis in 1923.[14]

One of the central issues raised by the 1460 legislation, whether or not the English parliament had the right to legislate for Ireland, was to be much debated in future centuries. During the controversy which it engendered in the seventeenth century, both sides looked back to the medieval Irish parliament in search of precedents to strengthen their arguments.[15]

Two of the protagonists of the view that Ireland was not bound by English legislation were the author of the *Declaration* of 1644 and William Molyneux in *The case of Ireland stated* (1698). Both claimed that the medieval Irish parliament had enacted that

> the statutes made in England should not be of force in the kingdom of Ireland unless they were allowed and published in that kingdom by parliament.[16]

This, it was averred, had first been enunciated in 1326–7 and had been repeated in 1408–9 and 1450–1.[17] However, as Molyneux himself admitted, these three enactments were not to be found in the parliament rolls. The authority for them was a marginal note in the collection of Irish statutes made by Sir Richard Bolton who acknowledged that the statutes did not appear in the official record but stated that he had

> seene the same exemplified under the great seale and the exemplification remayneth in the Treasury of the citie of Waterford.[18]

The evidence on which Bolton relied has now disappeared and modern constitutional historians, like Sir Samuel Mayart in his rejoinder to the *Declaration*, have tended to dismiss these examples as unsupported by sufficient evidence.[19] Nevertheless, it seems improbable that Bolton would simply have invented such statutes and there remains at least the possibility that precedents did exist for the declaration made in 1460, which, surprisingly, is not cited by either the author of the *Declaration* or Molyneux.

More solid evidence that the application of English legislation to Ireland was a matter for debate comes from a case tried in 1441 in the English Court of Exchequer Chamber. The case arose out of the efforts of John Pilkington to vindicate his right to the office of escheator of Ireland,[20] but because it raised much wider issues it was referred to the Exchequer Chamber, where particularly difficult points of law could be determined by an assembly of all the justices of England. One of the issues raised by *Pilkington's case* was the powers and position of the Irish parliament in relation to England, and in the course of the proceedings one of the serjeants[21] involved, John Fortescue, gave the following opinion:

> the territory of Ireland is separate from the kingdom of England, for if a tenth or fifteenth be granted here, it shall not bind the people of Ireland,

and if a statute be made here, it shall not bind those in Ireland unless they shall approve it in their own parliament, even though the king under his great seal shall send this same statute to Ireland.[22]

Fortescue was alone in his view that Ireland was separate and distinct from the realm of England; one of his fellow-serjeants argued that Ireland's position was analogous to the palatinates of Durham and Chester, which were not bound by parliamentary grants of taxation but were, nevertheless, part of the kingdom.[23]

In making the point that the people of Ireland were not bound by a tax granted in England, Fortescue was simply stating a fact. Equally, it was true that English people were not liable for taxes granted by the Irish parliament; in 1372 a Bristol merchant in New Ross was specifically exempted from Irish taxation on the grounds that he was not a resident of Ireland.[24]

The English parliament could not impose taxes on Ireland because it did not include Irish representatives who could consent to such an imposition. And in Ireland, as in England, it had been recognised since the thirteenth century that legitimate taxation demanded a form of consent, whether expressed by particular local communities or more generally through parliament.[25] The one serious challenge to the Irish parliament's control over general grants of taxation came in the 1370s. The efforts of the lieutenant, William of Windsor, to secure assent for increased taxation from Irish parliamentary representatives culminated in a summons to these representatives to appear in England in 1376. In most instances the summons was obeyed but it was made clear by the communities involved that they were under no obligation to send representatives to England since

according to the rights, privileges, liberties, laws and customs of the land of Ireland, in use since the time of the conquest and before, they are not bound to elect or send anyone from the aforesaid land to parliaments and councils to be held in England.[26]

And since most communities also witheld from their representatives the requisite power to consent to taxation in England, Windsor's ploy produced none of the hoped-for increase in revenue.[27]

It is easy to accept the validity of the argument that Irish representatives were not obliged to attend parliament in England and that, therefore, the English parliament could not impose taxes on Ireland. But the implication by Fortescue that there was a connection between the right to tax and the right to legislate, however convincing to modern ears, will not survive examination. It is clear that throughout the thirteenth and fourteenth centuries English legislation had been applied to Ireland without the approval of the Irish parliament. Apart from English legislation which dealt specifically with Ireland, there are a number of examples where laws passed in England were extended to Ireland simply on the order of the king.[28] As late as 1411 the English statutes against papal provisions were despatched to Ireland with a royal command that they be observed there. No mention is made of any need for approval by the Irish parliament. The writ accompanying the statutes simply ordered that they be enrolled in the records of the Irish chancery and courts and that they

> be publicly proclaimed in the several cities, boroughs and market towns and other places within the said land, where it shall be most fitting and needful.[29]

Fortescue, therefore, had, at most, thirty years of precedents on which to base his opinion that English statutes did not bind Ireland without the consent of the Irish parliament, even though the king should sent the statute to Ireland under his great seal. Nevertheless, although the balance of the evidence favours the view that English legislation did apply to Ireland without the need for confirmation by the Irish parliament, Fortescue's opinion demonstrates that the issue was not beyond dispute. It was the opinion of 'one of the most eminent of the common lawyers in the fifteenth century', a man who was to be appointed chief justice of the king's bench in 1442, and later to earn an enduring reputation as the author of classic works on English law and government.[30] Further, John Fortescue was probably better informed than most on the situation in Ireland since his elder brother, Henry, had acted as chief justice of the king's bench in Ireland between 1426 and 1429. During that period Henry Fortescue had twice been commissioned by the Irish parliament to convey its complaints to the king in England and he must, therefore, have been well aware of the attitudes of that body.[31] In making the case that the consent of the Irish parliament was necessary for valid legislation John Fortescue was probably reflecting at least a section of Anglo-Irish opinion and it would be unwise to dismiss the 1460 declaration as 'an aberration' or as 'a mere measure of protection devised by the duke of York'.[32]

The attribution to York of responsibility for the measure raises the issue of where the initiative lay in the framing of the declaration. It is true that one of the main purposes of the parliament was to protect York against Henry VI's government. And the emergency nature of some of the measures is made clear by the limitations placed upon their duration. Both the act which made it a treasonable offence to challenge York's authority and that providing for the recruitment of a force of archers for the duke were to remain in effect only for as long as York was resident in Ireland.[33] Significantly, no such limitation was placed upon the measure forbidding people from being summoned out of Ireland to answer charges unless such a summons was made under the great seal of Ireland. And this 'false usurpation or pretensed prescription' had to be formally revoked by Sir Edward Poynings in the parliament of 1494–5, where it was stated that it had been ratified by a parliament held before Richard, duke of York 'being then in rebellion and pretending himself lieutenant of the said land'.[34]

The declaration itself was not amenable to any restriction on the period of its validity since it was a bald assertion that Ireland was, and always had been, a separate entity, bound only by those laws which were accepted by its own parliament. The argument that the purpose of the declaration was solely to invalidate the English statute of attainder against York is not convincing. On the one hand, the measure was unnecessarily sweeping to cope with that particular difficulty; on the other, such an argument ignores the fact that the assertion of Ireland's separateness was repeated later in the parliament in a quite different context. In the act establishing a distinct Irish coinage, the justification for the measure was that the land of Ireland, though it was under the obedience of the realm of England, was separated from that realm and from all its statutes, except those that were freely accepted by Irish parliamentary assemblies.[35]

Obviously this measure was unconcerned with protecting York's position, and the initiative in its passage clearly lay with those members of the Anglo-Irish community who were anxious to remedy the shortage of coin within Ireland. The crown had always been reluctant to establish a separate mint in Ireland and a recent study has concluded that York 'in assenting to the act for the coinage as king's lieutenant, sacrificed the king's interests for the support of the Anglo-Irish'.[36] And, if this is true of the coinage act, it is probable that it is also true of the original declaration.

That York should be prepared to make concessions to the Anglo-Irish in 1460 is not surprising, given the difficulties in which he found himself; and, from the point of view of his immediate political advantage, the concessions paid off. In March 1460 the earl of Warwick sailed to Ireland and he and York celebrated St Patrick's Day together at Waterford. Warwick remained in Ireland until his return to Calais in late May, and presumably it was during this period that plans were made for Warwick's successful invasion of England in the following July.[37]

Henry VI's administration apparently attempted to counter Anglo-Irish support for York by appealing to the Gaelic Irish. In the session of parliament which met on 3 March it was claimed that four men had brought into Ireland many letters under the king's privy seal urging the Gaelic Irish enemies to oppose York. The statute which ordered the four accused to appear before York by 31 March and convicted them of treason if they failed to do so, exempted the king himself from any responsibility for such letters. They must have been dispatched without his knowledge since it was unprecedented that any king would take 'the said enemies into such confidence, favour or affection'.[38] It was this statute which formed the basis of the charge made in the Yorkist propaganda manifesto of July 1460:

> dyvers lordes have caused his hyghnesse to wryte letters under his privy seale unto his Yrysshe enemyes, whyche never kyng of England dyd heretofore, whereby they may have comfort to entre in to the conquest of the sayde land.[39]

Such an accusation suggests that in 1460 the government of Henry VI was prepared even to sacrifice control of Ireland in its bid to quash the threat from York. And in these circumstances it is hardly to be wondered at that York himself was willing to bow to Anglo-Irish demands in order to preserve his own position.

But if we allow that the declaration of ·1460 was influenced by earlier controversies about the application of English legislation to Ireland and that the initiative in framing it lay with the Anglo-Irish rather than with York himself, there remains the problem of understanding why the declaration should be made at all. To what extent does it reflect the wishes of that Anglo-Irish community which was represented in the Irish parliament?

Historians of the medieval Irish parliament have tended to stress, quite properly, the similarities between it and its English counterpart. But while acknowledging that the English institution formed the model for the Irish one, it is also fair to emphasise that all English institutions were, to a greater or lesser extent, modified by their passage across the Irish Sea into a much different environment. To concentrate, therefore, on the imitative character of the Irish parliament can obscure some of the distinctive characteristics of the Irish body.

Obvious differences in composition can be noted. It was a much smaller assembly than its English counterpart, particularly in the fifteenth century when the area under the effective control of the Dublin government had dwindled. From the later fourteenth century it included among its elected representatives proctors from the diocesan clergy who, in England, were now comprised within the provincial convocations of Canterbury and York. But perhaps the point on which most stress should be laid is that the Irish parliament was representative of only one of the two nations within medieval Ireland—the English nation. The occasional presence of a Gaelic Irish bishop by reason of his office prevents us from describing the personnel of the parliament as exclusively Anglo-Irish, but this does not invalidate the point that parliament was essentially an institution of the colonial population within Ireland.[40] The one attempt to include Gaelic Irish leaders within parliament, made by Richard II in 1395, did not succeed and there was no subsequent change in either the composition or function of the assembly.[41]

Thus when writs of summons to the Irish parliament mention matters which concern 'the community of our land of Ireland' (*communitatem terre nostre Hibernie*),[42] or assent is given to legislation 'by the whole community of the land of Ireland' (*per . . . totam communitatem terre Hibernie*),[43] the phrase, like its English equivalent, the community of the realm, may be open to differing interpretations as to whether or not it is synonymous with the elected representatives.[44] But in Ireland that *'communitas'* can be defined in a more certain if very different way—as the community of the king's loyal subjects within Ireland, those who thus plaintively described themselves in 1428:

> . . . we ever have and shall be your trewe liege men and myche sorrow suffre from day to day here of your enemyes for your sake . . .[45]

As a group the 'English lieges' were to be distinguished not only from the Gaelic Irish enemies but also from the 'English rebels', those of English descent who had forsaken their allegiance to the crown and degenerated by the adoption in varying degrees of the customs and traditions of the Irish enemies. Equally, however, these loyal subjects of English descent, 'the English by blood' were to be differentiated from native-born English, 'the English by birth'.[46]

An insight into how the 'English by blood' or Anglo-Irish regarded themselves can be gained from the account by the Dublin annalist of the opening phase of Lionel of Clarence's campaign in

Ireland in 1361. Shortly after his arrival in the country at the head of an English army, Clarence issued a proclamation that no one born in Ireland was to associate with his forces. But the result of 'going it alone' was that he lost 100 men in an engagement with the O'Byrnes of Wicklow. Thereupon, Clarence decided to bring the English and Anglo-Irish together and his cause prospered 'with the help of God and the people of Ireland'.[47]

The phrase itself is a telling one, for clearly the annalist took the view that the Anglo-Irish were the 'people of Ireland' and, as such, could be easily distinguished from the people of England. It was a distinction that had become increasingly apparent in the course of the fourteenth century. In the parliament of 1324 an Anglo-Irish lord could denounce an English-born bishop of Ossory as a 'foreigner'.[48] During 1341–2 royal directives to Ireland produced, according to the Dublin annalist, an unprecedented division 'between the English born in England and the English born in the land of Ireland'.[49] An ordinance of 1357 stated that both groups were true English but complained of the dissensions that had arisen between them,[50] and nine years later the Statute of Kilkenny had to enjoin that no difference of allegiance was to be made between the English born in Ireland and the English born in England.[51]

In the period following the Statute of Kilkenny the distinction between the two groups also became apparent within England, as a growing number of Anglo-Irish emigrated to the mother country, despite attempts to curb the exodus.[52] There they remained an identifiably separate group[53] and, as such, they faced certain restrictions and disabilities. From 1394 onwards they were subject to sporadic repatriation orders designed to secure either their return to Ireland or their payment of a fine for the right to remain in England. Students from Ireland, who wished to attend university at Oxford or Cambridge, were forced in the 1420s to provide proofs of their loyalty before admission, and the Inns of Court in London went further and banned Irish-born students altogether. These measures culminated in the formal classification of the Irish born as foreigners in 1440 so that they fell within the scope of the poll-tax imposed on aliens. Only after strong protests from the Dublin administration were the Irish subsequently exempted from this imposition.[54]

These measures can only have reinforced the sense of a separate Anglo-Irish identity, which, it has recently been argued, had already emerged 'out of the peculiar strains experienced by a colonial ruling elite, harassed by insecurity, and feeling itself neglected, misunderstood or undervalued by a ruler whose mind was of necessity elsewhere'.[55] And for this distinctive, if fragmented, Anglo-Irish community parliament provided a political and social focus. If the legislative and fiscal functions of the Irish parliament were less important than those of its English counterpart, it had another role as the mouthpiece of an increasingly embattled colonial population. And the petitions and protests emanating from the Irish parliament in the century before 1460 can be used as a guide to Anglo-Irish attitudes. Messages were sent to the king from 'the prelates, earls, barons and the community of the land of Ireland', from the 'prelates, lords and commons of Ireland' or simply from the 'community of the land of Ireland'.[56]

The extent to which these communications were influenced by the commons is difficult to determine. The charge was made in 1428 that 'those who are sent to parliaments and councils are chosen not for the good of the king and his lieges but at the will of the nobles and magnates'.[57] In 1441 the more specific accusation was levelled against the earl of Ormond that he had 'made and ordained Irishmen, grooms and pages of his household, knights of the shire'.[58] Doubtless magnates did attempt to influence the selection of parliamentary representatives in Ireland as they did in England, but it would be wrong, therefore, to conclude that the elected representatives were mere ciphers.[59] Their conduct in the face of William of Windsor's demands in the 1370s and their protests against unpopular impositions like coign and livery[60] demonstrate a capacity for independent action, and it is unlikely that complaints sent to England in their name would have been formulated without, at least, their tacit approval.

The main theme of many of these messages was that the king had a duty towards his lordship of Ireland and that failure to discharge it would have dire consequences. In 1385 the prediction was that

there will be made a conquest of the greater part of the land of Ireland,

in 1421 that

your said land and your lieges therein will within a short time be quite utterly ruined and destroyed for ever,

and the protest in 1455 spoke of

the great eminent danger that rests in the said land, by which this land is likely to be finally destroyed.[61]

Such statements clearly exaggerated the weakness of the colonists' position, presumably with the intention of arousing greater concern in England for their plight; but they also reflect a nagging fear among the 'English lieges' of Ireland that they might be overwhelmed both militarily and culturally by the Gaelic Irish enemies. The continuing animosity towards those enemies is reflected in one of the 1421 petitions to the king that he should request the pope to launch a crusade against the Gaelic Irish. The reasons advanced were that their leaders had broken the oaths of allegiance made to Richard II in 1395 and had not paid the sums pledged to the papacy if they defaulted on their obligations.[62] But whether the petitioners knew it or not, they were simply echoing a request made ninety years earlier in 1331.[63]

Among more practical remedies sought by Anglo-Irish petitioners was that the king himself should come to Ireland or, if that was not possible, that he should despatch a great lord from England.[64] No subsequent king of medieval England was prepared to follow Richard II's example and come to Ireland, but York's high rank among the English aristocracy made him an acceptable substitute and is one of the reasons for his marked popularity within Anglo-Ireland. In addition embassies to England usually sought military and financial assistance to deal with the Gaelic Irish threat by means which would not necessitate recourse to coign and livery, the much-resented billeting of troops on the local population.[65]

And yet, while the Anglo-Irish community looked to England to provide for its security and defence, it is also clear that English interference at certain levels was deeply resented. As early as 1342 parliamentary representatives complained to the king about those 'who are sent out of England to govern them, who themselves have little knowledge of your said land of Ireland'.[66] Friction between English and Anglo-Irish officials in the Dublin administration was one of the factors which contributed in the 1390s to the failure of Richard II's plans for Ireland,[67] and disputes over appointments to offices in the Irish administration continued to trouble relations between England and Anglo-Ireland in the fifteenth century.

Part of the problem lay in the fact that such appointments could be made by both the London and Dublin administrations, by letters patent under the great seal of either Ireland or England. But the rivalry thus engendered did little for efficiency in government, and one of the complaints made by the Irish parliament to the king in 1441 was that both methods had resulted in the appointment of unsuitable officials. The king was therefore requested to order that future appointees should undergo exmination by the chief govenor and council to ensure that they were 'sufficiente, able and connying to occupie suche offices'. If they failed to satisfy such criteria then the chief governor and council should have the power to remove them from office.[68] Agreement to such a scheme would effectively have given the chief governor of Ireland complete control over administrative appointments in Dublin and, unsurprisingly, the crown refused to surrender this area of patronage. Thus there were continuing allegations that petitioners in England secured official positions in Ireland 'by sinister information' or 'by craft',[69] and quarrels over minor offices in the Dublin administration could be pursued at great length and with remarkable tenacity.[70] The Irish parliament naturally tended to favour those officials who were appointed under the great seal of the Irish administration, and confirmation of such appointees in the face of rivals from England led to the specific charge in 1447 that parliament in Ireland was used to overthrow grants made 'to men born in England of any office in the said land of Ireland'.[71]

It is hard to resist the conclusion that, while the Anglo-Irish protested their loyalty to the English crown and expected the king to protect their interests, they nevertheless had little time for Englishmen in Ireland. Almost three centuries in Ireland had shaped them as a people clearly distinguishable from the English of England. In that sense they were, in the Dublin annalist's term, 'the people of Ireland'. Yet in their protest to the king in 1441 against their classification as aliens by the English parliament they claimed that they were 'Englishmen borne of his land of Irland' and that as such they should enjoy equality with the English born in England.[72] The peculiar circumstances of 1460 afforded an opportunity for the resolution of this dilemma. Parliament sought to maintain loyalty to the crown or dependence upon the realm of England while at the same time claiming a greater measure of autonomy for the lordship. Ireland, it was suggested, should have a status similar to that enjoyed by Guyenne and Normandy before these territories had been wrested from English control by the French.[73] This was no real solution for ultimately its implementation depended upon its acceptance by the holder of the English crown. The Anglo-Irish could not afford to be true separatists in the sense of openly rejecting the authority of the crown. To have done so would have undermined their position within Ireland by reducing them to the same level as the 'English rebels' or 'Irish enemies'. If faced with a stark choice between rule from England, even by Englishmen, and domination by the Gaelic Irish, there is little doubt that the 'king's English lieges' in Ireland would have chosen the former.

Notes

1. *Stat. Ire., Hen. VI*, p. 638. Subsequently parliament transferred to Dublin where it met on 23 February and was successively adjourned to 3 March, 28 April, 9 June, and 21 July. (Ibid., pp. 638, 740, 750, 758).
2. For a recent account of these events see R. A. Griffiths, *The reign of Henry VI; the exercise of royal authority 1422-61* (London, 1981), pp 820-3.
3. A. Cosgrove, *Late medieval Ireland 1370-1541* (Dublin, 1981), p. 45. See also G. L. Harriss, 'The struggle for Calais: an aspect of the rivalry between Lancaster and York', in *E.H.R.*, 75 (1960), pp 30-53.
4. *Rot. parl.*, v, 349.
5. *Cal. close rolls 1454-61*, p. 426, *Cal patent rolls 1452-61*, p. 563.
6. *Stat. Ire., Hen. VI*, pp 640-44. Subsequently William Overey was convicted of treason by parliament for inciting rebellion and disobedience to York as lieutenant (Ibid., pp 676-8).
7. Ibid., pp 644-6. In 1446 the earl of Ormond had been brought before the constable and marshal of England on a charge of treason made by Thomas Fitzgerald, prior of Kilmainham. See Griffiths, *Reign of Henry VI*, p. 418, J. G. Bellamy, *The law of treason in England in the later middle ages* (Cambridge, 1970), p. 146.
8. E. Curtis, *A history of medieval Ireland* (London, 1923), p. 369.
9. *Med. Ire.* (2nd ed., 1938), p. 322.
10. *Ir. parl. in middle ages*, pp 260, 263.
11. A. G. Donaldson, 'The application in Ireland of English, law and British legislation made before 1801', unpublished Ph.D. thesis, Queen's University, Belfast, 1952, p. 326, *Some comparative aspects of Irish law* (Cambridge, 1957), pp 41-2.
12. A. J. Otway-Ruthven, *A history of medieval Ireland* (1968), p. 190.
13. J. F. Lydon, *The lordship of Ireland in the middle ages* (Dublin, 1972), p. 265, *Ireland in the later middle ages* (Dublin, 1973), p. 145.
14. Recent historians of fifteenth-century England have tended to endorse this view. C. D. Ross wrote of York's 'clever appeal to the Anglo-Irish lords' desire for autonomy' (*Edward IV*, (1974), p. 22), and R. A. Griffiths thought that the Irish parliament of 1460 'was expressly exercising a legislative independence' and that the claims made in parliament reflect 'demands that were already current . . . for a wider measure of independent rule' (*Reign of Henry VI*, p. 855).
15. For a general review of the controversy see R. L. Schuyler, *Parliament and the British Empire* (New York, 1929), pp 40-101 and J. G. Simms, *Colonial nationalism* (Cork, 1976), pp 12-47.
16. *A declaration setting forth how, and by what means, the laws and statutes of England, from time to time, came to be of force in Ireland* (Dublin, 1644), printed by Walter Harris, *Hibernica* (Dublin, 1750), ii, 1-21. The quotation from p. 4 was subsequently repeated *verbatim* by William Molyneux, *The case of Ireland stated* (repr. from 1698 ed. with an introd. by J. G. Simms, Dublin, 1977), p. 63. The *Declaration*, sometimes attributed to Sir Richard Bolton, was probably the work of Patrick D'Arcy. Molyneux was clearly familar with the

Art Cosgrove

Declaration but not with the lengthy reply to it by Sir Samuel Mayart, an Englishman by birth and a justice of the court of common pleas of Ireland. *Serjeant Mayart's answer* was also published by Harris, *Hibernica*, ii, 23–131.

17. Molyneux, *The case of Ireland stated*, p. 63 gives all three instances. The author of the *Declaration* omits the 1408-9 example, Harris, *Hibernica*, ii, 4.

18. Richard Bolton, *The Statutes of Ireland beginning the third yere of K. Edward the second* . . . (Dublin, 1621), p. 67.

19. Harris, *Hibernica*, ii, 39, 61-2, 91, Donaldson, 'The application in Ireland of English law', pp 324-5, Schuyler op.cit., pp 57, 60-1, 71 and p. 85 where Molyneux's work is dismissed as 'a tissue of error, contradiction and fallacy'.

20. For the background see Richardson and Sayles, *Ir. parl. in middle ages*, pp 255-7.

21. A serjeant did not give judgements, but as a leading member of the legal profession his advice would be asked and the opinions of the serjeants, as well as those of the judges, are recorded in the proceedings of the exchequer chamber.

22. Le terre dirlande est severe del roialme dengleterre quar si une Xme ou XV me soit grante icy ceo ne liera ceux dirlande et si une statut soit fait icy ceo ne liera ceux dirlande mesque le roy maundera mesme celle statut en Irlande southe soun grant seale sinoun que eux voillent en lour parlement ceo approver . . . *Select cases in the exchequer chamber before all the justices of England 1377–1461*, ed. M. Hemmant (Selden Society, 1933), pp 82-3.

23. Ibid., p. 83. No decision in the case is recorded.

24. Richardson and Sayles, *Parl. and councils med. Ire.*, i, 48-9.

25. J. R. Strayer and George Rudisill Jr., 'Taxation and community in Wales and Ireland 1272-1327', *Speculum*, 29 (1954), pp 410-16; Richardson and Sayles, *Ir. parl. in middle ages*, pp 112-18.

26. 'Juxta iura privilegia libertates, leges et consuetudines terrae Hiberniae a tempore conquestus ejusdem et ante usitata non tenentur eligere nec mittere aliquos de terra predicta ad parliamenta nec consilia in Anglia tenenda' (T. Leland, *The history of Ireland* (Dublin, 1773), i, 378).

27. See J. F. Lydon, 'William of Windsor and the Irish parliament' in *E.H.R.*, 80 (1965), pp 252-67.

28. Donaldson, 'The application in Ireland of English law', pp 88-96, 102-34, Schuyler, op. cit., pp 29-30, 61-2.

29. 'Eos in singulis civitatibus burgis et villis mercatoriis ac aliis locis infra terram predictam ubi magis expediens fuerit et necesse ex parte nostra publice proclamari . . .' (*Stat. Ire. John—Hen. V*, pp 528-9).

30. Sir John Fortescue, *De laudibus legum Anglie*, ed. S. B. Chrimes (Cambridge, 1949), pp li, lix-lxxvii.

31. Ball, *Judges* i, 175; *Rot. pat. hib.*, pp 246-9, Betham, *Dignities*, p. 353. The link between John and Henry Fortescue was kindly brought to my attention by Dr Paul Brand.

32. Otway-Ruthven, *Med. Ire.*, p. 190, Richardson and Sayles, *Ir. parl. in middle ages*, p. 260.

33. *Stat. Ire., Hen. VI*, pp 644-5, 648-9.

34. *Stat. Ire., Hen. VI*, pp 646-7, *Statutes at large* . . . (Dublin, 1786), pp 43-4.

Equally no limitation was placed on the restriction of appeals of treason to the constable and marshal of Ireland; see Bellamy, op. cit., pp 158–63.

35. *Stat. Ire., Hen. VI*, pp 664–5.
36. S. G. Ellis, 'The struggle for the control of the Irish mint, 1460–c. 1506', in *R.I.A. Proc.*, 78 (1978), C, p. 18.
37. Cora L. Scofield, *The life and reign of Edward IV* (London, 1923), i, 59, 64.
38. *Stat. Ire., Hen. VI*, pp 742–3.
39. *An English chronicle of the reigns of Richard II, Henry IV, Henry V and Henry VI*, ed. J. S. Davies (Camden Society, 1856), p. 87.
40. See Richardson and Sayles, *Ir. parl. in middle ages*, esp. pp 78–80, 176–84, A. Cosgrove 'A century of decline' in Brian Farrell (ed.), *The Irish parliamentary tradition* (Dublin, 1973), pp 57–67.
41. E. Curtis, *Richard II in Ireland 1394–5 and submissions of the Irish Chiefs* (Oxford, 1927), pp 49, 58–9.
42. Richardson and Sayles, *Parl. and councils med. Ire.*, i, 26, 36–8.
43. Ibid., p. 9, and cf. ibid. pp 13, 71 and *Stat. Ire. John–Hen. V*, p. 482.
44. Above, pp 5–20
45. Betham, *Dignities*, p. 355.
46. For a general account of the divisions within Ireland see Cosgrove, *Late medieval Ireland*, pp 72–98.
47. 'cum adjutorio Dei et populi Hibernie'; (*Chartul. St Marys, Dublin*, ii, 395). The significance of the passage was noted by Robin Frame, *Colonial Ireland 1169–1369* (Dublin, 1981), pp 130–1.
48. *Proceedings against Dame Alice Kyteler*, ed. T. Wright (Camden Society, 1843), p. 17.
49. 'inter Anglicos in Anglia oriundos et Anglicos in terra Hibernie oriundos' (*Chartul. St Marys, Dublin*, ii, 383). For a recent re-examination of the conflict see Robin Frame, 'English policies and Anglo-Irish attitudes in the crisis of 1341–2' in James Lydon (ed.), *England and Ireland in the later middle ages* (Dublin, 1981), pp 86–103.
50. 'Item licet tam illi de Hibernia Anglici oriundi quam ipsi de Anglia nati et in Hibernia conversantes sint veri Anglici . . . varie tamen dissensiones et manutenencie ratione nacionis inter ipsos de Hibernia et illos de Anglia natos sunt suborte' (*Statutes of the realm* i, 363).
51. *Stat. Ire. John–Hen. V*, pp 436–7. Cf. Art Cosgrove, 'Hiberniores · ipsis Hibernis' in A. Cosgrove and D. McCartney (eds.), *Studies in Irish history presented to R. Dudley Edwards* (Dublin, 1979), pp 1–14.
52. The Statute of Kilkenny itself complained of the dearth of labourers because so many had left the country and ordered that 'no labourer shall pass beyond sea'. (*Stat. Ire. John–Hen. V*, pp 466–7). For later legislation against emigrants see ibid., pp 516–9, 568–9.
53. R. A. Griffiths's view that 'Irish and Welsh residents in England stood out from the mass of the king's subjects by their language, habits and historical associations' (*Reign of Henry VI*, p. 142) needs one qualification. The great majority of the Irish residents would have been English-speaking, though they were probably distinguished by dialect and accent.

54. Cosgrove, *Late medieval Ireland*, pp 32–6, 74–6, Griffiths, *Reign of Henry VI*, pp 131, 134–5, 142–3, 167–8, Sylvia L. Thrupp, 'A survey of the alien population of England in 1440', in *Speculum*, 32 (1957), pp 262–72.

55. Frame, 'English policies . . . in the crisis of 1341–2', p. 100.

56. Cf. *Stat. Ire., John–Hen. V*, pp 332–3, 484–5, 562–3, *Hen. VI*, p. 50.

57. *Rot. pat. hib.*, p. 248a, no. 13.

58. *Proc. privy council* v, 318.

59. Cf. J. R. Maddicott, 'The county community and the making of public opinion in fourteenth-century England', in *R. Hist. Soc. Trans.*, 5th series, 28 (1978), pp 27–43.

60. *Stat. Ire., John–Hen. V*, pp 520–1, 572–3, *Hen. VI*, pp 31, 168.

61. *Stat. Ire., John–Hen. V*, pp 484–5, 562–3, *Hen. VI*, pp 356–7.

62. *Stat. Ire., Hen. VI*, pp 564–7.

63. J. A. Watt, 'Negotiations between Edward II and John XXII concerning Ireland', *I.H.S.*, X (1956–7), pp 14, 20.

64. *Stat. Ire. John–Hen. V*, pp 484–7, 562–3, *Hen. VI*, p. 50.

65. C. A. Empey and Katharine Simms, 'The ordinances of the White Earl and the problem of coign in the later middle ages', in *R.I.A. Proc.*, 75 (1975), C, pp 161–87.

66. *Stat. Ire., John–Hen. V*, pp 344–5.

67. Dorothy Johnston, 'The interim years: Richard II and Ireland, 1395–1399', in James Lydon (ed.), *England and Ireland in the later middle ages* (Dublin, 1981), pp 185–8, 190–1.

68. N.L.I., Harris, *Collectanea*, iv, 336–7.

69. *Cal. pat. rolls 1446–52*, p. 204, *1452–61*, p. 245.

70. Cf. e.g. *Stat. Ire., Hen. VI*, pp 132–4, 590–5.

71. Ibid., pp 86–7.

72. N.L.I., Harris, *Collectanea*, iv, 337b.

73. *Stat. Ire., Hen. VI*, pp 662–5.

Parliament and community in Yorkist and Tudor Ireland

S. G. Ellis

An invitation to write on so novel a theme as parliament and community gives me a welcome opportunity for a partial reexamination of a familiar but little-studied problem of English rule in Ireland, the essential nature of government there. One of the principal features which distinguished government in Tudor England from the trend towards absolutism on the continent was the continued vitality of parliament.[1] In the 1530s fundamental changes in the structure and claims of government were implemented with parliamentary consent, as were all major changes in the law in the Tudor period, and in this way the government's legislative programme was adjusted to meet the interests of the political nation. Legislation reflected a consensus for change between crown and community, and in enacting laws for the common weal and more particular laws to serve individual interests, parliament was an important mechanism for maintaining the stability of the Tudor régime.[2]

In the lordship of Ireland, however, the institution of parliament evolved somewhat differently. The fifteenth-century Irish parliament has, with much truth, been characterized as an institution in decline, and in the sixteenth century the decreasing frequency with which parliaments were called betrayed a widening breach between crown and community.[3] Moreover, parliamentary legislation and conflict there have attracted attention as a convenient guide to the growth of Anglo-Irish separatism. Whereas fifteenth-century parliaments apparently promoted the interests of the community at the expense of the crown, after 1534 when the crown attempted to reverse this trend, it stimulated the growth of an organized constitutional opposition.[4] The differences between the two parliaments were emphasised and formalised by the passage of Poynings' Law; but since a connection has been established for England between parliament and government by consent, these differences call in question the nature of government in Ireland. It might appear that government there reflected no real consensus between crown and community but rather an unstable equilibrium which arose out of the crown's earlier lack of interest in Ireland but which was broken by the Reformation crisis and the revival in the power of central government in Henry VIII's later years. Yet, while there is much to recommend this view, it is not the whole story. It is questionable whether the interests of crown and community were irreconcilable, despite the much publicized clashes in the later fifteenth century, and it may be that the collapse of consensus politics in the mid-sixteenth century has been allowed to prejudge the issue for the earlier period. The Irish parliament was in fact more than just a mechanism for enacting laws and airing subjects' grievances. Shortage of space precludes a full treatment here of its development, but by concentrating on some lesser known aspects of its role in government I hope to throw further light on the nature of English rule in Ireland and of parliament's role in maintaining the rule of law.

Medieval Irish parliaments were chiefly remembered in a more democratic age for their intermittent support for two basic principles of constitutional monarchy, that of consent to taxation and the idea that legislative power should rest with the king, lords and commons of Ireland in parliament there. In practice, however, the king's high court of parliament came nearer after 1460 to realising that other misleading claim of medieval parliaments, to be a court, although it was never a court in the full sense. It is this aspect of parliament which I shall first consider.

Even a cursory glance at the parliament rolls discloses that parliament's legislative role was not very important. The reason for this was simple. The medieval lordship was considered to be a dependency of the realm of England and legislation of the English parliament was applicable to Ireland.[5] This left the Irish parliament the minor role of enacting statutes of purely local concern. Thus the pressures which led in England to the primacy of the legislative aspect of parliament, and the rerouting of administrative and judicial matters back to the ordinary sessions of the council, probably operated the other way in Ireland. Scrutinizing the fifteenth-century parliament rolls, Sir John Davies remarked on the extraordinary number of private bills and petitions answered and ordered in parliament, containing such mean and ordinary matters as, but for want of other business, were not fit to be handled in so high a court.[6]

In fact the years from 1460 saw a great expansion of parliament's role in government. Under Henry VI parliaments had usually met annually but there was rarely more than one sitting or session of each parliament and in the last fourteen years of the reign the tally of acts passed varied between twenty and forty.[7] Then in 1460 the parliament held by Richard duke of York ran to six sessions between February and July and passed 63 statutes. This set the pattern for Edward IV's reign. By custom confirmed by statute, the governor was restrained from summoning parliaments more frequently than once a year, but four or five sessions were frequently held, evenly scattered over ten or eleven months, and the number of acts passed normally reached about eighty or ninety. Precise information about parliamentary sessions is usually lacking but in 1463–4, when the earl of Desmond took parliament with him on a progress through the south–east, the four sessions lasted 23 days and no less than 106 acts were passed; in 1467–8 there were ten sessions lasting 65 days or more in which 84 acts were passed; and in 1471–2 five sessions lasted altogether 38 days during which 91 acts were passed.[9] Thus not only were parliaments convoked much more often than in England, where in the fifteenth century their frequency was decreasing, but under Edward IV they each sat for approximately the same number of weeks. It is true that some parliaments were dissolved after only one session with few acts passed, but in every case these early dissolutions can be linked to a change of governor or dynasty.[10]

Parliament's increasing role in government at this time stemmed entirely from the bulk of administrative and judicial matters which came before it. Much of this litigation might have been tried at common law and it has been well described by Mr Richardson and Professor Sayles in their book on the medieval Irish parliament.[11] Nevertheless, this upsurge in business was more than just a consequence of the decline of the common law courts brought about by the collapse of the lordship. The changes are in fact more readily explained in an English context than as yet another facet of an alleged process of gaelicization.

Already by the end of the fourteenth century the monopoly earlier enjoyed by the Dublin bench in the trial of real actions had been broken. Surviving plea rolls and later calendars show that very few of these actions or the possessory assizes over which the bench's jurisdiction was shared with king's bench now came before the common law courts.[12] In fact in the fifteenth century king's bench and common pleas were largely reduced like their English counterparts to the status of a debt-collecting agency.[13] Thus the dwindling length of the fifteenth-century plea rolls was not solely a consequence of the impotence of the traditional courts in the face of widespread disorder: rather, to a large extent it reflected changing patterns of litigation. From about 1450, to judge from the rolls, parliament began to supply the need for a court with power to override the form of the law in favour of justice, and within a decade it had become a sort of clearing house for disputes about land, many of which would under the three Edwards have come directly before the common law courts.[14] The normal remedy was to appoint a day in one of the common law courts for the determination of title, thus circumventing the weakness of mesne process at common law. Between 1470 and 1480, for example, the surviving parliament rolls alone record 36 such cases, seventeen of them from beyond the Pale.[15] And, as Richardson and Sayles have shown, almost any other matter in which the traditional courts offered no remedy or were powerless to enforce it might come before parliament.[16]

These facts, however, do not explain why in Ireland parliament became involved in the transformation of the legal system when in England similar difficulties had led to the development of chancery, nor why this occurred only after 1450. One minor consideration is the decision in the English court of king's bench in 1428 that that court had no authority to review the acts of the Irish parliament.[17] Now under Edward IV, the Irish parliament regularly reviewed process in the Irish king's bench and elsewhere,[18] and by then the intermittent trickle of Irish cases which until at least 1441 had come before the English king's bench seems to have dried up.[19] It looks therefore as if with the growing frequency of sessions of parliament under Edward IV the Irish parliament ousted the English king's bench as a court of review, being no doubt cheaper and speedier to Irish litigants. More generally, much of the parliamentary litigation under Edward IV had apparently been determined by the king's council under the Lancastrians, although further research is needed to establish this point with certainty.[20] In England some of this business had been remitted to the chancellor and was then determined in chancery; similarly in 1449 an Irish great council (the effective equivalent of a parliament at this period) ordained that petitions to the lieutenant should be remitted to chancery 'si il soit mater de consciens'.[21] Yet the king's council in Lancastrian Ireland was notoriously faction-ridden,[22] and it may be that parliament was felt by litigants—highly placed ones at first but very soon the nobility and gentry at large—to offer a more impartial and of course more prestigious tribunal for the settlement of private disputes. Parliament therefore became an instrument in the revival of crown government under Edward IV.

Excluding duplicates, fourteen parliament rolls of Edward IV's reign survived until 1922, including all but one of the rolls for the twenty years 1462–81, plus the roll of the 1462 great council. Although some were then incomplete, they recorded a total of 809 acts, of which the overwhelming majority apparently arose from private petitions.[23] In fact only 155 acts related to the lordship as a whole, and they included few which were in any sense important alterations of the law. Although a number of acts attempted to fix prices or to regulate the coinage,[24] and though a very few like the Statute of Archers remained in force until well into the sixteenth century,[25] it was not primarily to legislate that parliaments were called. Nor was it the government's need for taxation, though this might at first sight seem a more compelling reason. Until 1476, when it was revamped and confined to the English Pale, a parliamentary subsidy yielded only c.£300, and the government could in practice obtain more worthwhile sums by local taxation or a scutage, neither of which strictly required parliamentary consent.[26] Moreover, taxation might even act as an incentive to absent oneself from parliament, for silence by no means implied consent in the late medieval lordship. Power and government were much more decentralized than in lowland England, and as late as 1479 it was found necessary to enact that communities which sent no representatives to parliament should nonetheless be bound by its legislation.[27]

In practice the governor probably permitted such frequent sessions of parliament because they were a useful means of strengthening the Dublin administration's feeble control beyond the Pale and of dealing with disorders. Although parliament's work was at times hasty and perfunctory, the increased weight of business under the Yorkists suggests that it was on the whole relatively effective and popular. This suggestion receives some corroboration from the occasional practice of clerks of parliament who subsequently entered the word *vacatum* in the margin against certain acts to denote that they had achieved the desired effect or had been repealed.[28] No doubt the outlying communities continued to be represented, occasionally at least, because of the comparative effectiveness of parliamentary arbitration. It comes as no surprise to learn that 604 of the 886 acts on the 18 rolls which survived for the period 1462–93 arose out of particular interests of the Palesmen, but a further 112 acts, or $12\frac{1}{2}\%$ of the total, chiefly relate to the various communities beyond the Pale. All the late medieval counties except Kerry are included and all the major towns and cities from Carrickfergus round to Galway, although nearly 65% relate chiefly to counties Wexford (28 acts), Kilkenny, Waterford and Limerick and the cities of Waterford and Limerick.[29] While it has long been recognised that representation in the Irish parliament was never confined entirely to the Pale,[30] this evidence of legislation in favour of particular interests suggests that, overall, outside representation was in fact quite substantial even if, individually, only the shire of Wexford and the city of Waterford were regularly represented. It can be supported by evidence concerning the practice in Ireland of amercing those who absented themselves from parliament. This practice had been common in the fourteenth century, and was resumed under Henry VI, presumably in a bid to strengthen the Dublin administration's control over the outlying shires at a time when it seemed in danger of collapsing. The practice apparently continued until 1450 and the last recorded instance occurred in 1499.[31] This gap, however, seems to be more than just a quirk of the evidence. In 1494 Lord Deputy Poynings was for the first time explicitly empowered by his commission of appointment to amerce those absent from parliament. His successor, the earl of Kildare, received the same powers, and for the first time amercements were inflicted in 1499 on temporal lords and proctors of the clergy as well as on the commonalty and the lords spiritual.[32] It looks therefore as if the practice had been allowed to lapse after 1450 and was deliberately revived, a suggestion which accords well with the evidence outlined above, that under Edward IV representation in parliament was fairly wide because parliament's judicial role had expanded.

The surviving list of amercements inflicted for non-return of writs and absence from the 1499 parliament offers almost the only precise evidence concerning the level of representation in the late medieval period, and there is no reason to believe that it distorts the picture. In the fifteenth century representation in the three houses of the Irish parliament was fairly fixed and by correlation with earlier evidence the list indicates that in the first session at Dublin 32 out of a maximum of 46 members were present in the commons, falling to 27 for the second session at Castledermot, and that in the lords attendance was 29 at the first session out of 34 and 24 at the second session. The level of attendance by the clerical proctors is less clear because representation of some dioceses was increased from two to four proctors during the fifteenth century, and there is no evidence about how Cork and Cloyne were represented after the amalgamation of these dioceses in 1429.[33] The proctors' interests in parliament were in any case limited and in most cases their consent to legislation was unnecessary; but at the Dublin session eleven dioceses were apparently represented, falling to eight for the Castledermot session, and the total number of proctors present must have been at least 27 at the first session and 20 at the second.[34] By comparison we know that attendance in the convocation house in 1450 was 27, and in the 1491 parliament eight prelates plus ten temporal peers attended.[35]

In view of this relatively high level of attendance in parliaments of the later fifteenth century, it is unlikely that the preponderance of acts relating primarily to the Pale reflects no more than the ability of the Palesmen to secure their own interests at the expense of the outlying shires. Certainly the Pale was comparatively over-represented in parliament, and in the Lords Palesmen must normally have been in a majority, but in 1499 in both convocation and the commons the representatives of the outlying communities apparently had a comfortable majority. Only when attendance was exceptionally low can the Palesmen have been preponderant in all three houses. The implication, therefore, is that the enactments of the Irish parliament in the later fifteenth century reflected the interests of the political nation in Anglo-Ireland as a whole and not merely those of the Palesmen.

The diverging functions of parliament in kingdom and lordship in the fifteenth century probably had no direct influence on the passage of Poynings' Law, if indeed the king was conscious of this divergence. Poynings' Law was rather part of a reforming legislative programme of political and constitutional import and was designed to strengthen royal control over the Irish parliament as a legislature.[36] The weakness of this control had recently been high-lighted by the activities of Yorkist pretenders. Nevertheless, though conservative in aim, the law was revolutionary in application and brought the Irish parliament much more closely into line with its English counterpart. Whereas a parliament had met almost every year down to 1494, over the next forty years there were only seven parliaments, and only five more to the end of Elizabeth's reign.[37] Moreover in 1494 the medieval parliament rolls, which had recorded, in Norman–French, the results of parliamentary action, were replaced by statute rolls in English, recording only enactments which had previously been approved by the governor and council in Ireland and by the king and council in England.[38] This poses a problem for the historian because it is not entirely clear how far the role of parliament was changing and how far merely the character of its principal record. There is in fact some evidence that, initially at least, Poynings' Law was interpreted as not precluding parliament from determining minor administrative matters as before, even though these matters were no longer recorded on the roll. A licence of 1532 to found a chantry was granted 'on the requisition and assent of both houses of parliament, and at the solicitation of certain persons therein'; in 1541 the lords granted letters of protection to a man attainted of treason for complicity in the Kildare rebellion and a petition against an indictment for larceny in king's bench by a gypsy resident in Dublin was referred to the council. Arbitration in various disputes among the magnates also took place in that parliament.[39] Indeed, unless parliament were regularly so employed, it is hard to see why, for example, in 1508–9 parliament required four sessions to pass three bills and reject three more, or why in 1521–2 seven sessions totalling about twenty days were necessary to debate nine bills.[40] Nevertheless, the relative infrequency of parliaments after 1494 and, for most purposes, the need to obtain in advance the king's licence for each bill effectively deprived the institution of much of its value as a court and administrative board. Parliament in Ireland therefore became primarily a legislature, convened every five or six years mainly for a grant of taxation or in connection with the sporadic attempts at governmental reform through an English-born governor. The judicial and administrative duties of parliament largely devolved on the council aided by the development of chancery,[41] although not all the private bills considered by parliament were susceptible of remedy in this way. Yet in England the Tudor parliament's willingness to entertain private suits was an important factor in the maintenance of political stability:[42] the curtailment of a parallel role played by the Irish parliament deprived both the lordship of this stabilizing force and the Dublin government of a useful instrument for controlling the centrifugal forces at work there.

Yet neither parliament's legislative functions nor its role in the granting of taxation were as clearly defined as in England. Its claims to make law were in fact under attack from two different quarters. In a highly regionalized land many local ordinances were approved by local assemblies, very often the county court or an afforced council of the magnates and gentry of a particular locality; other ordinances were apparently imposed unilaterally by the magnates.[43] Such ordinances were a reflection of the comparative weakness of central government institutions: either they supplemented the existing law, or they were arbitrary infringements of the law, but under Elizabeth and James I they proved no real obstacle to the revival of the central government.[44] The more serious threat concerned the English parliament's claim to legislate for Ireland. In the fourteenth century it had sometimes legislated specifically for Ireland and much general legislation was also applied.[45] This in theory remained the position in the following century, but the issue was confused by the fact that English statutes were now usually proclaimed in the Irish parliament before enforcement, that in 1460 the Irish parliament had explicitly denied the principle that English legislation was applicable in Ireland, and that thereafter some English legislation was confirmed by the Irish parliament.[46] On the other hand, when the issue was raised in court in England, in 1441 and 1485, the judges eventually ruled that statutes made in England bound those in Ireland.[47] And that in general the lordship stood in an inferior relationship to the realm of England was seemingly acknowledged by the Irish parliament itself in 1474. In a neat attempt to turn the tables, parliament then argued that

> of very ryght the realme of England is bound to the defense of [the king's] land of Irland by resoun that it ys oon of the membres of his moost noble corone and eldest membre therof.[48]

It has been argued that doubts about the validity of English legislation were resolved by act of Poynings' parliament which allegedly declared 'that the statute law of England should be deemed good and effectual in law "and over that be accepted, used and executed within this land of Ireland"'.[49] In fact it is so ambiguously worded that its intention and effect are unclear, which is probably why the controversy surfaced again in the seventeenth century.[50] In its preamble the statute observed that 'many and diverse good and profitable statutes late made within the realm of England' had brought that realm 'to great wealth and prosperity, and by all likelyhood so would this land, if the said estatutes were used and executed in the same'. It enacted

> that all estatutes late made within the said realm of England concerning or belonging to the common and publique weal of the same from henceforth be deemed good and effectuall in the law, and over that be acceptyd used and executed within this land of Ireland in all points at all times requisite according to the tenor and effect of the same; and over

that by authority aforesaid, that they be and every of them be authorized, proved and confirmed in this said land of Ireland.[51]

The context seems to fit a particular application of English legislation to Ireland better than a general one. Although stress has been laid on the clause 'from henceforth' to suggest that English statutes should in future apply, the sense is rather that certain statutes for the common good *late made*, not all statutes past and future, should *from henceforth* apply, even though they had not hitherto been executed in Ireland. This did not necessarily raise the general issue, which the king no doubt regarded as settled by the judges' decision of 1485, if not before, for it had long been accepted that only statutes deemed suitable should be applied to Ireland. Moreover, the suggestion here advanced, that this was a particular measure which accorded with the general constitutional position as understood by the king and his advisers gains support from evidence of use. Within a few years actions in the Irish exchequer were being brought on foot of English statutes applied to Ireland by virtue of the act of 1494—for example a statute of 1442 restraining customs officials from keeping taverns, and one of 1490 permitting royal tenants who went on military service to convey their land to feoffees without payment of fines—but there is apparently no instance of a later statute being so applied.[52] Nevertheless, precisely because it did not address itself to the general issue, the effect of the act was to reinforce rather than resolve existing doubts. If certain English acts were now in force because the Irish parliament had confirmed them, did not this imply that English legislation not so confirmed was inapplicable to Ireland? In fact, the English parliament still legislated occasionally for Ireland. In 1495 it reversed the attainder of the eight earl of Kildare by Poynings' parliament; in 1534 it attainted the tenth earl of Kildare, and in 1536 it attainted two of the tenth earl's uncles.[53]

In 1534, therefore, the general issue was still unresolved, with important consequences for the future, but in the late medieval period this issue was more a minor irritant in Anglo-Irish relations than a source of deep resentment to the political community of the lordship. This was partly because the king rarely chose to legislate for Ireland through the English parliament. Although in the fifteenth century a weak king might have difficulty in preventing a governor from using parliament for his own ends, the king's overall control of parliament, when asserted, was never seriously questioned.[54] More especially, however, the interests of the Anglo-Irish political community, including legislative ones, were remarkably similar to those of the political nation in England, of which they were generally accepted as a part. Besides those lords resident in England who held lands in Ireland, at least six Irish peers and one or two others also held lands in England.[55] The Anglo-Irish community insisted on its Englishness and enjoyed the same laws and rights as the king's subjects in England.[56] Thus although in the modern context a greater significance has been attributed to the occasional conflicts, the existence of a separate parliament which offered mainly administrative solutions to particular problems within the framework of the common law did not necessarily promote separatist tendencies in the lordship.

Whatever the constitutional position about legislation, however, grants of general taxation undoubtedly required the consent of the local community, and this was most authoritatively given by the Irish parliament. Indirect taxation in Ireland, the great and petty customs and from 1499 poundage, which was granted in perpetuity, did not depend on a parliamentary grant, even though in Tudor England, parliament still retained some control over it by making a grant for life in the first parliament of each reign.[57] Local taxation had also been comparatively more important in Lancastrian Ireland, but the scanty evidence would seem to suggest that thereafter rather less was available to the governor from this source.[58] And until 1531 the crown occasionally levied scutages.[59] Nevertheless, these duties, though yielding a significant proportion of the total revenue, were from *c.* 1476 less valuable than the parliamentary subsidy. The growing importance of the subsidy in Irish finances may be explained by the cessation of regular financial and military subventions from England in the 1470s,[60] which in turn forced the Dublin administration to initiate a reform of the system of direct taxation. Thereafter the need to obtain regular grants of subsidies ensured frequent parliaments and so encouraged the government to seek parliamentary consent for other legislation, particularly measures to eke out the pitifully small hereditary crown revenues in Ireland. The common subsidy which was in theory worth 700 marks but in practice *c.*£300 was replaced by a more open-ended system involving the fixing *in parliament* of a rate per plough-land on which the subsidy was chiefly based, and the abandonment of a notional lump sum. In this way, parliament was induced in 1477 to grant a total of £1,357 15*s.* 4*d.* by way of two general subsidies and a local subsidy.[61] This is the context in which Edward IV issued his well-known order of 1479 that

in noo parliament to be holdyn herafter ther shall no subsidie be axed ne **graunted** in the same upon the commouns ne levied, but one in a yere **which** shall not excede the extent of vii^c mark as haith ben accustumed.[62]

It reflected a compromise between the needs of the governor, confronted by an empty treasury and no support from England, and what the Palesmen could fairly be expected to pay on a regular basis. There should be a regular levy of 700 marks based on a realistic extent, not a reversion to the previous *status quo*, and in fact the stipulated maximum was soon exceeded after Edward IV's death.[63]

So far as the government was concerned, the taxation system was further improved by the practice inaugurated under Poynings of making an annual grant for term of years, usually five or ten years, instead of the previous one-off grant. Since Poynings' grant was, exceptionally, at double the normal rate and calculated on a revised extent of ploughlands, the undertreasurer levied no less than £1,503 17*s*. 3¼*d*. for the year 1495–6, and no doubt similar sums annually down to 1499.[64] Thereafter the average yield exceeded £500 per annum to 1534 in a total revenue of *c.* £1,600 a year: the subsidy had become 'the substance of the kynges revenuous without the which the . . . lond may not be defended', and was levied every year until 1576 except in the years 1527 to 1532.[65]

Nevertheless, the central importance of parliamentary taxation to the Dublin government was again threatened by the series of administrative reforms initiated in the aftermath of the 1534 rebellion. Thomas Cromwell's interventions in Ireland had the indirect result of manoeuvring the king into agreeing to the resumption of English subventions for Ireland.[66] The cost of government mounted and by 1542 had reached £11,900 a year, of which less than £4,900 was found from the Irish revenues, principally ex-monastic lands and those forfeited by Kildare, leaving £7,000 to be supplied from England.[67] And in the years following the Irish revenue did not even expand in line with inflation. In the ten-and-a-half years to Michaelmas 1565, for example, the Irish revenues yielded on average less than £4,400 per annum, and there was a continuing tendency towards decline even in nominal terms.[68] An important reason for the stagnation of the revenue at this time was the failure of the parliamentary subsidy to expand from its pre-1534 level. Although in the later 1540s its yield rose to *c.*£750 per annum, this was only achieved by extending its incidence to the counties beyond the Pale, and thereafter the decline was fairly continuous. In Elizabeth's early years, for example, the subsidy was worth barely £300 a year.[69] The full implications of this development became apparent after Henry VIII's death.

In other respects too, neither the king nor his Irish subjects had reason to be satisfied with parliament's role in government. The history of Henry VIII's last two parliaments is too well known to require more than a few words here, but it has perhaps been too readily assumed that the opposition which emerged in the exceptionally well-documented Irish Reformation Parliament was without precedent.[70] On that occasion, it has been suggested, opposition was directed principally against a series of financial measures which threatened to increase the independence of the English governor and garrison and so to undermine the traditional role in government of the local community.[71] It is true that the Reformation and the governmental changes carried out in the aftermath of the 1534 rebellion introduced an important new dimension into Anglo-Irish politics but the discrepancies between the number of bills on transmisses for earlier parliaments and the acts on the respective statute rolls seem significant in this context. The parliaments of 1508-9, 1521-2 and 1531 apparently rejected far more bills than they passed, and it was the financial measures introduced by English-born governors which seem to have suffered most. The earl of Surrey failed in a bid to secure a royal salt monopoly and an act of resumption, and Sir William Skeffington was denied even a grant of subsidy and had to fall back on the much less satisfactory expedient of levying a scutage.[72]

In the circumstances the king can hardly have relished the prospect of regular parliaments, but down to 1534 seemingly the only alternative was to subsidize government there, which was even less acceptable. Nor were these parliaments very fruitful for the subject. The four parliaments of 1508-9, 1521-2, 1531 and 1533 passed about thirteen bills in all. Very probably the old saying to which a member alluded in the 1613-15 parliament—'Little said soon amended, a subsidy granted the parliament ended'—originated in this period.[73] Certainly it must have reflected all too closely the experience of members then.

Nevertheless the king persevered and in 1536-7 the need to enact for Ireland the measures of the English Reformation Parliament generated a legislative programme which was more important even than that of Poynings' parliament. At one stage the government was in serious danger of losing much of its programme, but a compromise was eventually agreed upon. The king obtained the consent of the lordship's political community to the main tenets of the Henrician Reformation and he also secured valuable new sources of revenue including some secular sources, although not all that had been demanded: in return the community secured indemnity for participation in the Kildare rebellion and, mainly by virtue of the suspension of Poynings' Law, sixteen of the 42 statutes were primarily aimed at promoting the common weal or gratifying particular interests.[74] In the 1541-3 parliament no less than nineteen of the 28 acts may be placed in this category, and parliament was seemingly concluded without any serious conflicts arising, although it is significant that no financial demands were made beyond the renewal of the subsidy.[75] In other respects too the two parliaments seem to mark a reversion to Yorkist practice. In 1536-7 nine sessions were held lasting 21 weeks in all, and in 1541-3 eight sessions of ten weeks altogether, and these included sessions at Kilkenny, Cashel and Limerick in 1536 and at Limerick and Trim in 1542.[76] Even though this has left no trace on the statute rolls, it would seem that a determined effort was being made to involve as many magnates as possible in the business of parliament and to utilise parliament's potential as a tribunal for the composition of feuds and disputes between them.[77]

In contrast, only four parliaments met between 1543 and 1613 and only the 1569-71 parliament passed a reasonable tally of acts—30 in all.[78] Those of 1557-8 and 1560 were called primarily to settle religion and did little else;[79] deadlock in the 1569-71 parliament was broken only when some opposition leaders switched their opposition to the battlefield and in 1585-6 the government lost its chief bills.[81] In fact under Elizabeth some of the expedients suggested or employed to secure acceptance of government policies sound distinctly ominous. The commons was packed with non-resident and unrepresentative Englishmen, despite the statutory obligation of residence which in Ireland had been confirmed in 1542, probably to prevent this.[82] For the 1560 parliament the government proposed to create new peers for the duration of parliament or for life and to summon opponents to court;[83] when it met the bills were passed and parliament dissolved within three weeks despite strong opposition to the religious bills; and subsequently it was claimed that they had passed on a date when opponents had previously been told that there would be no meeting.[84] Other measures were enforced without reference to parliament—the establishment of regional councils in 1569-70 for instance, and the related attempt to suppress the palatinates of Tipperary and Kerry.[85] The government was quick to resort to martial law to quell disorders, and not only in the face of rebellion.[86] And when in 1586 two acts of attainder were passed in the aftermath of the Desmond rebellion their terms were draconian by comparison with earlier attainders. Thirty-seven gentry supporters in the five south–western counties were attainted with the earl for 'many detestable and abominable treasons' committed, 'some of them by open rebellion in divers parts of your Majesties realm of Ireland, and the others, by sundrie confederacies and conspiracies, and other overt facts' yet some had received no trial by common or martial law. The second attainder, against a further 102 gentlemen of the same counties and similarly framed, also included all their unidentified associates.[87]

These developments betrayed a breakdown of consensus between crown and community. Indirectly this development should probably be linked with the revolution carried out in England in the 1530s, although it was a far from inevitable consequence. The establishment of the supremacy of the king in parliament and the vast expansion in the scope of parliament's legislative activity which this involved subjected to increasing pressure the traditional arrangements for the maintenance of both a separate parliament in Ireland and a common law. Yet, as Professor R. Dudley Edwards has argued, from the 1530s 'the Tudor government regarded parliament in Ireland as a means of securing a public endorsement for a policy already approved in England, and already operating in Ireland without reference to any necessity of securing the prior sanction of the Irish parliament'.[88] Even before parliament met in 1536 the Dublin administration had moved to implement the Reformation legislation,[89] and at a time when the extent and importance of legislation were increasing it required not only very careful management but also extreme circumspection on the government's part if this public endorsement were to be obtained by the consent of the community freely given.

It is to Henry's credit that he persisted with this difficult strategy. Even so, he was forced in 1537 to moderate substantially his plans for revenge in the aftermath of the Kildare rebellion in order to retain the support of the Pale gentry both in general and for his parliamentary programme. Without this the crown would have had to pay for a substantial army to maintain his interests there.[90] But whether because he was reluctant to increase still further expenditure on Ireland or because he felt that attempts to coerce the Anglo-Irish political community might have adverse effects on the acceptance of his policies in England, Henry baulked at this alternative. Nevertheless, it is not altogether surprising that his successors tried a different approach. Edward VI's government dispensed with the Irish parliament altogether, relying on the applicability of English legislation to Ireland in order to introduce the Edwardian Reformation by proclamation. Although a licence to hold parliament was issued in 1548 none met and by the time a parliament next sat in Ireland, in 1557, Mary's government had long since restored catholicism by proclamation.[91] Since Henry VIII had claimed that his supremacy was a personal one, there was perhaps more justification for proceeding without reference to parliament in religious matters than in secular,[92] but the contrast with the position in England remains significant. Elizabeth secured parliamentary consent before enforcing ecclesiastical changes in Ireland, but there is a strong suspicion that this consent was not freely given.[93]

Thus at first sight the history of the Irish parliament under the Yorkists and early Tudors appears to provide corroboration for the view that English rule in Ireland was by nature despotic. It seems that the Tudors steadily reduced the initiative and independence of the Irish parliament until under Elizabeth it became largely irrelevant to government. Certainly the frequent clashes in parliament illustrate the difficulties faced by successive governors in managing parliament in accordance with English policies which took little account of problems peculiar to the lordship. In fact, however, these clashes and the changing role of parliament in government constitute evidence of a sustained effort by the crown to adapt existing institutions in order to reach a compromise with the local community which would safeguard both its traditional role in government and the crown's vital interests in Ireland. Yet the government's difficulties were greatly exacerbated by the refusal of the local community to make realistic grants of taxation, especially after 1534, and in the longer term these circumstances contributed to the radical change in policy inaugurated after 1547. Although parliament had met only every five or six years between 1495 and 1547 the evidence about money bills shows that it remained an important instrument through which the local community could exert an often decisive influence on government: thereafter its influence was much reduced and largely negative. It remains to consider why this change came about.

Briefly it happened because the Edwardian government changed its mind about the crown's Irish problem and ceased to regard it as essentially similar to the problems which it faced in governing the north or Wales: instead it embarked on a military solution to the problem. In the fifteenth century, the difficulties of maintaining law and order in a region far from the centre of government had been tackled by the delegation of authority to local nobles, and from the 1470s this strategy was combined with the creation of special governmental structures for the north and the marches of Wales in line with those already established for Ireland and the Principality of Wales.[94] Again in the 1530s, the powers of the local magnates were further curbed, the councils in Ireland, the north and the marches of Wales were reorganized and efforts were made to bring these areas more closely under the control of Westminster.[95] Yet from 1547 a more radical strategy of conquest was adopted for Ireland, entailing greater reliance on military force and also plantation. During the duke of Somerset's protectorate the army there was reinforced, a series of English garrisons was established at Ballyadams in Leix, Daingean in Offaly, Nenagh, Athlone and Leighlin Bridge, two English captains were posted at Newry and in Lecale, and the first tentative steps were taken towards the plantation of Leix and Offaly.[96] Of course none of these steps was entirely unprecedented: since 1534 the govenor had had a permanent retinue of English troops at his disposal, plantations had frequently been suggested as a means of extending and strengthening the Pale, and garrisons had occasionally been left for a time in forts captured from Gaelic chiefs.[97] Moreover, Henry VIII and the privy council had of late come to accept that the difficulties of controlling the English districts stemmed in large measure from the survival of an independent Gaelic polity beyond, which had hitherto been largely ignored.[98] Thus the government's conception of the problem as a whole was changing. Nevertheless, the decisive event was the gradual realization by the Edwardian government that the traditional restraints on policy-making which had been imposed by the need to obtain the consent of the Anglo-Irish community did not necessarily apply. This greatly widened the range of options available and allowed the government to work out a new solution to the problem.

With regard to Edward VI's reign, it is highly relevant that Protector Somerset broke generally with traditional crown policy and made the solution of the Scottish problem his top priority. On the basis of the English crown's ancient claim to suzerainty over the Scottish kingdom and in pursuit of its dynastic desire to take complete possession of that realm, Somerset resumed Henry VIII's Scottish war: but relying on his previous military experiences there he now sought to control the country by the more costly strategy of garrisons throughout lowland Scotland where the old king had relied principally on periodic, large-scale military expeditions to chastise the Scots.[99] In Ireland too the government was prepared to pay for results and a soldier-administrator and privy councillor was appointed to apply a military solution to the similar problem posed by Gaelic Ireland.[100] In both regions, therefore, previous policies of peaceful coexistence or incorporation by consent were abandoned in favour of more coercive methods. In Scotland the new strategy was rendered futile by the arrival of a French army and much later the problem was solved by the union of the two crowns, but in Ireland the government decided that the augmentation of the army from 500 to 2,000 men gave it a new freedom of manoeuvre in its dealings both with the Gaelic Irish and the king's subjects there. This evidently outweighed earlier financial considerations and any additional benefits to be gained through the whole-hearted support of the Anglo-Irish community. Thus the question of the crown's relations with the latter gradually became subordinated to the problem of Gaelic Ireland, whereas in England the problem of the north and that of Scotland, though interacting on one other, were kept largely separate.[101]

From 1547, therefore, Tudor policy in Ireland was frequently pursued without reference to the wishes of the king's subjects there and the way was open for military conquest and colonization on a scale which would otherwise have been impossible. The growing contrast between government in England and Ireland is therefore very instructive concerning the more general problem of the rule of law in the Tudor state. Indeed, in certain respects government in Tudor Ireland seems to follow a pattern which is more familiar to continental historians of the sixteenth century—the growing infrequency of parliament, the establishment of a standing army, and the building up of financial resources which, if rarely adequate for the policies which successive governors wished to pursue, were largely independent of taxation granted by parliament.[102]

Although from 1534 a permanent English garrison had been maintained in Ireland, until 1547 it rarely exceeded 500 men, and this was little larger than the private army which the earl of Kildare had previously kept for the defence of the Pale. Under Edward VI, however, the garrison was increased to 800 men in July 1547 and to 2,134 English troops plus 484 Irish by May 1551; it was reduced to 2,024 in October 1551 and to 1,060 late in 1553, but by 1558 it again exceeded 2,000 men and rarely fell below 1,500 throughout the 1560s.[103] With a force of 1,500 men or more, the government was much less reliant on the support of the local community, particularly if the troops were quartered in or around the Pale.

Moreover, the increase in the size of the garrison was accompanied by a vast extension in a series of military exactions which both undermined the ability of the population to pay increased taxation in parliament and lessened the government's dependence on this. Purveyance, or cess as it was known in Ireland, was levied for the provisioning not only of the governor's household but of his retinue too; the duty of able-bodied men between the ages of 16 and 60 to serve in the defence of their country was extended so that the governor by advice of an afforced council could compel inhabitants to serve without payment in hostings upon the king's enemies for up to forty days two or three times a year, or exact a fine in lieu; he could likewise compel them to provide carts to carry provisions, or labourers for building projects connected with defence; and at need he could quarter Irish troops on the marches for defence.[104] These exactions had originated in the circumstances of the medieval lordship when successive governors had faced a growing problem of defence with less than adequate financial and military resources. Despite occasional disputes about them,[106] in general they had allowed a more flexible and economical approach to governmental problems which benefited both crown and subject. After 1534, however, the increasing commutation of these services and their more systematic exploitation began to challenge the principle of consent to taxation. Holdings of kerne and galloglass on the Pale became more frequent in the 1540s. In November 1546, for example, the five counties of the Pale contributed £306 13s. 4d. towards the wages of 400 galloglass for six weeks.[107] In 1543 the military service of seven counties for a general hosting was for the first time commuted for £971 15s. to allow the government to pay 420 kerne for three months, and the cartage owing from two more counties was commuted for a further £496; in 1547 the cartage for the Pale was commuted for £695 1s. 4d.; and in 1554 the entire hosting was commuted to finance an expedition to Limerick.[108] Purveyance was put on a more regular footing under Lord Deputy Bellingham (1548–9) when the system of garrisons was established and the army increased. In October 1549, 10,720 pecks of wheat and malt and 2,120 cattle were purveyed for the provisioning of Fort Protector in Leix and fixed prices were agreed.[109] Initially it was the increased incidence of purveyance to feed an enlarged army which caused friction. The garrison in Fort Protector was 300 strong but corn and cattle sufficient for 1,000 men for a year were purveyed, though until 1566 the annual levies made about Michaelmas were rather under the levels of 1549.[110] In the 1550s, however, the queen's price for victual began to lag behind the market price even in years of reasonable harvest and by 1566, when the levy was substantially increased to feed a larger army, the government in effect admitted this by allowing counties to compound for their corn quotas at rates which indicate that this aspect of purveyance was then worth £1,950 per annum to the government.[111]

In these circumstances the government could obtain far more by the systematic extension of what amounted to a system of military taxation than was grudgingly granted by parliament. Moreover, with an army of 1,500 men in pay there was no immediate possibility of achieving financial self-sufficiency, and the moneys available through increased taxation fell far short of the overall deficit which had to be met by English subventions. Between April 1555 and Michaelmas 1565, for example, expenditure on Ireland averaged £24,326 st. per annum, of which £21,413 st. had to be sent over from England:[112] this meant that government policy was tailored primarily to interests at court rather than the interests of the local community. The Palesmen at least saw the implications of all this and pleaded for the appointment of a governor who would defer to their interests and reduce the garrison.[113] Purveyance caused great resentment and when, in 1577, the governor tried to enforce a general composition instead, the Palesmen argued that purveyance was illegal because 'all the lawes for purveyors in England were lawes in this land' and 'without parliament or graund counsell ther cold be noe imposition layd uppon the subjecte'.[114] The Irish council replied that purveyance was a royal prerogative but supported its argument with misleading citations of medieval great council rolls and levies of scutage, plus some more apposite and recent precedents from Lord Deputy Bellingham's time.[115] By 1577, however, the custom was well established and the government was in no mood to relinquish its ill-gotten gains. It is true that purveyance was usually authorized by a great council, but this was only the privy council well-stocked with unrepresentative English-born officials and afforced by such nobles as the governor chose to summon, not the representative great council of the medieval lordship, and it is doubtful whether its consent was more than a formality.[116]

By 1547, therefore, the benefit to the crown of regular meetings of the Irish parliament had been substantially eroded and this facilitated the pronounced shift towards more coercive methods of government from 1547. Nevertheless, had the Irish parliament countenanced a realistic level of taxation in Henry VIII's later years when there was some possibility of making a revitalized Dublin administration financially self-sufficient, the temptation to extract the money willy-nilly by extra-parliamentary methods would probably have been resisted. That in 1536 and 1541 parliaments were called to discuss important legislative programmes and again used to promote unity and cooperation from the magnates shows that Henry VIII was fully aware of parliament's potential role in government. Though Poynings' Law had been necessary to safeguard royal control, it does not follow that the cumbersome procedure prescribed for holding parliament was intended to restrict its role merely to the ratification of pre-existing measures. Rather parliament was looked upon, in Ireland too, as a forum in which the interests of crown and subject could be harmonized. Yet the consensus which was apparently achieved in 1494, and intermittently down to 1543, eventually broke down. Perhaps this was partly because in the Reformation crisis the difficult task of securing change by consent required a more pliable instrument than Poynings' Law, but it was clearly also because the representatives of the local community were less than generous in meeting the needs of the crown. In these circumstances the crown began to see the Irish parliament less as an instrument of policy than as a vexatious and largely superfluous tribunal. And in Ireland certain weaknesses and ambiguities in the constitutional position of parliament could be exploited to circumvent it. Thus the shift towards more coercive forms of government lends no real support to the view that Tudor rule in Ireland had always been potentially despotic, rather circumstances largely accidental—the need for a standing army and the comparatively small value of parliamentary taxation to the government—suggested a possible alternative method of rule which was not generally applicable in England, and local intransigence provided the spur to use it. Thus if post-Henrician Ireland provides an exception to the rule of law in the Tudor state, an examination of the circumstances surrounding the creation of this exception also provides a useful illustration of why this remained no more than an exception.

Notes

1. See Penry Williams, 'The Tudor state' in *Past and Present*, no. 25 (July 1963), pp 39–41 and the references there cited.
2. Cf. G. R. Elton, 'Tudor government: the points of contact: I. Parliament', in *R. Hist. Soc. Trans.*, 5th ser., xxiv (1974), pp 183–200.
3. Art Cosgrove, 'A century of decline' in Brian Farrell (ed.), *The Irish parliamentary tradition* (Dublin, 1973), ch. 4; T. W. Moody, 'The Irish parliament

under Elizabeth and James I: a general survey' in *R.I.A. Proc.*, xlv (1939), sect. C, pp 42–9.

4. For example, J. F. Lydon, *The lordship of Ireland in the middle ages* (Dublin, 1972), pp 262–5; R. D. Edwards, 'The Irish Reformation Parliament of Henry VIII, 1536–7' in *Hist. St.*, vi (London, 1968), pp 59–84, esp. pp 79–80.

5. Richardson & Sayles, *Ir. parl. in middle ages*, pp 61–2, 248–51, 260.

6. Sir John Davies, *Historical tracts* (Dublin, 1787), pp 297–8.

7. No meaningful distinction was made in the Irish parliaments of this period between sittings after an adjournment and after a prorogation: see D. B. Quinn, 'Parliaments and great councils in Ireland, 1461–1586' in *I.H.S.*, iii (1942–3), p. 62. Only three parliament rolls from before 1447 were extant in 1922 and these did not include private bills which had been recorded among the chancery warrants: Richardson & Sayles, *Ir. parl. in middle ages*, pp 198–9.

8. Parliament rolls, 29 Henry VI c. 5, 34 Henry VI c. 6 (*Stat. Ire., Hen. VI*, pp 258, 354).

9. *Stat. Ire., Hen. VI*, passim; *Stat. Ire., Edw. IV*, i, ii, passim.

10. *New hist. Ire.*, ix; F. M. Powicke & E. B. Fryde (ed.) *Handbook of British chronology* (2nd ed., London, 1961), pp 532–4.

11. *Ir. parl. in middle ages*, ch. 14.

12. De Banco rolls, Hilary 1 Henry V (P.R.O.I., CB 1/5), Michaelmas 32 Henry VI (P.R.O.I., Ferguson coll., iii, ff 199–203v); Coram Rege roll, 1 Henry VII (P.R.O.I., RC 8/43, pp 1–47). Cf. G. J. Hand, *English law in Ireland 1290–1324* (Cambridge, 1967), pp 40–103, 233–46.

13. Cf. Margaret Hastings, *The court of common pleas in fifteenth century England* (Cornell, 1947); Marjorie Blatcher, *The court of king's bench 1450–1550* (London, 1978).

14. Cf. Richardson & Sayles, *Ir. parl. in middle ages*, pp 174–5, 196–7.

15. *Stat. Ire., 1–12 Edw. IV*, 650ff, *12–22 Edw. IV*, passim, Cf. *Ir. parl. in middle ages*, pp 215–21.

16. Ibid., pp 215–24.

17. Ibid., pp 174–5, 254–5. Richardson and Sayles (cf. pp 174–5) have over-estimated the element of continuity in parliament's administrative and judicial development in the fifteenth century at the expense of change under Edward IV.

18. For example, Parliament rolls, 11 & 12 Edward IV c. 78, 15 & 16 Edward IV c. 37 (*Stat. Ire., 1–12 Edw. IV*, 868–70, *12–22 Edw. IV*, 338–40), 1 Richard III c. 16 (P.R.O.I., RC 13/8).

19. *Ir. parl. in middle ages*, p. 257.

20. Ibid., p. 199.

21. Parliament roll, 28 Henry VI c. 6 (*Stat. Ire., Hen. VI*, p. 169). Cf. W. S. Holdsworth, *A history of English law*, i (7th rev. ed., London, 1956), 53*–7*.

22. See especially, M. C. Griffith, 'The Talbot–Ormond struggle for control of the Anglo-Irish government, 1414–47' in *I.H.S.*, ii (1940–41), pp 376–97. Cf. *Ir. parl. in middle ages*, pp 171–2.

23. Calculated from *Stat. Ire., 1–12 Edw. IV*, and *12–22 Edw. IV*. I am aware that the provenance of statutes cannot reliably be identified merely from their wording, but in default of other evidence this method is of value as a rough guide.

24. Parliament rolls, 10 Edward IV c. 10, 11 & 12 Edward IV c. 17 (*Stat. Ire., 1–12 Edw. IV*, 656–60, 746–50); S. G. Ellis, 'The struggle for control of the Irish mint, 1460–c. 1506' in *R.I.A. Proc.*, lxxviii (1978), sect. C, pp 17–36.

25. Parliament roll, 12 & 13 Edward IV c. 45 (*Stat. Ire., 12–22 Edw. IV*, 98–100); Coram Rege roll, 13 Edward IV (T.C.D., MS 1731, p. 6); *Stat. Ire., Hen. VII & VIII*, pp 113, 115. For examples of prosecutions under the statute, see Memoranda rolls, 23 Henry VII m. 17 (P.R.O.I., RC 8/43, pp 245–6), 19 Henry VIII m. 16d (P.R.O.I., Ferguson coll., iv, f. 126). Cf. *Ir. parl. in middle ages*, pp 225–6.

26. B.L., Royal MS 18C, XIV, f. 108 (see below, note 61); *Ir. parl. in middle ages*, pp 154–8, 238–43; S. G. Ellis, 'Taxation and defence in late medieval Ireland: the survival of scutage' in *R.S.A.I. Jn.*, cvii (1977), pp 11–18.

27. Parliament roll, 19 & 20 Edward IV c. 20 (*Stat. Ire., 12–22 Edw. IV*, 728–30).

28. The rolls of 3, 11 & 12, and 18 (I) Edward IV were frequently so marked: *Stat. Ire., Edw. IV*, passim.

29. Calculated from *Stat. Ire., Edw. IV,*; Parliament rolls, 1, and 2 & 3 Richard III (P.R.O.I., RC 13/8; P.R.O.I., transcript), 8 Henry VII (P.R.O.I., RC 13/9).

30. For example, H. G. Richardson, 'The Irish parliament rolls of the fifteenth century' in *E.H.R.*, lviii (1943), p. 457; *Ir. parl. in middle ages*, pp 179–81.

31. Ibid., ch. 10.

32. Close roll, 10–15 Henry VII art. 46 (B.L., Add. MS 4797, ff 109v–10, printed with commentary in *Galvia*, xiii (1981), pp 56–62); *Cal. pat. rolls, 1494–1509*, pp 12, 62; *Ir. parl. in middle ages*, ch. 10 esp. pp 143–4 and note 50.

33. *Handbook Brit. chron.*, p. 326.

34. Cf. *Ir. parl. in middle ages*, pp 183–6. A statute of 1537 denied the claim of the proctors to a voice in parliament, but a subsidy commission of Mary's reign mentions them as assenting to its levy (T.C.D., MS 588, f. 174); Statute roll, 28 & 29 Henry VIII c.M(P.R.O.I., CH 1/1). This would tend to support the suggestion of R. D. Edwards (*Church and state in Tudor Ireland*, Dublin, 1935, p. 180 n. 2) that the proctors continued to sit after 1537.

35. *Rot. pat. Hib.*, p. 265 no. 13; *L. & P. Ric. III & Hen. VII*, i, 377–82.

36. *Ir. parl. in middle ages*, ch. 17.

37. See the table in *New hist. Ire.*, ix.

38. Cf. Richardson, 'Irish parliament rolls', pp 448–50; *Stat. Ire., Hen. VII & VIII*, pp 73–4.

39. J. D'Alton, *The history of the county of Dublin* (Dublin, 1838), p. 577 (quoting an inquisition of 1613); *Cal. pat. rolls Ire., Hen. VIII–Eliz.*, pp 71–2; N.L.I., D.2349 (*Ormond deeds, 1509–47*, no. 261); Brendan Bradshaw, *The Irish constitutional revolution of the sixteenth century* (Cambridge, 1979), pp 238–42. Cf. *Fiants Ire., Hen. VIII*, no. 264; D. B. Quinn, 'The early interpretation of Poynings' Law, 1494–1534' in *I.H.S.*, ii (1940–41), pp 252–3.

40. *Stat. Ire., Hen. VII & VIII*, pp 104, 108, 116, 123.

41. See S. G. Ellis, 'Henry VII and Ireland, 1491–6' in James Lydon (ed.), *England and Ireland in the later middle ages* (Dublin, 1981), pp 248–9.

42. Cf. Elton, 'Tudor government: parliament', pp 183–200.

43. C. A. Empey & K. Simms, 'The ordinances of the White Earl and the problem of coign in the later middle ages' in *R.I.A. Proc.*, lxxv (1975), pp 162–78; *Liber primus Kilkenn.*, pp 156–60; Patent roll, 14 Henry VII (P.R.O.I., Lodge MS 'Articles', i, f. 221); Hore, *Southern & eastern counties*, p. 164.

44. Cf. Empey & Simms, loc. cit., pp 163, 172 n.51.

45. *Ir. parl. in middle ages*, pp 92–3, ch. 16.

46. Lydon, *Lordship*, pp 263–5. Cf. William Molyneux, *The case of Ireland stated* (ed. J. G. Simms, Dublin, 1977), pp 62–7.

47. For example, Lydon, *Lordship*, pp 263–5.

48. P.R.O., C.47/10/29, printed in Donough Bryan, *The Great Earl of Kildare* (Dublin, 1933), p. 22.
49. Statute roll, 10 Henry VII cc 7, 39 (*Stat. Ire.*, i, 43–4, 56–7); Richardson & Sayles, *Ir. parl. in middle ages*, pp 266, 273–4 (quotation at p. 273); Lydon, *Lordship*, p. 265.
50. See Molyneux, *Case of Ireland*, pp 7–14.
51. The quotation in Lydon, *Lordship*, p. 265 is in fact from Edmund Curtis, 'The acts of the Drogheda parliament, 1494–5, or "Poynings' Laws"' in Agnes Conway, *Henry VII's relations with Scotland and Ireland, 1485–98* (Cambridge, 1932), p. 129, not from the statute.
52. Memoranda rolls, 17 Henry VIII m. 19, 23 Henry VIII m. 26 (P.R.O.I., Ferguson coll., iv, ff 106, 158). Cf. J. M. W. Bean, *The decline of English feudalism, 1215–1540* (Manchester, 1968), p. 146 and note.
53. *Rot. parl.* (6 vols., London, 1761–83), vi, 481–2; *Stat. of realm*, 26 Henry VIII c. 25, 28 Henry VIII c. 18. See also S. G. Ellis, 'Henry VIII, rebellion and the rule of law' in *Hist. Jn.*, xxiv (1981), pp 513–31.
54. *Ir. parl. in middle ages*, pp 263–8.
55. P.R.O., S.P.65/1/2; *Alen's reg.*, pp 286, 307–12; *Cal. close rolls, 1500–09*, no. 243; *L. & P. Ric. III & Hen. VII*, i, 75; *L. & P. Hen. VIII*, i (1st ed.), nos. 1299, 4254, ii, no. 1277, iv, no. 6135 (26); *Gormanston reg.*, pp 87–110, 165–8; Parliament rolls, 16 & 17 Edward IV c. 8, 19 & 20 Edward IV c. 50 (*Stat. Ire., 12–22 Edw. IV*, 468, 812); J. A. Guy, *The Cardinal's court* (Hassocks, 1977), pp 128–30; Gearóid Mac Niocaill, *Na Buirgéisí* (2 vols., Dublin, 1964), ii, 485–6n; S. G. Ellis, 'Thomas Cromwell and Ireland, 1532–40' in *Hist. Jn.*, xxiii (1980), p. 508.
56. E.g. Otway-Ruthven, *Med. Ire.*, chs. 3, 5.
57. See V. W. Treadwell, 'The Irish customs administration in the sixteenth century' in *I.H.S.*, xx (1976–7), pp 387–8; S. G. Ellis, 'The Irish customs administration under the early Tudors' in *I.H.S.*, xxii (1980–81), pp 271–7. Cf. G. R. Elton, *The Tudor constitution* (Cambridge, 1960), pp 39–40.
58. Cf. D. B. Quinn, 'The Irish parliamentary subsidy in the fifteenth and sixteenth centuries' in *R.I.A. Proc.*, xlii (1935), sect. C, pp 220–21, 231; *Ir. parl. in middle ages*, pp 238–43.
59. Ellis, 'Taxation and defence', pp 5–28.
60. *Ir. parl. in middle ages*, pp 228–9.
61. B.L., Royal MS 18C, XIV, ff 105–5v; Parliament roll, 16 & 17 Edward IV cc 4, 45. These documents and the changes in the parliamentary subsidy in the later fifteenth century are discussed in S. G. Ellis, 'The administration of the lordship of Ireland under the early Tudors' (unpublished Ph.D. thesis, Belfast, 1979), ch. 2, app. iii. Except where otherwise stated, moneys are given in pounds Irish. At this date, IR£1 = 1 mark st.
62. Close roll, 19 Edward IV m. 7d (Gilbert, *Viceroys*, p. 599; *P.R.I. rep. D.K. 57*, p. 569).
63. Parliament roll, 2 & 3 Richard III c. 17 (P.R.O.I., transcript). Cf. B.L., Royal MS 18C, XIV, ff 105–5v, 107v.
64. Ellis, 'Henry VII and Ireland', p. 244.
65. *Stat. Ire., Hen. VII & VIII*, p. 110; Pipe roll, 18 Henry VII (N.L.I., MS 761, pp 327–39); *S.P. Hen. VIII*, ii, 78; P.R.O., E. 101/248/21, S.P. 65/1/2; Quinn, *Guide finan. rec.*, pp 17–27; 'Irish parliamentary subsidy', pp 230–31.
66. Ellis, 'Thomas Cromwell and Ireland', pp 507–17.
67. B.L., Add. MS 4767, f. 71; ibid., pp 508, 515, 517.

68. *Cal. Carew MSS 1515–74*, no. 250; N. P. Canny, *The Elizabethan conquest of Ireland* (Hassocks, 1976), p. 37.
69. Quinn, 'Irish parliamentary subsidy', p. 231.
70. Cf. Edwards, 'Irish Reformation Parliament', p. 80; Brendan Bradshaw, 'The beginnings of modern Ireland' in Brian Farrell (ed.), *The Irish parliamentary tradition* (Dublin, 1973), pp 72–5.
71. Brendan Bradshaw, 'The opposition to the ecclesiastical legislation in the Irish Reformation Parliament' in *I.H.S.*, xvi (1968–9), pp 285–303; *The dissolution of the religious orders in Ireland under Henry VIII* (Cambridge, 1974), pp 47–65.
72. *Stat. Ire., Hen. VII & VIII*, pp 96–138 passim; S. G. Ellis, 'Parliaments and great councils, 1483–99: addenda et corrigenda' in *Anal. Hib.*, xxix (1980), pp 110–11; Quinn, 'Early interpretation of Poynings' Law', pp 250–51; Ellis, 'Taxation and defence', pp 9–11.
73. *Stat. Ire., Hen. VII & VII*, pp 108–38 passim; Moody, 'Irish parliament under Elizabeth and James I', p. 61.
74. Edwards, 'Irish Reformation Parliament', pp 59–80; Bradshaw, 'Opposition to the ecclesiastical legislation in the Irish Reformation Parliament', pp 285–303.
75. *Stat. Ire., Hen. VII & VIII*, pp 157–69; Bradshaw, *Irish constitutional revolution*, pp 238–42, 252–3.
76. *New hist. Ire.*, ix.
77. Bradshaw, op. cit., pp 238–42; above, p. 46.
78. V. W. Treadwell, 'The Irish parliament of 1569–71' in *R.I.A. Proc.*, lxv (1966), sect. C, pp 55–89.
79. *Stat. Ire.*, i, 239–312.
80. Treadwell, loc. cit., p. 75.
81. Moody, 'Irish parliament under Elizabeth and James I', pp 47–8.
82. Treadwell, 'Irish parliament of 1569–71', p. 68; J. Hardiman (ed.), 'Statutes of Kilkenny' in *Tracts relating to Ireland*, ii (Dublin, 1842), app. 2–3.
83. *H.M.C., Cecil MSS*, iii, 459–60 (misdated, r. 1559).
84. Edwards, *Church and state in Tudor Ireland*, pp 178–80; *New hist. Ire.*, ix.
85. Canny, *Elizabethan conquest*, pp 99–100.
86. *Proc. privy council, Ire., 1556–71*, p. 137. The comparison between the English and Irish parliaments might usefully be extended by examining the extent to which proclamations and judge-made law undermined the role of parliament in Ireland.
87. Statute roll, 28 Elizabeth cc 4, 5 (*Stat. Ire.*, i, 418–28).
88. Edwards, 'Irish Reformation Parliament', p. 64.
89. *S.P. Hen. VIII*, ii, 215; Gwynn, *Med. province Armagh*, p. 211; Edwards, 'Irish Reformation Parliament', p. 64.
90. Ellis, 'Henry VIII, rebellion and the rule of law', pp 523–4.
91. Edwards, *Church and state*, pp 126, 160, 165.
92. Elton, *Tudor constitution*, pp 333–5.
93. Edwards, *Church and state*, pp 173–81.
94. For example, R. R. Reid, *The king's council in the north* (London, 1921), pt. i; Penry Williams, *The council in the marches of Wales under Elizabeth I* (Cardiff, 1958), ch. 1; R. A. Griffiths, *The principality of Wales in the later middle ages: the structure and personnel of government I. South Wales, 1277–1536* (Cardiff, 1972), pt. i; Ellis, 'Henry VII and Ireland', pp 237–8.
95. G. R. Elton, *Reform and reformation: England 1509–58* (London, 1977), pp 201–20, 271–2.

96. D. G. White, 'The reign of Edward VI in Ireland: some political, social and economic aspects' in *I.H.S.*, xiv (1964–5), pp 199–204.
97. For example, *S.P. Hen. VIII*, ii, 337–40, 350–51.
98. For example, Canny, *Elizabethan conquest*, pp 31–3.
99. For Scotland, see M. L. Bush, *The government policy of Protector Somerset* (London, 1975), ch. 2.
100. White, 'Reign of Edward VI in Ireland', pp 198–9.
101. Below, p. 62; Bush, *Government policy of Protector Somerset*, ch. 2; Reid, *King's council in the north*, pt. ii.
102. Cf. J. Hurstfield, 'Was there a Tudor despotism after all?' in *R. Hist. Soc. Trans.*, 5th ser., xvii (1967), pp 83–108; Williams, 'The Tudor state', pp 39–41.
103. *Cal. S.P. Ire., 1509–73*, pp 132, 137, 143; *Cal. Carew MSS 1515–74*, nos. 214, 220; *Proc. privy council Ire., 1556–71*, p. 281; B.L., Add. MS 4767, ff 71, 80–0v, 114vff; Ellis, 'Thomas Cromwell and Ireland', pp 502, 510, 516.
104. Ellis, 'Taxation and defence', pp 6–8, 18–19; Quinn, 'Irish parliamentary subsidy', p. 225; Parliament roll, 1 Richard III cc 4, 18 (P.R.O.I., RC 13/8).
106. Otway–Ruthven, *Med. Ire.*, p. 299.
107. B.L., Add. MS 4763, f. 230v.
108. Ibid., ff 229v, 231, 233v.
109. Ibid., ff 231v–2. Cf. *Anal. Hib.*, ii, 140–41, 160, 161.
110. *Proc. privy council Ire., 1556–71*, pp 22, 66–8, 73–4, 108–9, 123–4, 125–6, 143, 168–9; Bagwell, *Tudors*, i, 373, 405, ii, 51.
111. Ibid. Cf. N. P. Canny, *The formation of the Old English elite in Ireland* (Dublin, 1975), p. 35, n. 8.
112. *Cal. Carew MSS 1515–74*, no. 250.
113. Canny, *Elizabethan conquest*, pp 36–9.
114. *Anal. Hib.*, ii, 132; D. B. Quinn, 'Calendar of the Irish council book, 1581–6' in *Anal. Hib.*, xxiv (1967), pp 101–2.
115. *Anal. Hib.*, ii, 104–5, 109; Ellis, 'Taxation and defence', pp 18–19.
116. Quinn, loc. cit., p. 101.

The English parliament in the sixteenth century: estates and statutes

G. R. Elton

I have before this attempted to present a general framework for the study of the English parliament in the Tudor century.[1] On this occasion I should therefore like to turn towards the general theme of this book—parliaments and communities—by discussing two things: the manner in which the composition of parliament and its relationship to the whole community were viewed at the time, and the manner in which that community came to regard its acquisition of a supreme lawgiving institution. Everyone agreed that parliament formed the apex of the king's courts: here errors of the other courts could be amended while its own errors were remediable by itself alone. This, no doubt, represents a rather limited lawyer's view, but few except lawyers thought or spoke on such constitutional matters. For that very reason, what those few had to say becomes the more significant. Historians, following a tradition established by the Whig victory of the seventeenth century and impressed by the fact that the meetings of representative assemblies inevitably bring together varied and often rival interests, have habitually concentrated on a political function; to them the parliament has been primarily the embodiment of that 'politic' principle which, as Fortescue explained in the fifteenth century,[2] distinguished the otherwise 'regal' monarchy of England from the purely royal despotism that, rather uncertainly, he discerned in France. Thus its history has been written around the occassional clashes between the crown and other politically influential elements, and this is true of the whole history of the parliament from its beginnings down to, at any rate, the Revolution of 1688. Yet even for so intermittent an institution those clashes were exceptional rather than normal. It should be remarked that, even though one should keep in mind the times between particular parliaments and the advisability of looking at those meetings as particular occasions, there was nevertheless an institution to be called the parliament, continuous in its rights, claims, practices and records, at any rate from 1529 onwards. Since, however, it came into active existence only at the will of the crown, without whose decision to issue the summons it could not even meet, the primary attention given to its constitutional role in limiting the power of the executive must from the start seem misplaced. We therefore need to become clear about two things both of which bear on the constitutional relations between the institution and the monarchy: what were supposed to be the component parts of parliament, and what was at the time thought to be its normal role in the government of England?

Regarding the composition of the parliament, we find a certain fundamental confusion throughout the century which complicates what was yet the main accepted conviction. Earlier ages had entertained no such doubts: to them the parliament was the king's court of which he was, as it were, the president but not a member. Its members, instead, were the 'three estates' of nobility, spirituality and commonalty assembled in two houses, though of the two the upper or house of lords occupied a superior position as the conciliar part of the parliament (a council of the realm), while the lower or house of commons acted as the petitioners on behalf of the realm. The institutional discrepancy between the houses had been in process of disappearing between about 1484 and 1523. During the sittings of the Reformation Parliament (1529–36) a new concept of a high court consisting of three parts equally participant in its work—king, lords and commons—began to gain general currency. It was adumbrated quite unselfconsciously by Christopher St German in 1531, stated plainly in the Dispensations Act of 1534, and endorsed by Henry VIII in 1542 when he described a parliament in which he as head and the houses as members formed one 'body politic'.[3] This doctrine, which placed the king inside the parliament, was accepted by Sir Thomas Smith when he defined the institution as embodying the realm in time of peace and as consisting of the prince, the 'barony', the commonalty and the bishops, though he left some room for debate because he seemed to hint at a structure by estates rather than houses.[4] Smith's opinion had something authoritative about it, not only because he was an experienced member of several governments but also because even the office of the secretary of state regarded his treatise as the best guide to the English constitution.[5] It is important to note that his remarks about parliament were written in the early 1560s and thus described practice and concepts as they stood at the beginning of Elizabeth's reign at the latest.[6] By 1559, the best opinion held that in England the supreme lawmaking power was vested in 'the king in parliament'.

However, as Smith's choice of words indicates, some room remained for uncertainty. The older concept, which separated the monarch from the parliament, could still crop up, especially when the misleading notion intervened which viewed the parliament as composed of estates. In England, the medieval concept of the three estates had always been better suited to political and social theory than to institutional analysis. After all, while one might just possibly regard the king, in his capacity as a corporation sole, as an estate, this was not the usual meaning of the word; and neither house of parliament fitted the estates terminology at all. The lords spiritual presented there no separate existence; they were only members of one constituent part of parliament and were held to sit there, being summoned individually by the crown, as tenants-in-chief, not as members of the spiritual estate. The lords temporal did even worse because, according to the doctrine of estates, they should have included not only the peerage but also the knights: thus they appeared to be distributed between two houses. And the commons of the realm, the conventional third estate, even if one were to allow citizens and burgesses in parliament (who in personal status often belonged to the lesser nobility) to represent them, shared a house with the knights for the shires, very definitely by convention regarded as noble rather than common. The truth, of course, was that since at the latest the reign of Edward II the English parliament had never owed anything to any attempt to gather together a representation of the estates, so that the use of the term produced only mental and verbal confusion; but used it was nevertheless, with the result, among other things, that the medieval definition which treated the prince as separate from the parliament could survive. But it should be recognized that this survival was unreal and that the true doctrine looked upon him as a member of the parliamentary trinity.

Not surprisingly, princes themselves were liable to use language which could mislead. Thus Queen Elizabeth, right at the start of her reign, signed a proclamation which asked the realm to postpone religious innovation 'until consultation may be had by parliament, by her majesty and her three estates of this realm';[7] and when James I informed the nation of the Gunpowder Plot he declared that the plotters had meant to blow up 'us, our children, and all three estates in parliament assembled'.[8] William Harrison, who did not respect monarchy all that highly, noted that the law governing the ordination of ministers was made 'by the three estates of the realm in the high court of parliament' and later defined this court in such a way as to make it plain that to him the king was not one of the estates, namely as consisting of 'several sort of people, that is to say, the nobility, clergy and commons of this realm'—good old-fashioned estates doctrine.[9] Up to a point this view later received the favourable support of John Selden who in one of his *obiter dicta* declared that 'the king is not one of the three estates, as some would have it (take heed of that!), for if two agree the third is involved: but he is king of the three estates'.[10] Just what he meant by this is far from clear, for he cannot have supposed either that an agreement between his three estates in parliament bound the king to consent (which would have denied the power of the veto) or that the king took no share in the decisions of the parliament. Perhaps he had in mind that the king must not be bound by a majority decision which yet would exist if the three estates included him; perhaps—since he does not mention it—he was not thinking of the parliament at all and preferred to use the estates terminology for its original, non-parliamentary, purposes. If so, he helped to lead others away from an identification of the elements of parliament with the three estates, an identification which, however unsatisfactory to a scholar, had great use in clarifying the nature of the parliament and its powers. The revolution of the mid-century, when parliament had by stages dispensed with two of its three 'estates', inclined some people against any teaching which failed to raise the king above any of his subjects, even in parliament, a change of mind from Tudor practice—and indeed from Charles I's famous declaration in 1642[11]—which was fully espoused by so careful a lawyer as Sir Matthew Hale. Writing after the restoration of the monarchy, Hale expressly denied that the king was one of the estates of the realm and spoke of 'the "three estates of the realm" assembled in parliament, viz. the lords spiritual, lords temporal and commons'.[12] But Hale's confidence covered up a very dubious argument. For his first point he cited no evidence later than 1484, which meant that he simply ignored the drastic change which had come over the definition of parliament from about 1530 onwards—thus proving himself a sort of medievaliser common among seventeenth-century lawyers (and twentieth-century historians). His second point he claimed to prove by reference to Elizabeth's Act of Supremacy in which, according to him, the three estates had recognized the queen's title, but what 1 Elizabeth I, c.1, actually says is 'your faithful and obedient subjects, the lords spiritual and temporal, and the commons in your present parliament assembled', which was the conventional description of the two houses and had nothing to do with any three estates. It was Hale who by inserting a second 'lords' before 'spiritual' managed to create the semblance of an estates structure.

In fact, those of the queen's faithful subjects who looked at reality knew better than to set her apart from the parliament or to confuse the truth—three partners in the parliament—with the fiction, a parliament of estates. That the parliament consisted of queen, lords and commons conjoined, to cite Henry VIII, in one body politic, was the view of Lord Burghley who sat in and supervised probably more parliaments than any man before the eighteenth century.[13] Arthur Hall, member for Grantham, trouble-maker in the sessions of 1576 and 1581, quarrelled violently with Sir Walter Mildmay, chancellor of the exchequer, over the antiquity of parliament, but both men firmly agreed on this definition of the parliament, as did William Lambarde.[14] All these four also demonstrated how quickly realism could absorb the fiction when they applied the term 'the three estates' to prince, lords and commons—of which estates, as Burghley put it, 'consisteth the whole body of the parliament able to make laws'. Not unexpectedly, such easy and harmless confusion would not do for Richard Hooker who yet agreed with what Burghley and the rest were trying to say, though in his anxiety to grant authority also to the church he annexed convocation to the parliament, a dubious proceeding in law, however convenient in practice. (He was concerned to show that the parliament was not 'so merely temporal as if it might meddle with nothing but leather and wool'). His definition, therefore, made of parliament 'the body of the whole realm' consisting of 'the king and of all that within the land are subject to him: for they are all present, either in person or by such as they voluntarily have derived their very personal right unto'—the last sentence being pure Thomas Smith.[15]

There were, in fact, three ways of coping with the confusing concept of estates. You could use it without justification, as these exponents of the true mixed-sovereign concept did; you could, like Smith and Hooker, take care to avoid the word; or you could simply pretend that the term fitted the real situation well. Almost predictably, this solution—riding sovereignly and idiosyncratically over all the difficulties—was adopted by Sir Edward Coke according to whom parliament consisted of the king 'sitting there in his royal politic capacity' and 'the three estates of the realm' (lords spiritual, temporal and commons); those four parts 'are the great corporation or body politic of the kingdom and do sit in two houses'— the king and the lords in one, the knights and burgesses in the other.[16] Coke's fence-sitting act enabled David Jenkins, imprisoned by parliament during the civil wars, to deny Prynne's insistence that the king was but one estate of the parliament: he pointed out that even Coke, 'their oracle', had confined the term estates to the two kinds of peers and the commons.[17] Even so, Jenkins held that 'the king is the head of the parliament, the lords the principal members, the commons the inferior members, and so the whole body is composed'—a definition which, by placing the king inside the parliament, came much closer to Tudor doctrine than to Hale's swerving from it.[18]

Perhaps it is not surprising that Hale, after the experience of a parliament which had done without the king, should have revived an estates-based doctrine which set the monarch apart from the parliament, but Coke's ruthless carpentering job described much better what was really practised and held under Elizabeth. Then the legislative authority rested with an institution consisting of three parts—the king and two houses—each separately deciding whether or not to agree in the threefold consensus which alone could make laws. If they had to be called estates, let them by all means take the name: it meant nothing in practice but seemed to satisfy some sort of philosophy. The point was well made by William Camden with that accidental skill which distinguishes the good historian. In the first edition of his *Britannia* (1586) he defined parliament as consisting of three estates and as representing the whole body of the realm: *'ex tribus enim Angliae ordinibus constat et totius Angliae corpus repraesentat'*. The subsequent Latin editions retained this succinct and inadequate description. But when Camden supervised the English translation, to which he added new passages, he put forward a significantly expanded definition for home consumption: 'it consisteth of the king, the clergy, the superior nobles, the elect knights and burgesses; or to speak more significantly after the lawyers' phrase, of the king, the lords spiritual and temporal, and the commons, which states represent the body of all England'.[19] After the lawyers' phrase: the right legal view spoke of the king-in-parliament. And he added words to underline the primacy of that view: 'It has the sovereign and sacred authority in making, confirming, repealing and expounding laws, in restoring such as be attainted or outlawed in their former estates, in deciding of the hardest controversies between private persons, and, to speak at a word, in all causes which may concern either the state or any private person whatsoever'. The English parliament, which included the king, was above all a sovereign lawmaking body.

This leads to the question how clear contemporaries may have been, even before Camden wrote, about this supreme lawmaking power vested in parliament. Definitions tend to result from argument; it is only differences of opinion that produce attempts at clarification. The function of the Tudor parliament was thus liable to be more precisely analysed during the years of disputation which Stuart methods of government unleashed, and it will serve to start off after the event. That reflective and much too talkative king, James I, once offered an interpretation which showed that he understood his second kingdom rather better than historians have done who nevertheless used to speak of his ignorance and his need to be taught better.[20] In March 1609, addressing the parliament, he explained the need for reform.[21] Much as he respected the common law, he could not avoid recognizing that it required improvement, 'but always by the advice of parliament, for the king with his parliament here are absolute in making or forming any sort of laws'. After running over the kind of revision required—replacing the use of French by English, codification, a review of statutes to remove illogical confusions—he added that furthermore parliament, as 'the representative body of the whole realm', was the means for bringing the nation's grievances to the king's notice. It is not that James displayed high originality or insight; what signifies is the manner in which he understood the commonplaces of the position. Parliament had a definite role to play in the running of the country: it provided a forum for opening up matters requiring attention, and it possessed the power to remedy such matters by the making of laws. To him, as to the Tudors, parliament was thus an extension of the royal means of government, not a restriction upon them: he thought in terms of habitual cooperation, even harmony—and again this was a commonplace, not perhaps merely a momentary need to appear conciliatory. As a 'Discourse concerning the success of former parliaments', published in 1642 (the year of final disruption) rather wistfully put it:

> It was ever heretofore seen that our parliaments were rather a strength and advantage to an honourable wise prince than a remedy against a bad and weak one; or, if we change the expression, they were rather an excellent diet to keep a good reign in strength than physic to cure a bad one.[22]

This plea for cooperation between the king, the lords and the commons, coming from a supporter of the Long Parliament who wisely confined his historical examples to the years before 1399, correctly stated the role of the institution in the hundred years before he came to write.

Remedying grievances and deficiencies by the making of law: a chorus of Tudor pronouncements lies behind this Stuart definition. St German said so even before the Reformation Parliament demonstrated the consequences that could arise from permitting the law to be enlarged by statute: as he knew, the ultimate source of law in England 'standeth in diverse statutes' made by the king, the lords and the commons.[23] It was Elizabethan doctrine that the making of law must always have been vested in parliament, a doctrine maintained even when the evidence of the past appeared to contradict it. That sensible antiquary, William Lambarde, denied any independent lawmaking power in the king alone by blatantly demanding that the evidence for it be ignored:

> If you shall find any acts of parliament seeming to pass under the name and authority of the king only, as there be some that have that show indeed, yet you must not by and by judge that it was established without the assent of the estates.[24]

William Camden, even when engaged in very properly analysing the high claims of the royal prerogative, yet emphasized that revision of the law did not belong to the king alone because lawmaking was a parliamentary function; and he found a good recent example: 'whereof yet if any man doubt let him see the statutes made in the time of King Henry VIII: and let no king desire to be accounted worse than Henry VIII'.[25] A brief note on the courts of the realm, jotted down late in Elizabeth's reign, summed it all up succinctly: 'Parliament: to make new laws and abolish old'.[26]

However, as James I indicated, the matter could not be left so simply at the level of defining a function: what laws were to be made? As James again indicated, the answer lay in the reception and resolution of 'grievances'—of anything that troubled the subject. The petitions that were received and tried in Plantagenet parliaments for the king's answer had their successors in the petitions and bills brought into Tudor parliaments for legislative answers from the parliamentary trinity. However, if parliament was to bring such matters to public attention, its function extended clearly beyond the purely legislative one: it was seen, and also described, as advising on action, as a council. Even Matthew Hale, writing about the prerogative in full awareness of what revolution had done to it a few years earlier, admitted that parliament was a great council whose advice should be followed unless there is 'clear reason to the contrary'; and its advice could cover 'all matters concerning the state'. He hastened to add that kings were not constitutionally bound to follow such advice, but he clearly allowed that parliament had also a political function.[27] By 1660 it would have been hard to avoid seeing that fact, but the notions are much older and lie, for instance, behind the claims that even the commons on their own were a council of the realm, able and indeed bound to advise the crown on political issues, which Paul and Peter Wentworth were fond of putting forward in Elizabethan parliaments. The semi-public platform of a parliament—in either house—offered a suitable stage for political argument and general debate, and the inclination to engage in such debate was much stimulated by the decisions taken in the 1530s which demanded from both lords and commons a deep involvement in the affairs of state and church. It is, however, important to understand that conceptually the political function was seen as essentially subordinate to the legislative one: discussion was merely a preparatory stage towards the making of statutes designed to improve the law and remedy grievances (the primary purpose for which parliament assembled), and a meeting which failed to move from the preliminary to the essential stage, as the parliament of 1614 did, caused not only frustration but astonishment. 'Bills', as John Pym noted in his first year in the house (1621), 'are the end of a parliament'. An admirable and memorable definition.[28]

One thing that any modern commentator would surely expect to find mentioned here has so far had no airing: in contemporary discussion we hear virtually nothing about the granting of money to the crown, that famour chief pillar for the continued existence of representative institutions. Neither those eager to elevate monarchy nor those concerned to mollify a parliament would, it is true, be much inclined to remind their hearers of that tiresome subject. Only Francis Bacon, reviewing the first two parliaments of James I and trying to ascertain why they had been such messy failures, adverted to taxation, and he did so because in his view too open an insistence on it had been a chief reason for the difficulties encountered.[29] He may have been right, but the way in which one of the most constant preoccupations of any meeting of parliament is passed over by the commentators remains striking—and a warning against equating their comment too readily with the truth and the whole truth. Even those writers who, trying for a systematic treatment, list the uses of parliament in some detail—writers like Sir Thomas Smith or Richard Robinson[30]—slip the matter of money in very casually and concentrate on activities which require legislation. Doing things that no one else could do, and doing them by producing laws: that, in the all but universal view of constitutional theorists, was what parliaments were for.

Generally speaking, this line of thought also characterizes the views expressed by people called upon on given occasions to explain why a particular parliament had been called. By the early sixteenth century at the latest, it had become customary to open a new parliament with what in effect was a speech from the throne—an oration in which the speaker (nearly always the lord chancellor or keeper of the great seal) laid out the reasons for the meeting about to start and justified the burden placed on members of both houses by their obedience to the royal summons. As long as chancellors were chosen from among prominent clerics, these speeches were in fact and purport sermons which tended to concentrate on turning the assembled lords' and commons' minds to their spiritual duties and gave remarkably little attention to the real reasons for the meeting of parliament. In 1483, preparing an address to the parliament of Edward V which was never delivered, and one for that of Richard III which was, Bishop Russell of Lincoln, chancellor, talked a good deal about Christian virtue and spread himself quite interestingly on problems of good governance, but found little else to say.[31] For the first occasion he meant to explain that the sole purpose of the parliament was to confirm the duke of Gloucester's protectorship, while on the second he lamely concluded by reminding the assembly that their task lay in the advancement of the commonwealth.

This medieval tradition, which emphasized rather the need to maintain a godly frame of mind than deal with practical problems or put forward a programme, continued into the reign of Henry VIII, though a small change was coming over these set pieces in the hands of Archbishop Warham who as chancellor opened three parliaments with sermons summarized by the clerk of the lords in his Journal Book. In 1510, he said much about the needful fear of God and the excellence of the new king, but also added that the parliament was invited to consider the existing laws with a view to amending what was amiss and repealing what was wrong;[32] the parliament followed instructions by passing measures intended to prevent a recurrence of the alleged abuses committed by the late king's administration.[33] In 1511, when Henry was planning to join in European war, Warham expressly 'declared the cause of the summons of parliament' by drawing attention to that prospect, but in spite of the obvious implications he does not seem to have spoken specifically about supply; after justifying the rapid calling of a second parliament in the reign with a tedious catalogue of Roman and Jewish assemblies, he merely emphasized the need to prepare for war by seeking the advice of the realm.[34] There are, however, reasons for thinking that in that context 'advice' stood as a euphemism for finding the money. And in 1514 (reminding one of Russell's preoccupations) he spent most of his time in reflecting on the qualities needed in a good ruler and a good system of justice, before perfunctorily telling the parliament to remedy whatever needed attention.[35] They—that is, the commons—were in effect (in the medieval manner) to be responsible for bringing up the agenda of the meeting. Next time, in 1523, Wolsey was chancellor, but he apparently extended his dislike of parliaments to the point of suppressing his normal delight in the sound of his own voice. The sermon was instead preached by the bishop of London, Cuthbert Tunstall, who, so far as he was recorded, confined himself to the moral duty of man and the need for good kingship ('where there is no ruler the people shall perish'); however, perhaps he became more specific thereafter, for 'in a wise and devout fashion the said bishop of London added many things more fully, more penetratingly and more elegantly than is here entered'.[36] On balance, this still sounds as though he elaborated his points of edification rather than presented some list of practical purposes.

The chancellor who opened the Reformation Parliament was Sir Thomas More, more devout than most bishops but a layman and a lawyer, and moreover a conscious and practised orator. From this time, the opening of parliament usually necessitated a sermon in Westminster Abbey and a speech to all the parliament in the house of lords.[37] More's speech abandoned the sermonising of tradition and concentrated on the reasons for the summons.[38] As he explained these, they were the misgovernment of his predecessor, Wolsey, whom he attacked with the abusive severity that he usually reserved for heretics, and the need to provide new remedies for newly arisen 'enormities'—in the context, almost certainly only the problem of heresy. This was More's programme and not either the king's or the parliament's, which in the event found itself preoccupied with the deficiencies of the church and the breach with Rome, but at least the chancellor presented a plain reason for the meeting.[39] Since such addresses remained confined to the opening of new parliaments, none being delivered at the start of prorogued sessions, there was now an intermission, but in 1536 Lord Chancellor Audley completed the secularization of the speech when he explained at length that the sole purpose of the parliament was to provide for the succession to the crown, in total disarray after the annulment of Henry VIII's first two marriages.[40] Audley's speech is a fascinating mixture of king-worship and frankness about this particular king.

At this point unfortunately the clerk ceased to enter summaries of the opening address in the Journal, and until 1559 we lack all knowledge of what was said.[41] He did, however, note the speeches in the house of lords with which Audley and Thomas Cromwell introduced the prorogued session of 1540, and although these were addressed to one house only they concern us here because they amounted to statements of government policy. Audley in fact spoke twice, on the first day praising good religion but on the second, more significantly, calling for law and reform and specifying the measures he wanted. Cromwell, in a passionate oration, looked for unity in religion (supposedly settled by the Act of Six Articles in the previous year) and asked for a new formulary as well as less contentious disputing.[42] At this point, therefore, we find ourselves in the presence of parliaments called to carry out a legislative programme submitted by government, but it is necessary to remember that the preparing of such programmes was peculiar to the era of Cromwell's ascendancy and rarely followed so vigorously at other times. Naturally, when government wanted certain laws enacted it reminded parliament that its function lay in the enacting of laws. We cannot even conjecture what may have been said to the nine parliaments that met between Cromwell's fall and the accession of Elizabeth—and they included the parliaments that made England protestant and turned her back to Rome. All that can safely be said is this: in the course of Henry VIII's reign it became customary to tell the parliament that it shared in the tasks of government and was there to be consulted, but that its advice was meant to lead to the making of such laws as the occasion required. Even when supply was to be got and reference made to the needs of the crown, the actual mention of money was apparently avoided. In the Cromwell era, with the council in charge of the proceedings and engaged in pushing through a planned policy, reference to new laws became specific rather than vague.

Information comes to us again with the beginning of Elizabeth's reign and is full for the first three of her parliaments—1559, 1563, 1571. Prorogued sessions, of course, still witnessed no opening speeches. The reason for this happy state of the evidence lies in the high oratorical reputation of Nicholas Bacon who as lord keeper opened them all. His speeches in an out of parliament, collected and frequently copied, survive in several manuscripts and thus became available also to Simonds D'Ewes who used them with some confusion.[43] Bacon's addresses, artfully put together and manifestly effective, followed a pattern. He liked to begin by explaining his lack of skill, a proem which must by stages have both amused and exasperated his audience; he always claimed to be conveying the mind of the queen; and he carefully parcelled his matter in numbered sections with subdivisions. Thus he gave much clarity to the information and instruction expressed.

In 1559,[44] Bacon made it plain that the parliament was to do three things: to establish uniformity of religion, to attend to 'the enormities and mischiefs that do or might hurt or hinder the civil orders and policies of this realm', and to consider the effect upon the realm of the recent 'losses and decays' inflicted upon 'the imperial crown of this realm' to the end that they might 'advise the best remedies to supply and relieve the same'. The last point referred especially to the loss of Calais and the possible cost of measures to recover it. The rest of the address elaborated each section at length. Parliament was given a very broad hint that the religious settlement must avoid either extreme; it was told that remedying mischiefs involved both new problems requiring legislation and a consideration of the existing laws; the request for supply was wrapped up in a long declamation about the excellence of the queen and the miserable state of her inheritance from the previous reign.

Having once found his formula, Bacon varied it only to suit the situation. In 1563,[45] he divided the business of the session into matters of religion and matters of policy, the former 'for the better maintenance and setting forth of God's honour and glory', the latter 'for the more perfect upholding and establishing the queen's majesty's honour and royal estate and the preservation of the commonweal committed to her charge'. The first in turn involved two things—doctrine (that is, the enforcement of uniform practices) and discipline (the spiritual improvement of clergy and laity), but so far as the clergy were concerned he emphasized that both were to be attended to by 'my lords the bishops . . . and that as speedily, diligently and carefully as can be'. This was the supreme governor speaking, of course. The only thing here left to the legislature was the problem of making 'the common people' attend church more regularly—unless indeed the bishops, having obeyed the queen's demand that they should devise remedies for the church, decided that they wanted an act of parliament. Here, I think, we hear the lord keeper's own voice. Commonwealth matters Bacon also divided into two sorts—'good governance' and 'defence against the enemy abroad'. Good governance in turn was declared to consist of two branches: a revision of the existing laws (are there too many, especially too many dealing with the same things?) and better provision for their execution. This last point, we learn, calls for three steps: a careful choice of agents (ministers of the crown at all levels), 'sharp laws' to put an end to 'sloth, corruption and fear of them' (quite probably a reference to the Statute of Artificers planned for this session), and—what he calls an idea of his own over which he will defer to the judgment of parliament—a regular enquiry every third or second year into the conduct of lay officials, similar to ecclesiastical visitations. Bacon recalled the old general commission of oyer and terminer (used by Henry VII and early in his son's reign) but with reason doubted whether it was adequate for the task he had in mind. Admitting that such a check applied to 'the great and open courts of the realm' would make his own burden in the chancery 'equal with the greatest', he disarmingly declared that he 'would gladly every year hear and feel such a controller'. Lastly he turned to defence, justifying the need for further taxation by once more reviewing the state of affairs encountered at the queen's accession and the costs incurred in gaining a peace and repairing the inherited deficiencies. The queen's treasure had been spent, her lands sold, and her credit committed to the limit at home and abroad—'and all this for your surety and quietness'. Referring to the costs of the expeditions to Leith and Le Havre, he slid over the facts by explaining that the details were not yet available: a trick not unknown in later debates on supply. The queen, he added, would much rather not have called the parliament and burdened the subject, but there was no help for it. This address, so far as our evidence goes, came much closer to being a detailed programme for the parliament than anything previously delivered, and the emphasis, supply apart, was once again exclusively on legislation.

Since Bacon's two remaining speeches were very similar in general structure and particular import there is no need to discuss them at length. In 1571 he concentrated on the reform of the laws both ecclesiastical and temporal, again reminding his hearers that the former were in the first place the concern of the bishops. There then followed yet another call for money justified both by the debt of gratitude owed to the queen for ten years of successful rule, and by the special needs created by the upheavals of 1569–71 (with no reference to actual or possible war).[46] For 1572, the collections let us down and we have no text preserved; instead we must rely on the notes made by private diarists.[47] Such notes offer more problematic evidence, but it would appear that Bacon tried to preempt discussion of the really contentious issues—the fate of the duke of Norfolk and of Mary queen of Scots—by suggesting that a short session would be wise for a meeting which took place in mid-summer, with the danger of plague about, rather than in the usual winter time. After apologizing, on the queen's behalf, for a summons issued at so risky a season, he declared the purpose of the parliament to be first the making of laws touching the queen's safety (called for by the detection 'since the last parliament' of various treasons and conspiracies), and secondly 'an old common cause in all parliaments', namely reviewing the existing state of the laws and remedying any deficiencies in them. He concluded with a warning that 'when they had once begun to deal with matters for the queen's safety they should as little as might be intermeddle with other matter until the despatch of them'. This attempt to prevent official bills from being swamped by private ones backfired: since to the commons the queen's safety seemed likely to profit more from the removal of Norfolk and Queen Mary than from penal laws, they waded enthusiastically into just those issues that Elizabeth did not wish to see debated.

Bacon's speeches thus came truly from the throne, expressing the desires and purposes of queen and council, and they overwhelmingly identified the purpose and function of every meeting as taxation (on which he said most because it needed most justification) and the making of laws which, as he made plain, would occupy the bulk of parliament's time. Like his predecessors, so far as we can discover their views, the lord keeper thought of parliament as an instrument of legislation and of its business as contained in the making, mending and repealing of statutes. Its so-called capacity to advise was to be expressed in those ways. This, of course, is a view pronounced by those who ruled, and the alternative opinion that parliament was a political council engaged in the conduct and super-vision of public affairs can also be found; but in the reign of Elizabeth at least it was held by very few men and must be called eccentric.[48]

From the recognition that parliament stood at the head of the hierarchy of courts, and from the fact that its chief function was the making of law, there sprang the doctrine of the supremacy and omnicompetence of parliamentary statute. By 1558, opinion generally agreed on this; even those occasional judges who still treated parliament as just another court and its pronouncements in consequence as no more than the ultimate judgments available in the system testified to the universal range of statute and the universal obedience due to it.[49] Even the problem of judicial interpretation, which of necessity arose in the course of applying acts of parliament to cases litigated, would have looked very different if the authority of statute had not been so high as to impose obedience even on judges. Interpretation meant making sense of what blind obedience would have turned into nonsense, or it meant avoiding confusion arising from the equal authority of all acts of parliament even when they conflicted with one another. If statute had still been regarded much like the judgment of any court, such difficulties would have been resolved by ignoring the statute, not by seeking to give it a meaning which would work. Thus interpretation sprang from the judges' position as servants of the statute, not from any sovereignty over it that they might wish to claim.[50]

In fact, statute was remediable only by another statute, and there was no appeal against any act of parliament against which not even a writ of error could be brought. As the Queen's Bench explained in Trinity term 1571: though a writ of error would lie against commissioners of oyer and terminer in a judgment of treason, the writ ceased to be available once the judgment had been confirmed by act of attainder. 'That which is confirmed by parliament is made indefeasible, although it were defeasible before'.[51] The same litigation (*Earl of Leicester* v. *Heydon*: a case brought by bill of Middlesex concerning lands obtained from a forfeiture arising out of a conviction for treason since reversed) also provides an excellent example of the contortions to which the judges could be reduced in their efforts to combine the provision of justice with absolute respect for the supremacy of statute.[52] It being argued that the confirmatory act under discussion contained misstatements of fact, it was admitted that parliament 'may be misinformed as well as other courts' but held that 'when they have recited a thing which is not true, it cannot be otherwise taken but that they were misinformed, for none can imagine that they would purposely recite a false thing to be true, for it is a court of the greatest honour and justice of which none can imagine a dishonourable thing'. Thus far can legal doctrine depart from experience. Establishing an error in an act was thus no insult to the supremacy of parliament which, having been merely misinformed, cannot be supposed to have intended the unfortunate consequence of an erroneous allegation because, had it been better informed, it would have ruled otherwise. Rather daringly, it was therefore held by the court

> that when an act of parliament confirms a thing which is and wants force, the act shall give force to it and shall make it to be of effect where it was not before; but if an act of parliament is referred to that which is not, and confirms it, as in our case, there the act shall be void to all intents.

The Bench could even cite a recent precedent. The act of 1 Edward VI, c. 12, which repealed treasons and felonies created in the previous reign, in sect. 18 meant to exempt from repeal the Henrician act against servants who stole from their masters. However, the passage by mistake described the session during which this earlier act had passed as extending from 4 February to 24 April, whereas it had really ended on 14 April: for which error the exception was held void, and an act which opinion generally thought valuable stood repealed. In this way, parliament's immunity to a writ of error could actually be by-passed, and while the writ provided a remedy only for errors in the record (under which heading the case of 1 Edward VI. c. 12 could be classified) this judicial doctrine could extend to errors of fact. However, as the precedent shows, the doctrine was used to frustrate government rather than enhance its powers.[53]

It must again be emphasized that such encroachments upon the sovereignty of statute arose solely from the tenet that statute was supreme and omnicompetent: there would have been no need for these complications if the judges had felt able to treat the judgments of parliament as they treated other judgments—as guides but not as binding guides. This high position, however, statute had acquired only recently, mainly as the result of the events of the 1530s. Even the virtue of an act confirming a title obtained in the usual way, by donor's grant, had not always been recognized, as is shown by the legal opinion of 1510 which thought it 'not expedient' (not required for better security) to obtain such an act to confirm the testamentary bequests of the Lady Margaret Beaufort upon which the existence of St John's and Christ's Colleges, Cambridge, depended. A confirmation, 'at leisure', by royal patent was then thought sufficient.[54] A few years later, a confirmatory act was welcomed in court as validating letters patent in themselves dubious because the king, though possessed only of a reversionary right, had conveyed the estate itself.[55] But even then, doubts (not resolved in the report) could be expressed whether a subsequent confirmatory act would not void even the effects of the attainder it confirmed, and thus become inadvisable.[56] In the course of the 1530s, Thomas Cromwell's and Thomas Audley's predilection for settling the property deals of the crown in statutes would seem to have terminated these hesitations with regard to both the desirability and the effectiveness of this use of statutory supremacy: confirming acts become quite customary as the best guardians of secure possession.

Of more general significance is the ability of statute to override and abrogate rights established at law. In Hilary term 1529, the courts doubted parliament's capacity to legislate in matters spiritual;[57] a few months later, the meeting of the Reformation Parliament by stages terminated the immunity of the spiritual realm from statute. There really was no escaping this, though the efforts to do so help to underline the novelty of the transformation. Even towards the end of the century, Hooker (as we have seen) still tried to save something by including convocation—contrary to all the evidence of the statute book—within the body that sovereignly ruled the church, but even he could not avoid the conclusion that parliament could by itself legislate for such spiritual matters as the definition of heresy.[58] As the *Discourse upon the statutes* had noted a generation earlier, 'though an act of parliament pass without [convocation's] consent, yet it is firm and good'.[59] The triumph of statute over the law of the church was complete but recent, and so (despite earlier pointers) was its triumph over the law of the realm. In 1527, John More, J. (father of Thomas More) unhesitatingly denied that parliament could alter established customs such as gavelkind;[60] twelve years later, the act of 31 Henry VIII, c. 3, entitled 'An Act for Changing the Custom of Gavelkind', obligingly did precisely that.

Judicial preconceptions clearly changed as a consequence of the work done in parliament during that decade, a change resulting not only from facts accomplished but also from policy enunciated. If it became accepted that matters spiritual (including the settlement of true religion) were suitable material for acts of parliament, opinions of the kind that Thomas Cromwell in 1537 expressed in public surely played their part. Presiding over a meeting of bishops convened to discuss the nature of the sacraments, he exhorted his audience to argue the controversies thoroughly (though also 'friendly and lovingly') and to arrive at their conclusions solely on grounds of scripture, 'as God commandeth you in Deuteronomy'. The king, Cromwell explained, would not 'suffer the scripture to be wrested and defaced by any glosses, any papistical law, or by any authority of doctors or councils', not a very accurate representation of Henry's attitudes but highly revealing of the viceregent's. In addition the bishops learned that in their own persons they served as investigators and advisers only, for the king would not allow 'any common alteration but by the consent of you and of his whole parliament,.[61] The outcome suggests that in this, too, Cromwell expressed his own views rather than Henry's. The formulary which resulted from that meeting (the *Bishops' book*) may have failed to receive parliamentary endorsement only because Henry did not like it, but the successor of 1543 (the *King's book*), of which he approved, was held to be authoritative without an act of parliament. However, by 1549 when the first Act of Uniformity formally enacted the Book of Common Prayer, Cromwell's desire for parliamentary authorization had triumphed.

Thus the statutes of the 1530s initiated the change in standing from a high regard to an acceptance of omnicompetent supremacy, a change which, of course, reflects a similar change in the standing of parliament itself. More particularly, those statutes directly affected the law at its heart—in the training of its practitioners. By its bulk and importance this legislation called forth a new style of reporting, designed to assist the absorption of the statutes by the profession, while by mid-century the Henrician acts had replaced those of earlier periods as the chief subject of instruction at the Inns of Court.[62] In the reign of Elizabeth, readers at the Inns could express high regard even for acts that more recent opinion has tended to despise as poorly made: thus Francis Bacon thought the Statute of Uses absolutely marvellous.[63] By the beginning of that reign the transformation was in fact complete and statute had acquired unquestioned supremacy. In the words of the *Discourse upon the statutes*, acts of parliament ruled common law, being able to add to it, abridge or abolish it.[64] That is to confer absolute supremacy in the law of England.

As we have seen, the novelty of that doctrine raised practical problems; quite apart from the need for interpretation, there remained unsettled questions. One such touched the endurance of a statute: did it lose its force with time? A curious question, perhaps, but not unimportant because limitation in prescription applied in so many branches of jurisprudence; it was therefore briefly considered in the *Discourse upon the statutes*. What was at issue was neither the power of parliament to alter what its predecessors had done—no one doubted that—nor the effect of limitations of time fixed in the statutes themselves, a common practice in the sixteenth century, but simply the possibility that the passage of time by itself eroded the meaning and effect of a statute. (The very fact that the issue was raised shows how wrong the influential historians are who deny that sixteenth-century common lawyers had any appreciation of historical change). The *Discourse* thought it did: true, 'no continuance of time can gain any prescription against' acts of parliament (mere age would not be an acceptable plea in court for ignoring a statute), but yet time can weaken them—as Livy says, who calls laws as mortal as man.[65] However, determined not to be subject to out-of-date laws, the author got himself into a tangle. He pointed out that Magna Carta had by an act of Edward III been declared unalterable for all time and had yet through age ('which all can fret and bite') lost force in many of its clauses. What he really proved here was the impossibility of binding future parliaments, for insofar as Magna Carta had lost force this was the result only of alteration by statute. No doubt, some of its clauses were no longer applicable and raised no litigation (which may have been in the mind of the author of the *Discourse*), but that disuse had not done away with them: anyone willing to employ them in litigation would still have found them in existence. I incline to thinking that the courts would in the sixteenth century have enforced any statute, however ancient, that had not been repealed, but until we know more about the application of acts of parliament in actual litigation, a subject little studied so far, the question must remain open.

What, lastly, about the monarch's relation to statute law? How sovereign was this law with respect to our sovereign lord or lady? Were the king *solus* and the queen *sola* as subject to the edicts of the king-in-parliament as were all other inhabitants of the realm? This question really contains two issues within itself: whether the king could free himself from the constraints of statute law, and whether he could convey a similar freedom to others. As to the first, it was generally held that the royal prerogative had been defined by the common law,[66] so that, in view of statute's superiority over that law, there could be no doubt that parliament could legislate for the prerogative—both enlarging and diminishing it. It did so freely in Henry VIII's reign, for instance in the notorious case of the Act of Proclamations (31 Henry VIII, c. 10) which legislated for the validity of one of the crown's undoubted prerogatives. Elizabeth several times confronted the problem when she did not wish parliament to interfere, and the fact that she adopted political solutions—avoiding rather than forbidding acts trenching on the prerogative—sufficiently confirms where the right answer lay. If so high a defender of the prerogative (much higher than her father) could never claim that prerogative matters must not be handled in statute and had to rest content with reserving acts on such topics to her own initiative, the fact that statute was recognized as governing prerogative is confirmed. In 1562 it was laid down in the Bench (in *Willions* v. *Berkeley*, decided against a crown patentee in favour of some rather distant remaindermen) that where the king claimed an estate governed by common and statute law he himself was 'restrained along with the estate'.[67] Opinion went the same way on a different issue altogether. In the Easter term of 1582, Serjeant Gawdy, in Common Pleas, raised a question on the act of 13 Elizabeth I, c. 12, 'An Act to Reform Certain Disorders Touching the Ministers of the Church'. Suppose an incumbent had been deprived for failing to read the Articles of Religion from his pulpit and, the living standing vacant, the ordinary failed to inform the patron of the fact, so that no successor was presented and the advowson reverted to the queen: could she present, even though the notice stipulated in the act (sect. 7) had not been issued? The court held that the queen was bound by the proviso and would have to give notice, as under the statute. Gawdy, it appears, was preparing his ground, for a little later an actual case was brought which was decided in accordance with this opinion.[68]

However, we know of at least one attempt to restrict the subjection of the monarch to statute; it is curious and occurs in the *Discourse upon the statutes*, a treatise not as a rule concerned to decry the powers of acts of parliament.[69] It is there alleged that all the inhabitants of the realm are automatically bound by an act, but the king only if he is expressly named in it, though conversely 'he shall take advantage of a statute though he be not named'. Just what this reservation may mean is not certain: so far I have come across no case in which the prerogative was declared free of statute on the grounds that there was no mention of the king or queen in the act. Such mention might occur either because royal interests were directly involved (as in a private act for crown lands, a grant of taxation, or an act defining the royal supremacy); it might be impersonal and allusive (as in a reference to royal commissioners or the queen's dominions); or it might be purely formal as when the 'be it therefore enacted' formula mentioned all three parts of the parliament. I have therefore before this suggested that the surprising practice in Elizabeth's reign by which officially sponsored bills tended to avoid express mention of the queen in the enacting clause may have been intended to take advantage of the rule adumbrated in the *Discourse*.[70] Since, however, no other treatise or opinion seems to exist to support the *Discourse* in its view, and since once again no case is so far known in which the question arose to be judicially settled, it is not possible to say how well accepted or practicable that exception might have been. In practice, the crown allowed that its rights and claims lived under statute, not above it.

There remains the royal power to render an act void by prerogative action. In the reign of Henry VIII, for instance, the act laying down standards of cloth-making was at the request of the parties affected several times suspended by proclamation, but it would seem that in the reign of Elizabeth the only approximately similar action occurred in May 1559 when merchants travelling abroad were exempted from the strict statutory prohibition against the export of coin and bullion (to the tune of £4 per man).[72] It can be stated with some confidence that in this reign no power was ever claimed or exercised by the crown to suspend the law made in parliament, except of course in cases where the statute specifically authorized such action. On the other hand, the crown claimed and exercised the right to except individuals from the operation of particular statutes—the so-called dispensing power embodied in licences *non obstante* under the great seal. Since many laws were framed categorically, on the assumption that their application would be suitably varied by means of government licences, this power was very necessary to the running of the whole system and never seriously questioned until James II brought it into disrepute. Moreover, it too was governed by a species of rules of interpretation. In its subheading ('how the king may dispense with statutes, for he is above his laws and may dispense with his laws') the *Discourse* seems to take a high prerogative view of the royal power, but the text actually points out that this superiority above the law is strictly limited by the law.[73] It applied only to *mala prohibita*—individual actions in themselves lawful which had been expressly barred by parliament.

> But for such statutes that have the force of a law and bind men generally and every man specially . . . , that are made, as you would say, for a commonwealth, with such things he cannot dispense.

What this appears to mean is that the crown could license exceptions from the essentially temporary and very variable statutory regulations governing, for instance, trade and industry but licences *non obstante* were not valid against the main bulk of parliamentary legislation. Even if she had wished to do so, Elizabeth could not by the prerogative have licensed anyone to avoid the use of the Book of Common Prayer in the services of the church, or to absent himself from such services without fear of a recusancy fine, nor could she have found a litigant harmless against a successful defendant's claims for costs (8 Elizabeth I, c. 2) or permitted anyone to practise usury (13 Elizabeth I, c. 8). By this interpretation, James II's evasion of the Test Act in fact offended against Tudor principles, and the Bill of Rights' seemingly vague phrase about the dispensing power 'as of late exercised' becomes precise.

Thus the developments of the sixteenth century made parliament into a supreme legislator, unhampered by other laws positive (but presumably not free of the obligations of piety and morality supposedly embodied in the laws of God and nature); parliament stood dominant over the executors of the law—the crown and its courts. The doctrine of estates, however handled, arose from the conviction that the institution embraced all members of the realm. The community of England therefore related directly to its parliament and there expressed itself in communal sovereign action. Though earlier parliaments had manifestly pointed towards such a development, they had not achieved it. The sixteenth century parliament testified to a fundamental restructuring not only of itself but also of the state and its functions, and in consequence also of its impact upon the nation.

Notes

1. G. R. Elton, 'Parliament in the sixteenth century: functions and fortunes', in *Hist. Jn.*, 22 (1979), pp 255 ff.
2. Sir John Fortescue, *The governance of England*, ed. C. Plummer (Oxford, 1885), pp 113–4. I have throughout modernised the spelling in all quotations.
3. For all this cf. my articles, 'The body of the whole realm', *Studies in Tudor and Stuart politics and government*, ii, esp. pp 32–6, 38–40; and 'The rolls of parliament, 1449–1547', in *Hist. Jn.*, 22 (1979), pp 1 ff.
4. Sir Thomas Smith, *De Republica Anglorum*, ed. Mary Dewar (Cambridge, 1982), p. 78.
5. Conyers Read, *Mr Secretary Walsingham and the policy of Queen Elizabeth* (Oxford, 1925), i, 428 (where Robert Beale advises that the book, though in some respects out of date, should be regarded as the fundamental instruction).
6. In her edition of the *De Republica*, Dr Dewar has conclusively proved that Smith's chapters on parliament were completed by 1565 and not perhaps inserted or revised for the first printing in 1583, as Sir John Neale, convinced that the pre-Elizabethan parliaments were too 'primitive' to fit that description, always imagined.
7. *Tudor royal proclamations*, ed. P. Hughes and J. F. Larkin (New Haven, 1969), ii, 103 (27 Dec. 1558).
8. *Stuart royal proclamations*, ed. J. F. Larkin (Oxford, 1973), i, 143.
9. William Harrison, *The description of England*, ed. G. Edelen (Folger Library, 1968), pp 27, 170.

10. B. L., Harleian MS 1315, p. 70.
11. In his 'Answer to the nineteen propositions' which enunciated the 'classic' doctrine of the mixed sovereign, the king-in-parliament: C. C. Weston, 'The theory of mixed monarchy under Charles I and after', in *E.H.R.*, 75 (1960), pp 426–43.
12. Sir Matthew Hale, *The prerogatives of the king*, ed. D. C. E. Yale (Selden Society, 1975), pp 11, 134.
13. Simonds D'Ewes, *The journals of all the parliaments during the reign of Queen Elizabeth* (London, 1682), p. 350.
14. For Hall and Mildmay see my 'Arthur Hall, Lord Burghley and the antiquity of parliament', in *History and imagination*, ed. Hugh Lloyd-Jones, Valerie Pearl and Blair Worden (London, 1981), pp 88ff; for Lambarde see *Archeion*, ed. C. H. McIlwain and P. L. Ward (1957), p. 123.
15. *The works of . . . Mr Richard Hooker*, ed. J. Keble (Oxford, 1888), iii, 408–9.
16. Edward Coke, *Fourth institute of the laws of England* (1644), pp 1–2.
17. David Jenkins, *Works* (1648), p. 49.
18. Ibid. p. 19. Yet ibid. p. 50 we learn that 'the king, as king, is present in his parliament as well as in his other courts of justice, howbeit he is not there', a statement which by equating parliament with, e.g., the king's bench implicitly makes the king the 'owner' of the parliament rather than a member of it.
19. *Britannia* (1586), p. 83; (1610), p. 177.
20. Cf. J. R. Tanner, *Constitutional documents of the reign of James I* (Cambridge, 1930), p. 202: 'a lecture to a foreign king on the constitutional customs of his realm'. Of course, this applied to 1604, and it could, I suppose, be argued that James dutifully learned his lesson. Current views of the king are growing daily more respectful of his astuteness and sense.
21. *Harleian miscellany* (1744 ed.), i, 12.
22. Ibid. vi, 377–81.
23. *Doctor and student*, ed. T. F. T. Pluckett and J. L. Barton (Selden Society, 1974), pp 30–1, 73.
24. *Archeion*, p. 139.
25. 'William Camden's "Discourse concerning the prerogative of the crown",' ed. F. S. Fussner (*Proceedings of the American Philosophical Society*, 101 [1957]), p. 215.
26. Inner Temple, Petyt MS 538/54.
27. Hale, *Prerogatives*, pp 140–1.
28. Cited by C. Russell in *The English commonwealth 1547–1640*, ed. P. Clark *et al.* (Leicester, 1979), p. 150. It has recently been argued that a doctrine of estates and a proper recognition of parliament's legislative functions are not to be found before the middle of the seventeenth century: C. C. Weston and J. Greenberg, *Subjects and sovereigns: the grand controversy over legal sovereignty in Stuart England* (Cambridge, 1981), esp. ch. 1. The authors have in fact identified a special stage in the debate, provoked by the events of the 1640s, but they err in supposing that the central concepts were then formulated for the first time.
29. Cf his analysis (1615) in *The letters and the life of Francis Bacon*, ed. J. Spedding, (1869), v, 176–91.
30. Cf my remarks in *Hist. Jn.*, 22 (1979), p. 258.
31. S. B. Chrimes, *English constitutional ideas in the fifteenth century* (Cambridge 1936), pp 168–91.
32. *Lords' jn.*, i, 3.

33. Cf my remarks in *Studies*, i, 92–5.
34. *Lords' jn.*, i. 10.
35. Ibid., p. 18.
36. Ibid., p. lxxv (taken from the roll, the journal being lost).
37. E.g. in 1563, Alexander Nowell, dean of St Paul's, preached on the queen's marriage before the lord keeper got the chance to direct parliament's thoughts to less contentious matters (J. E. Neale, *Elizabeth I and her parliaments*, [London, 1953], i, 92–5); in 1571, Edwyn Sandys, bishop of London, choosing for his text the words of Sam. xii (*'Timete deum et ei servite in veritate'*) showed how religion 'is chiefly to be sought in virtue and truth' and reminded princes that they 'ought to direct their doings in true religion and to govern their people in truth, equity and justice' before Bacon once again brought things back to reality (*Proceedings in the parliaments of Elizabeth I*, ed. T. E. Hartley, [Leicester, 1981], i, 243).
38. Esp. Edward Hall, *The union . . . of Lancaster and York* (ed. 1809), p. 764; and cf. J. R. Guy, *The public career of Sir Thomas More* (Brighton, 1980), pp 113–5.
39. S. E. Lehmberg, *The reformation parliament 1529–1536* (Cambridge, 1970), pp 78–9. Professor Lehmberg's studies of Henrician parliaments provide a good account of these speeches, as well as a handy guide to the evidence.
40. S. E. Lehmberg, *The later parliaments of Henry VIII, 1536–1547* (Cambridge, 1977), p. 84.
41. As Professor Lehmberg notes (ibid., p. 56), on the authority of William Dugdale's *Summons to parliament* (1685), 502–3, the parliament of 1539 seems to have been opened by neither the chancellor nor any bishop but by the earl of Sussex, lord chamberlain, who is stated to have explained the reasons for the assembly. Dugdale cites a manuscript in the College of Heralds which is likely to have got it right: the heralds kept accounts of the proceedings at the start of parliaments. The most likely explanation for this surprising intrusion lies in Cromwell's illness at the beginning of the session. As vicegerent in spirituals he could have claimed the right to deliver the address. Perhaps Audley refused to stand in at short notice. Dugdale's evidence shows that 'speeches from the throne' continued to be delivered and that the silence of the journal represents only a change in record-keeping.
42. G. R. Elton, *Reform and renewal: Thomas Cromwell and the common weal* (Cambridge, 1973), pp 152–3; Lehmberg, *Later parliaments*, pp 90–1.
43. E.g. for 1563 D'Ewes (pp 59–61) printed a speech which differs very considerably in phrasing and detail, though not in substance, from that found in British Library, Harl. MS 5176, ff 89–92 and there dated 1563. He printed the main part of this latter text as the address of 1572 (pp 192–5), adding to it a lengthy passage taken from another version of what he correctly printed as the address of 1571. As for 1563, all MSS are later copies and neither version is included in the best collection of Bacon's speeches (Harl. MS 398). D'Ewes's variant version, taken from British Library, Cotton MSS, Titus F.i, fos. 66 seqq, was called by Neale 'a lengthy report'; it may well have been an earlier draft of the speech. While these confusions are now cleared up in Dr Hartley's edition of *Proceedings in the parliaments of Elizabeth I*, it is as well to remember that we cannot be absolutely sure that we know exactly what was said and must not argue too confidently about precise words.
44. *Proceedings*, i, 33–9.
45. Ibid., pp 80–6.
46. Ibid., pp 183–7.

47. Ibid., pp 317, 336.
48. The view was advanced by Paul and Peter Wentworth, but they got so little support in the house that the customary concentration on their interventions (e.g. Neale, *Elizabeth I and her parliaments*, i, 152 ff., 318 ff.) distorts reality.
49. Cf L. W. Abbott, *Law-reporting in England 1485–1585* (London, 1973), pp 228–9.
50. For general discussions of this point cf [T. Egerton], *A discourse upon the exposicion and understanding of statutes*, ed. S. E. Thorne (San Marino, 1942), especially the introduction; and Abbott, *Law-reporting*, pp 229–39.
51. *Plowden's reports* (Dublin, 1792 ed.), p. 394.
52. Ibid., p. 399.
53. According to the sensible views expressed in the *Discourse upon the statutes*, p. 114, errors mattered only if they occurred in the enactment: 'for it is not the words of the preamble that have the effect of an act of parliament but it is the body of the statute that has the force'.
54. St John's College, Cambridge, Archives 6.12.
55. *The reports of Sir John Spelman*, ed. J. H. Baker (Selden Society, 1977), i, 149.
56. Ibid., p. 151. An obscure difficulty. Buckingham's attainder had led to an inquest which found him seised of the lordship of Holderness; by the attainder and as a result of the office the lordship reverted to the king who, thus seised, granted the stewardship to Sir Robert Constable. The act confirming the attainder declared all Buckingham's property forfeit, which appears to have been taken as rendering the office doubtful and as freeing the king (now seised under the act) to regrant the stewardship a few years later to the earl of Northumberland.
57. *Spelman's reports*, ii, 44, n.2.
58. *Hooker's works*, iii, 357–8, 408–9.
59. *Discourse upon the statutes*, p. 110.
60. *Spelman's reports*, ii, 44–5.
61. Alexander Alesius, *Of the word of God against the bishop of London* (1537: *STC*, 292), ff 1v–2r.
62. Abbott, *Law-reporting*, 67–8; W. R. Prest, *The inns of court under Elizabeth and the early Stuarts 1590–1640* (London, 1972), p. 120.
63. B.L., Harl. MS 1853, ff 125 seqq.
64. *Discourse upon the statutes*, p. 143.
65. Ibid., pp 165–6.
66. William Staunford, *An exposicion of the kinges prerogative* (1563: *STC*, 23213), f. 5.
67. *Plowden's reports*, pp 246–8, 322.
68. B.L., Harl. MS 1699 (an Elizabethan commonplace book of the law), ff 140r, 141v.
69. *Discourse upon the statutes*, p. 110.
70. Cf. G. R. Elton, 'Enacting clauses and legislative initiative, 1559–71 [i.e. 81], in *I.H.R. Bull.*, 53 (1980), esp. p. 191, n. 34.
71. It is of some interest to note that the act cited in the advowson case just mentioned referred to the queen four times: the preamble speaks of 'the churches of the queen's majesty's dominions', and the enactment mentions 'true religion put forth by the queen's authority', 'the queen's highness' commissioners in causes ecclesiastical', and the valuation of livings 'in the queen's books'. I.e. the queen is not once made the subject matter of the act in her own person but puts in these four adjectival appearances. She is not put into the enacting clause. Was she then no party to the act, in the sense intended in the

Discourse upon the statutes? The judges held that the act applied to her, which must throw some doubt upon the idiosyncratic views of the *Discourse*—though it must be plain that counsel in this case was anxious to get the judges to decide as they did and would thus be unlikely to put this point of law—if it was one.

72. *Tudor royal proclamations*, i, 258, 291, 300, 306; ii, 113–4. The Elizabethan proclamation merely repeated one issued by Mary: ibid., ii, 62–3.
73. *Discourse upon the statutes*, pp 168–9.

Parliament, 'party' and 'community' during the English civil war 1642–46

Brian Manning

The great Victorian historian S. R. Gardiner thought that after the outbreak of the English civil war in 1642 those M.P.s who remained at Westminster—the parliamentarians—became divided into two parties—the peace party and the war party.[1] This idea governed accounts of the politics of the Long Parliament until it was challenged in 1941 by J. H. Hexter. He argued that there were not two parties but three—the peace party, the war party, and the middle party. The middle party held the balance of power, voting with the war party for the more vigorous prosecution of the war and with the peace party for the re-opening of negotiations with the king.[2] Hexter's notion was endorsed and developed in a series of articles by Lotte Glow (Mulligan) and Valerie Pearl,[3] and it provided the model for the major studies of the politics of parliament during the civil war—David Underdown's *Pride's purge*, Clive Holmes's *The eastern association* and, more recently, Patricia Crawford's biography of Denzil Holles.[4] The idea of a middle party became an orthodoxy. Christopher Thompson wrote in 1972: 'No one now doubts the existence of that body of trimmers, led at first by Pym and later by St John, whose course between the policies of the two extremes of the peace and war parties was so often decisive'.[5]

This orthodoxy rests on the assumption that there were in fact parties in parliament between 1642 and 1646. Not of course parties in a more modern sense, for Hexter noted in his original formulation: 'Several elements characteristic of the later developments of parliamentary parties did not exist . . . There was no organisation in the counties and boroughs, no elaborate system of patronage, no ministry dependent on a continuous majority in the lower house, and no party discipline'.[6] Valerie Pearl warned against regarding the middle party 'as a latter-day party with a programme and a platform'. With reference to parties in general in the politics of the mid-seventeenth century, she observed instability and fragmentation, as M.P.s shifted constantly from one party to another.[7] David Underdown and Clive Holmes noted the ephemeral and transitory nature of parties, coming together on one issue and then splitting up and re-forming on another. 'Civil war parties . . . were at best loose, amorphous, and transient, . . . vaguely identifiable groups of men who happened for a time to think alike on one or more of the major issues of the day'.[8] 'Parties were the products of immediate circumstances, ephemeral and kaleidoscopic groupings of M.P.s seeking common ends, dissolving into new patterns when those ends were obtained, or the circumstances which appertained at their creation were altered'.[9] Nevertheless Underdown still maintained: '. . . ephemeral and transitory as they may have been, and affecting only a minority of the politically conscious, groups recognisable as parties did exist'. 'Loose in structure, lacking in cohesion . . . the parties were there, and were becoming more clear-cut'.[10] Recently Robert Ashton has expressed some unease about using the term 'party', which, he has written, 'is likely to beget some confusion unless it is realised that the word "party" is not here employed to describe a firm and cohesive political organisation with disciplined membership and consistent political behaviour. No such organisation existed in the Long Parliament . . .' Yet he still found it 'convenient, if not altogether appropriate' to describe 'the rather amorphous political groupings' as 'parties'.[11] Indeed Hexter and his followers have never been quite sure that 'party' is the appropriate title, and they have shifted uncertainly between the designations 'party' and 'group'. John Morrill, having referred in one place—rather surprisingly—to 'organised parties', a few pages later changed his terminology to 'groups' and 'alliances'. 'There existed a number of small groups of members . . . These groups made working alliances with one another on major issues . . . At most periods of the war, there were three such alliances . . .'[12]

Historians, however, have found it impossible to fit most M.P.s into these 'parties', 'groups' or 'alliances'. Hexter wrote:

> . . . Parliament was not divided into three sharply separated parties, but into three clusters, shading off from the cluster in the centre to the two clusters at the extremes . . . We can point out typical members of peace, middle, and war party . . . but as we move out from . . . the middle or in

from . . . the extremes we come to areas of shadow and uncertainty, where we hesitate to say of a member he is this, or he is that. Knowing full well that what we can hope to find is not a compact, solid, easily ponderable body, but rather a vague, shifting, unstable mass . . .[13]

Underdown went further and concluded that the majority of the members of parliament could not be associated with peace, war or middle party. In a house of just under two hundred active members, before the recruiting to vacant seats began in August 1645, he estimated that each of the three parties had about thirty identifiable adherents. He guessed that the rest—just over one hundred members—voted on the merits of the issue rather than for a party, and 'did not think of themselves as party men, and indeed regarded the whole concept of party as factious and reprehensible'.[14] Morrill agreed that 'only a minority of M.P.s were "party" men',[15] and Ashton concluded that '. . . the majority of M.P.s probably had no affiliation, however vague and indefinite . . .' with the parties.[16] Thus the parties have been cut down to size, and the usefulness of the concept for explaining the decisions of parliament has been reduced by the discovery that it did not apply to the majority of active members.

Does the middle party, on which accounts of the civil war politics of parliament have depended for the last forty years, really exist at all? It has often been regarded as somewhat less of a party than the war or peace party. Patricia Crawford wrote of the latter having 'leaders and a hard core of devoted adherents' but of 'the middle group' being 'less stable in composition'.[17] Robert Ashton admitted that the middle group was 'more nebulous and less consistent' than the war or peace party.[18] Valerie Pearl described the 'lack of organisation', 'fragility', and 'fissiparous nature' of the middle group. '. . . The views of many of its members were governed by what seemed to them both expedient and right and it was extremely difficult to keep them united . . .'[19] Thus the middle group fades. It disappears altogether in the formulation which Underdown employed in an article in 1968. 'Between these two factions [the war and peace parties] lay an undefined middle group, which is another name for the majority of non-partisan M.P.s'.[20] If the middle group is identical with the majority of M.P.s who voted on the merit of each issue rather than in support of a leader, or of a group, or of a party, then it is certainly not any sort of party, and it is difficult to see what meaning there is in calling it a group. It is no more than individuals who did not consistently support either the peace party or the war party.

Hexter's original notion of a moderate centre party between two extremes provided no certain criteria for identifying its adherents, for the composition of such a centre party varies in accordance with where the extremes are placed: St John is a moderate between the extremes of Holles and Vane, but Vane is a moderate between the extremes of Holles and Marten.[21] James E. Farnell has questioned the reality of Hexter's middle group and has pointed out that the discussions of parties and groups in parliament during the civil war have referred only to the house of commons and have ignored the house of lords.[22] One of the few studies of the upper house in this period—G. F. Trevallyn Jones's biography of Lord Wharton—did not find it easy to apply Hexter's model to the peers and reverted to Gardiner's two-party model.[23] John R. MacCormack has suggested that the centre consisted merely of 'floating voters'.[24] More recently, Mark A. Kishlansky has argued that the centre, which embraced the majority of M.P.s, was composed of men who were uncertain whether to support the peace or the war party and reluctant to commit themselves totally to either, and so they ended up by voting for both.[25]

The dichotomy of war party and peace party did at least have the advantage of focussing on the issues that divided M.P.s. Once the civil war had broken out politics were dominated by the overriding issue of peace or war: whether to enter into negotiations with the king and if so, on what terms; whether to fight a limited, defensive war or a total, aggresive war; whether to seek an end to the war by compromise or by unconditional surrender. On these interrelated questions the M.P.s at Westminster clearly became divided. Some consistently pressed for negotiations for peace, sought to moderate parliament's demands, and supported military action only in so far as it was necessary to prevent the complete defeat of parliament; while others consistently demanded more vigorous and effective prosecution of the war and pursued total victory over the king and power to dictate the peace.[26] Broadly speaking the crucial divide was between, on the one hand, those who thought that complete victory for either side would result in extremist solutions to the constitutional and religious disputes which had caused the war, and so wanted the war ended by negotiation and compromise on those disputes, and, on the other hand, those who saw the differences as irreconcilable and sought a military solution by conquest. Thus there were two policies and members supported one or the other, or voted for both, for many different reasons and with many variations of emphasis. But even if it were appropriate to speak of those who consistently supported one policy as a party, it would not be legitimate to see such a party as continuing to exist beyond the issue which gave rise to it.

In 1645, according to Patricia Crawford, the peace party became the presbyterian party and the war party became the Independent party.[27] David Underdown, noting in the same year that the terms presbyterians and Independents came into use to describe the divisions at Westminster, concluded that the peace party was 'the main component' of the presbyterian party and that the war party formed the nucleus of the Independent party.[28] Subscribers to Hexter's thesis maintained that in 1645 the middle party split and the three parties polarised into two—presbyterians and Independents. 'The tripartite division between peace, war and middle groups', wrote Robert Ashton, 'gave way to a two-party dichotomy' with the middle group losing its separate identity. 'In the course of 1645 these two groups became increasingly known as presbyterians and Independents'.[29] It is tempting to see a direct line of development from peace and war parties to presbyterian and Independent parties. But the use of the terms presbyterians and Independents points to issues. As parliament came under growing pressure to restore order in the church and to settle religion, and as it became increasingly assured of outright military victory, the overriding issue ceased to be that of peace or war but of the form of the ecclesiastical system that the victors would impose on the king and the kingdom. Underdown contradicted his own thesis that the peace party was 'the main component' of the presbyterian party and the war party was the nucleus of the Independent party, when he observed that 'on a political issue such as conduct of the war or the presentation of peace terms to the king . . . the members . . . would divide in one way; on religious issues the same members would divide in quite another'. 'If we examine the members in one way they divide into war, peace and middle groups . . . , but if we look at them in another way they divide into Independents, presbyterians, moderate episcopalians and erastians'.[30] That being so, it is difficult to see why Underdown continues to use the term 'parties' and to accept an evolution from peace and war parties to presbyterian and Independent parties. But he persists: 'Although the two terms came only gradually into general usage in the course of the year 1645, and although both remained loose confederations of groups rather than close-knit parties, . . . it is now possible . . . to speak of the presbyterian and Independent parties'. Only if 'loose confederations of groups' are the same thing as 'parties'; even so, most members of parliament did not belong, or were 'only tenuously attached', to either loose confederation.[31] But there is a problem about describing these 'parties' as presbyterian and Independent. 'These religious labels, misnomers from the start, have actually done more to obscure the issues than to clarify them'.[32] Many members of the presbyterian party were not presbyterians, and many members of the Independent party were not Independents; indeed the Independent party contained presbyterians and moderate episcopalians as well as Independents.[33] Ashton concluded unhappily that '. . . there must have been a good deal of cross-party voting on religious issues in parliament'.[34] By which he must mean that the parties were not generated by religious issues; and Valerie Pearl said just that: 'One can assume that loyalty to one form of church government was not the cause that bound them'.[35] The solution to this difficulty has been to rename the groups 'political presbyterians' and 'political Independents'. In that case the issues around which the groupings formed were not religious but political and it would be better to abandon the religious labels altogether.

Clearly, however, there were religious issues which did divide parliament. The members came under intense pressure from 1644 onwards to suppress the radical religious sects which had grown in numbers and influence since the outbreak of the civil war, and to re-establish a uniform national church from which dissent or separation would not be allowed. Since episcopacy had been abolished, it seemed to many M.P.s that only a more or less presbyterian system would be capable of meeting the need.[36] Against this the sects struggled for toleration: they did not necessarily reject a state church to which the mass of the people would be compelled to belong, provided that they themselves were permitted to separate from it and to form their own congregations, subject to their own discipline in matters of religion. The Independents, while favouring a national church, were desirous of obtaining for the sects toleration within it or, if that were not possible, permission to separate from it.[37] At the same time parliament was divided between the allies and opponents of the Scots,[38] and over the terms of the settlement in the state as well as in the church that was to be imposed on the king now that the war was won. Thus parliament was divided not over one but several issues. The terms 'religious presbyterian', 'political presbyterian', 'religious Independent', 'political Independent', indicate that members polarised in one way on political issues and in another way on religious issues. There was not an invariable correspondence between a member's political attitudes and his religious beliefs:

moderation in politics did not always go with moderation in religion, nor radicalism in religion with radicalism in politics. Members distinguished between secular and ecclesiastical matters, and secular considerations might pull a member in one direction and ecclesiastical considerations in another. In so far as a group of members developed a common outlook over a range of issues, both political and religious, that did not create a party. A party requires by definition more than a common outlook, it comprehends leadership, organisation, programme, and membership.[39] The historians who have analysed the politics of parliament during the civil war in terms of parties have not, on the basis of their own evidence and formulations, proved their case. They have established the existence of groups, providing that these are defined in terms of common attitudes towards specific issues and not in terms of following a leader, creating an organisation, subscribing to a programme, and accepting the obligations of membership. Parliament was composed of individuals each with 'his own preferences and prejudices which might incline him one way or the other as a host of considerations influenced him at any given time'.[40] '... An individual's choice at Westminster was the result of a complex calculus of inputs—religious conviction, constitutional principles, and ... local, familial or personal interests and ties'.[41] The formation of groups was the response of individuals to the impact of issues which ironed out the differences between them, by subjecting them to pressures from their constituents, or their neighbours and friends, or their interests, and by instilling in them fears such as the danger to the social order from the growth of the sects, or hopes such as the prospect of promoting godliness and creating a more godly society.

The religious issue was crucial and it was expressed by the labels presbyterian and Independent, but it cannot be properly understood or fully explained by reference to Westminster alone. It is necessary to relate it to what was happening in the provinces. Consideration has to be given to the localities, both rural and urban, and to the relationship between 'national' issues and 'local' issues. In this context historical study has been dominated at the local level for at least two decades by the notion of the 'county community', just as it has been dominated at the national level by Hexter's notion of 'parties'.

'In many respects, despite its ancient centralised government, the England of 1640 resembled a union of partially independent county-states or communities, each with its own distinct ethos and loyalty'.

So wrote Alan Everitt in 1966 in his very influential study of Kent. He entitled his book *The community of Kent and the great rebellion*, and in his subsequent essay *The local community and the great rebellion* 'the local community' is the county. In that essay he declared:

> The allegiance of the provincial gentry to the community of their native shire is one of the basic facts of English history in the seventeenth and eighteenth centuries. Though the sense of national identity had been increasing since the early Tudors, so too had the sense of county identity, and the latter was normally . . . the more powerful sentiment in 1640-60.

He regarded the county as the administrative and social unit upon which the interests and loyalties of the gentry focussed: the members of this community were not the mass of the inhabitants of the shire but its ruling elite, the greater or county gentry.[42]

Counties, however, were not geographical unities. Everitt himself referred to the 'six Kents'—the six different geographical regions of the county.[43] John Morrill in his study of Cheshire, having observed that '. . . Cheshire men referred to the county, not to the kingdom, as their "country", and this primary allegiance is of fundamental importance in the understanding of the early modern period', went on to point out that this was 'not the whole of the story; there was nothing unitary in the geography of Cheshire for example'. 'There were . . . varied agrarian interests within the county; indeed, nine distinct regions have been identified', and parts of Cheshire had more in common with parts of neighbouring counties than with the rest of Cheshire.[44]

It is fundamental to Everitt's concept of the county as a community that it is united by its institutions of government, notably the quarter-sessions. But in Lincolnshire there were eight administrative districts, each with its own quarter-sessions and its own justices of the peace. 'Quarter-sessions were not a county event . . .'. Clive Holmes concluded that 'most of the Lincolnshire gentry's administrative experience was forged in units smaller than the county, and it may be argued that their loyalties focussed upon these sub-divisions as much as upon the county itself'.[45] In Cheshire the Epiphany sessions were held at Chester, the Easter sessions at Knutsford, the Midsummer sessions at Nantwich, and the Michaelmas sessions at Northwich or Middlewich. Some justices attended only the sessions nearest their homes and no justices appeared regularly at all the sessions.[46] In Sussex there were two separate benches of J.P.s, one for West Sussex and the other for East Sussex.

At Epiphany, Easter and Michaelmas, quarter-sessions were held separately in both the eastern and western divisions of the county. At Midsummer the quarter-sessions were held only at Lewes, but even then only the J.P.s from East Sussex attended and it was not a county assembly. This reflected the fact that Sussex was divided into two by geography, and its gentry moved in two separate social circles.[47] Here there was no county community.

The fact that the county was for some purposes a governmental and administrative unit did not necessarily make it a community. If parliamentary elections and some offices and administrative duties did from time to time cause the elite of the gentry to think in county terms, that did not invariably unite them, for the county was as often as not the focus of feuds and struggles for power between its leading families. In Leicestershire from the middle of the sixteenth century down to the civil war there was 'rivalry for the control of the county' between the Hastings and the Greys, and the gentry were divided by allegiance to one family or the other.[48] In Wiltshire there was a similar situation on the eve of the civil war. The ancient rivalry between the Seymours and the Herberts appeared in struggles for control of the lieutenancy and the commissions of the peace. The gentry of Wiltshire were allied traditionally with one or other of these two great families.[49] In Somerset in the 1620s and 1630s there was a struggle for supremacy in the county between Sir Robert Phelips and Lord Poulet, and the gentry were divided into two factions by kinship or friendship or alliance with one or other of the contenders.[50] Caernarfonshire was split before the civil war by the rivalry for power and pre-eminence between the Griffiths of Cefnamwlch and the Glynnes of Glynllifon.[51] In Cheshire there was antagonism between the 'party of the barons' and the 'party of the baronets'.[52]

By concentrating on the reactions of the province to the policies and demands of central authorities, whether king or parliament, Everitt, Morrill and others can find counties utilising their institutions to defend local autonomy, but the fact that local interests and local loyalties found in the county a convenient shield against outside interference does not mean necessarily that those interests were co-extensive with the county, or that those loyalties were attached to the county as such. By looking at the civil war in terms of the conflict between royalists and parliamentarians, the division within a county appears more important than any unity of a county in defence of its autonomy. In Leicestershire the 'great majority' of the parliamentarian gentry were in the north and west—in the hundreds of East Goscote, West Goscote, and Sparkenhoe.[53] In Somerset the western parts tended towards royalism, while parliamentarianism was strongest in the north-east and in Taunton, Wellington, Martock and Frome.[54] In Sussex the lack of unity between east and west became the dividing-line between the parties in the civil war: the parliamentarians came mostly from the east and the royalists were heavily concentrated in the west.[55] As regards party affiliation in the civil war the significant area was a unit smaller than the county.

Everitt and Morill identified 'local community' with 'county community', but much of their evidence for localism did not refer to the county at all but to the village, the parish, and the town. Everitt concluded that for at least three-quarters of the gentry of Kent 'their sphere was the parish rather than the county . . .' Most of the Kentish gentry had their estates concentrated in a few parishes and they married amongst their neighbours. 'The great majority of the gentry spent their lives within a few miles of their manor houses in a circle almost as narrow as that of their tenants'. Everitt wrote that even a member of the small elite of greater gentry, whose political sphere was the county rather than the parish, '. . . remained embedded in that circle of cousins and neighbours . . .' around his home.[56] But the vast majority of the inhabitants of a county were not gentry and studies of Cambridgeshire by Margaret Spufford, of Kent by Peter Clark, and of Lincolnshire by Clive Holmes, have stressed that for most people their community was a village or parish.[57] Other studies have emphasized that for urban dwellers their community was the town.[58] Wallace T. MacCaffrey described Exeter as 'a tightly knit and self-contained society. For most of its inhabitants this little world embraced the whole range of their hopes and cares. Almost all the important events of their lives transpired within it. The city was the political and economic unit within which their daily existence was carried on'. Exeter was '. . . a semi-autonomous community, with its own corporate life and its own special interests', and the average citizen 'found his prime social identification in the community of Exeter, while his identity as an Englishman was only secondary'. This contradicts Morrill's notion that the 'primary allegiance' of people in the early modern period was to their county: that did not apply, acording to MacCaffrey, to the people of such towns as Exeter. Such a town was a community in the sense that the county was not, for unlike the county it was not defined just by territorial boundaries, it also possessed its own values and its own social order which distinguished and divided it from the world outside. 'The counties were merely separate geographic areas,' wrote MacCaffrey, 'while the walls of a city enclosed not only territory but another social world'.[59]

The idea of the town as a community is qualified, however, by MacCaffrey's further observation that 'the civic community' of Exeter was confined to the small oligarchy of merchants among whom the offices of government in the city circulated.[60] This raises the question whether the mass of the inhabitants or only a small elite found their identity as members of the community of Exeter. And some historians have also expressed doubts whether the rural village did in fact form a community, on the grounds that it was deeply involved economically and socially with an area much wider than its own boundaries, that the turnover of its population was very rapid as its inhabitants regularly migrated elsewhere and were replaced by a steady stream of newcomers, and that the ties between most of the villagers were few or fragile.[61] However those factors were not sufficient to prevent a village or town from being a community in the sense of feeling distinct from other villages and towns, having its own interests and its own customs and norms of behaviour. But a community was undermined fundamentally when social division and social conflict within it reached a point at which there were mutually hostile groups with antagonistic interests and conflicting values and norms of behaviour. For a community is defined as being held together, not by inhabiting the same place and sharing the same experiences, but by possessing values in common and subscribing to the same modes of conduct and rules of behaviour.[62]

The civil war has been studied intensively within the context of the localities and the local issues involved in the struggle have been revealed and emphasized. But, as Derek Hirst has pointed out, this has resulted in two kinds of history: one which confines itself to Westminster and the court, and another which scarcely hints at what passes outside the town wall or beyond the county boundary.[63] This raises the question of the relationship between the national and the local issues in the civil war. In Leicestershire the pre-war rivals for local power continued their struggle into the civil war, but now in the name of king or parliament—the Hastings became royalists and the Greys became parliamentarians.[64] Similarly in Wiltshire the pre-war struggle for supremacy continued when the Seymours adhered to the king and the Herberts adhered to the parliament.[65] Everitt regarded the conflicts in these counties as mainly local contests for local power rather than as struggles over national issues about the constitution and the church. The local power-struggle, he concluded, was more important than the conflict 'between puritan and cavalier', and the civil war was 'simply a further stage in the long drawn-out battle for local dominion'.[66] This provides one model for analysing the relationship between local and national issues: the local issues are the real issues; the national issues are either merely cloaks for the local issues or subordinate to them. There is much evidence that fits this hypothesis. A. H. Dodd, the historian of the civil war in Caernarfonshire, judged that '. . . it is in family feud, rather than in political or religious principles, that we must seek the origin of these divisions . . .'[67] '. . . The struggle between Glynllifon and Cefnamwlch . . . was still a more present reality than the struggle between cavalier and roundhead . . .'[68] In Newcastle-upon-Tyne before the civil war there was a conflict between, on the one hand, the small group of perhaps twenty wealthy merchants who controlled the coal trade and the municipal government—the 'inner ring'—and, on the other hand, some members of the trading and manufacturing companies who wanted a share of the profits of the coal trade and of power in the town, and desired to widen the ruling clique to include themselves. The split between royalists and parliamentarians in the civil war conformed to this local cleavage, for the 'inner ring' supported the king and their opponents supported the parliament. 'It is merely an older struggle now disguised by new names', wrote Roger Howell, 'and fought out in terms of a national struggle with which it had little positive connection'. The local struggle was continued under the cover of the causes of king and parliament. '. . . Entirely local battles were being fought under the banner of these national issues'. The local political factions took advantage of the national conflict to work out local rivalries.[69] Also in Chester during the first four decades of the seventeenth century the assembly was divided into opposing factions. A small group within the Company of Merchants, led by the Gamulls, succeeded in controlling the most lucrative areas of external trade, and they were opposed by a group led by William Edwards. 'The split between royalist and parliamentarian in Chester in 1642 . . .', wrote A. M. Johnson, 'was for most of the principals the expression and outgrowth under national labels of the local political struggle in which they had been engaged throughout the early seventeenth century'.[70] But this model fails to explain why or how the national issues arise at all—they appear to be generated artificially at Whitehall and Westminster without roots in or connection with society at large; it ignores, or does not explain, or plays down the religious issues and movements; it does not allow sufficiently for the influence of the national issues on the local issues; and it does not tell the whole story or fit all the facts.

In many cases the pre-war structures of power and patterns of conflict did not survive into the civil war, or at least were temporarily re-arranged and subordinated by the national crisis and struggle. Although at one point John Morrill maintained that '. . . the prior sub-political divisions within each shire or borough were reflected in the line-up of forces by early 1643', and that 'polarisation then usually followed the lines of purely local groupings . . .', elsewhere he admitted that 'the pre-existent power groupings within each county buckled under the pressure and tensions of national events . . .'[71] In Somerset the local conflict for local power between the two factions of the gentry did not continue: they were re-united in opposition to the king in 1640 and to the parliament in 1642.[72] In Caernarfonshire the rivalry between Cefnamwlch and Glynllifon was suppressed by the civil war: both factions became royalists, even though less enthusiastically on the part of Glynllifon than on the part of Cefnamwlch. A. H. Dodd saw the civil war as delaying the triumph of the Glynnes over their rivals.[73] In Chester, although the Gamulls did become royalists and William Edwards did become an active parliamentarian, Johnson's conclusion that the civil war parties corresponded to the pre-war factions is weakened by his own evidence that most of Edwards's old faction acquiesced during the civil war in the rule of the Gamulls and the royalists.[74] Religion must be taken into account, for after all Edwards was a puritan. Howell, in his conclusion that the civil war conflict in Newcastle was merely a continuation of the pre-war struggle between the 'inner ring' and its rivals, left out of account his own evidence that 'there was another sort of opposition in the town, a religious one', which was not identical with the opposition to the 'inner ring'. It was Henry Dawson, one of the leaders of the puritans in Newcastle in the 1630s, who came to power there as a result of parliament's victory in the civil war. He and his circle only temporarily replaced the old oligarchy, which returned to power at the restoration. But the puritan movement emerged stronger after the civil war than before; religious dissent could not be suppressed at the restoration; and the religious pattern of the town was changed radically and permanently.[75] Thus the local power-struggle between the 'inner ring' and its rivals may have been less important, and was certainly less profound in its consequences, than the struggle between the puritans and their opponents.

John Morrill, despite some contradictions arising from his reluctance to reject Everitt's thesis totally, has offered an alternative model. He observed that provincialism did not exclude 'concern for general or national political and constitutional issues' and argued that 'such issues took on local colours and were articulated within local contexts'. People across the country 'shared many assumptions about the nature of the crisis', but 'their response was largely conditioned by local events and local power structures'.[76] In this model the national issues are given more importance and their impact on the localities more significance: the national issues take on local colours rather than the local issues taking on national colours. This model may be extended by adding that the crisis and conflict at the centre worked upon local power structures and struggles, modifying them, intensifying them, and directing them into the national context. In the period 1600–1640 the merchant oligarchy of Chichester was at odds with the clergy of the cathedral— a common type of conflict in early Stuart England.[77] It was worsened by the Laudianism of Bishop Montagu. In the 1630s the corporation sought to bring under its jurisdiction the cathedral close, which occupied nearly a quarter of the area of the city, but the king supported the clergy and counter-attacked against the charter of the city. In the civil war the merchant oligarchy inclined towards parliament and the clergy and gentry of the close tended towards the king. Although Anthony Fletcher concluded from this that 'the alignments of the previous decades formed the basis of civil war allegiances in Chichester...', the real significance of what he called 'parochial parliamentarianism' was that the local conflict was intensified by the injection into it of a new national ecclesiastical policy and by the revelation of the hostility of the central government to the interests of the corporation.[78] That made the merchants aware of national issues, caused them to relate those issues to their own local situation, and led them to take sides in the national struggle. At Norwich before the civil war the municipal government was sympathetic towards puritanism: it brought puritan ministers to the town, set up lectureships, encouraged sermons, and enforced observance of the sabbath. But in 1635 Matthew Wren became bishop of Norwich and launched a campaign against the puritans. He suspended eight Norwich ministers and suppressed sermons. The significant point is that the eruption of Laudianism into Norwich split the corporation. A majority of the aldermen supported Wren or acquiesced in his actions, but a minority of the aldermen, backed by most of the common council, opposed him. This generated a power struggle in which the puritans were successful and aligned Norwich with parliament in the civil war. It is true that the grievances of the Norwich puritans were against Wren rather than against episcopacy, and that their aim was to regain control over religion within their own city, eliminating Laudian practices and restoring puritan ministers and puritan worship in their own community, rather than to change national religious policy and the general ecclesiastical system. But the Norwich puritans were aware that their grievances were not peculiar to themselves and that their struggle with their bishop could not be won within the city. 'Thus they became intensely interested in the developing hostility between parliament and the crown and they exerted their energies once war became a reality to encourage their town to support parliament. If parliament lost, their hopes were destroyed'.[79] They did not just react to national events, they participated in them actively. As Paul Slack found at Salisbury, 'the national political crisis' increased local disputes and divisions and 'concern with national political issues arose out of local controversies'.[80]

But how localised and particularised was the religious issue in the civil war? The puritans felt themselves to be part of a national and a general movement; they felt a sense of kinship and solidarity with 'godly people' everywhere; they were intent upon establishing a godly nation or commonwealth. Puritanism united large numbers of people from different and diverse neighbourhoods in common sympathies and antagonisms.[81] Puritanism grew as a result of contacts beyond the locality and puritans knew that they could not survive nor succeed without such contacts. Although Howell concluded that the puritan movement in Newcastle was a response to a local situation, he also provided evidence that it depended for its existence and continuance on contacts through trade with London and the continent. 'Many of the men who were later to emerge as leaders in the puritan movement in Newcastle . . . had established trading contacts outside the conservative north for extensive periods of time'. Above all the puritan movement in Newcastle drew strength from contacts with the Scots.[82] Like the Norwich puritans, the Newcastle puritans knew that they could not achieve their local aims without the support of a national movement and without participating in a national struggle on the side of parliament.

Religious grievances and religious conflicts were local. Petitions against the clergy showed that the parishioners were concerned primarily with the conduct of their own minister, his performance of his duties and the quality of his ministry.[83] Parishioners were also divided: some attacked their minister, others defended him; some assaulted altars and stained-glass windows and images, others defended them. Some parishioners wanted changes in the government of their parish church, with a shift in power from the squire and the parson to the congregation, others did not.[84] Some parishioners wanted a greater role for 'the godly' in their local church and stricter discipline over 'the ungodly': 'the ungodly' did not. These were local issues, but they were also national issues, and it was from these local issues that the national puritan movement grew. Thus a third model may be suggested: the national issues grew out of the local issues. Robert Ashton has written recently that 'historians have paid, and are paying, too much attention to the imagined dichotomy between the local and the national, as opposed to studying the process whereby the latter emerged out of the former...'[85] This model removes the artificial separation of local from national issues and, unlike the other two models, provides an explanation of the origins of the national issues.

The fundamental division that occurred in parliament in 1645–1646, which contemporaries termed a conflict between presbyterians and Independents, was at root a dispute about whether the parochial system should continue intact and be strengthened. The parish was not merely a unit of ecclesiastical government, it had become an increasingly important unit of civil government and social control.[86] The sects believed that a true church consisted only of the godly and, since most people (at least for the present) were not godly, a national church could not be a true church. This also involved rejection of the parish church which, in comprising all the people of a locality, included both godly and ungodly. So the sects formed their congregations of only the godly people in a parish or of the godly people from different parishes. Thus the congregation of a sect was not co-extensive with the parish nor confined by its boundaries nor subject to its control. This above all distinguished the sects from the presbyterians and the Independents. 'In the presbyterian and Independent schemes there was still to be a national church, though it was to be a federation of parishes with a greater or less degree of independence. So the sectaries, in refusing to communicate in parish churches . . . were rejecting the state as well as the church'.[87] Erastians, moderate episcopalians, presbyterians and Independents, all defended the parish system, and presbyterians and Independents disagreed on the degree of freedom from central control to be allowed to the parish. But when the Independents went further and showed willingness to permit the sects to separate from the parish churches and to form their own autonomous congregations outside the parochial system, the split with the presbyterians became irreconcilable. It was this issue that '...proved to be the deepest and most fundamental point of conflict between Independents and the most moderate and accommodating of the English presbyterians, and that doomed to failure the parliamentary accommodation committee's attempt to find a compromise'.[88]

The split between the puritans/presbyterians and the sects was not new. It was not a consequence of the civil war. It went back at least to the Elizabethan period and was related to long-term changes in English society and the attendant intensification of social antagonisms. Numerous local studies have recorded in the decades before the civil war an acceleration of the differentiation of the rural population and an increase of the polarisation between rich and poor in the localities. Land and control of economic resources passed from smaller and middling farmers to a few big farmers, and the numbers of landless, or almost landless, labourers increased. A polarisation grew, in the words of Alan Macfarlane, between those 'who owned the farms and shops' and those 'who worked for them'.[89] The wealthier villagers—farmers for the market and the more prosperous tradesmen—formed the ruling groups of the parishes.[90] They were fearful that the increase of the poor would result in the growth of irreligion, discontent and disorder, and they were frightened, in times of dearth and depression, by unemployment, vagrancy, crime and riot. They responded, not only as individuals but as the groups which faced these problems and pressures, by seeking to strengthen their own position as the ruling elite and to improve social control, by compelling attendance at church, by enforcing observation of the sabbath, by suppressing alehouses and disorderly popular recreations, and by imposing a strict moral discipline in order to control the birth-rate and to prevent drunkenness and idleness, to which they attributed much of the poverty. These aims they articulated individually and collectively as the puritan movement.[91] At Terling in Essex the gulf between the richer villagers and their poorer neighbours had widened before the civil war. The more substantial inhabitants formed the ruling group of the parish. Wealth, status and power coincided in this group and differentiated them from the mass of the villagers, and on to these distinctions grew differences of education, culture and religion. They became puritans and sought to impose on the poor new values and new standards of behaviour, and incidentally to reinforce their own dominant position.[92] But it must be remembered that such local puritan elites fought on two fronts, not only against the 'ungodly' masses but also against governments, bishops, aristocrats and local gentry, who were unsympathetic to the godly discipline and resisted loss of their control over the ecclesiastical system, parish churches and local society, to the village elites.[93] The victory of parliament in the civil war, to which the local puritans contributed so much, and the defeat of the royalists, which weakened monarchical and aristocratic power, gave them the opportunity and the necessity to push harder. In Cheshire the godly elites of the parishes asserted and strengthened themselves both against the poor and against the local gentry and county rulers.[94] But sectarianism, which began in Elizabeth's reign and earlier and came to a climax in the civil war, rejected the parish and articulated a community based, not on ties of neighbourhood, or kinship, or wealth, or status, or power, but on spiritual brotherhood and on its own norms of behaviour and outlook. The sectarian congregations—voluntary and exclusive—provided an alternative community or focus for some of the smaller farmers, poorer tradesmen and artisans, who were excluded from the elites which had taken power in rural or urban parishes: it gave them the means to escape from the domination of their richer neighbours and at the same time to differentiate themselves by their godliness from the mass of labourers, paupers, vagrants and criminals.[95]

A form of ecclesiastical system based on the parish and dominated by the leaders of the parish, to which all would have been compelled to belong and to submit to its discipline, would have suited well many of the local elites, and at the end of the civil war the slogan used to describe such a system was 'presbyterianism'.[96] The Independents took up a middle position between presbyterianism and sectarianism and sought to combine a parochial discipline for the ungodly masses with permission for the godly—the sects—to separate from the parish churches and form their own autonomous congregations. This was unacceptable to the presbyterians, by whose hostility the Independents were driven into closer association with the sects. The conflict over the national religious settlement and the form of the national church was a reflection of the struggle for control of the parishes; and in that struggle there was involved the question whether the richer farmers and tradesmen would continue to advance in wealth, status and power at the expense of smaller men, or whether the latter would develop the institutions by which they could reassert their status and regain a share of power, and so stem the erosion of their economic independence.

The class-consciousness of the aristocracy and gentry has not been doubted by historians, but they have been represented as being the only class in seventeenth-century society, because they alone felt conscious of belonging to a social formation that transcended local boundaries and embraced the nation.[97] It has been argued that other groups in society did not form classes because their consciousness of the group to which they belonged was confined to their own locality, and they did not identify with people of similar status in other localities but only with their peers in their own neighbourhood. In pre-industrial society class-consciousness was localised, but it was nonetheless class-consciousness for that and nonetheless productive of class conflicts, though generally on a local scale.[98] Keith Wrightson and David Levine have shown that the more substantial villagers of Terling 'formed a local ruling group that possessed a distinct social identity', which, although it did not extend beyond the bounds of the parish, did exhibit itself in a growing desire to differentiate themselves in every sort of way from their lesser neighbours, and in a growing hostility towards the poor.[99] Philip Pettit found that at Briggstock in Northamptonshire 'a definite cleavage existed in the village community between " the rich and mighty men . . ." and "others to be pitied for their beggarly estates".'[100] W. G. Hoskins detected at Wigston Magna in Leicestershire in the seventeenth century '. . the emergence of a rudimentary class-structure . . .', with an 'upper class' of wealthy villagers and a lower class of labourers.[101] At Kirkby Lonsdale in Westmoreland in the seventeenth century Macfarlane discovered '. . . traces of a growing separation between the rich and the poor, which turned into a permanent class barrier . . .'[102] Buchanan Sharp found in the west of England evidence of 'class hatred' between the poor rural artisans and the rich villagers.[103] Thus there is evidence that at a local level the elites of villages and small towns became conscious of themselves as a class, and so did the poor; and also evidence that at a local level there were conflicts and differences of norms and values between these classes. Squeezed between rich and poor, the smaller farmers and artisans also became conscious of themselves as a class, and in differentiating and defending themselves surpassed local boundaries, co-operating with others in a similar position and developing 'a consciousness of membership of a group whose interest transcended parish boundaries'.[104] This consciousness enabled many of them to become sectaries and some of them to become levellers.

The county community either did not exist or was restricted to a tiny fraction of the population. If towns and villages were communities only a small minority of the inhabitants belonged to such communities. The most important fact about the localities was not that the people were united in a community but that they were deeply divided into antagonistic local classes. This explains why the issues of the civil war could not be settled by votes at Westminster but only by a multitude of local struggles. This localisation of class conflict also had the effect in the end of limiting and reducing the impact of the revolution on the existing social and economic order.

Notes

1. S. R. Gardiner, *History of the great civil war 1642–1649* (4 vols., London, 1893), i, 53–7, 61–3, 79–80.
2. J. H. Hexter, *The reign of King Pym* (Cambridge, Mass., 1941).
3. Lotte Glow, 'Pym and parliament: the methods of moderation' in *Jn. Mod. Hist.*, 36 (1964); 'The committee of safety', in *E.H.R.*, 80 (1965); 'Political affiliations in the house of commons after Pym's death' in *I.H.R. Bull.*, 38 (1965); Lotte Mulligan (Glow), 'Property and parliamentary politics in the English civil war, 1642-6' in *Historical Studies* (Melbourne), 16 (1975); Valerie Pearl, 'Oliver St John and the "middle group" in the Long Parliament' in *E.H.R.*, 81 (1966); 'The "royal Independents" in the English civil war' in *R. Hist. Soc. Trans.*, 5th series, 18 (1968).
4. David Underdown, *Pride's purge: politics in the puritan revolution* (Oxford, 1971); Clive Holmes, *The eastern association in the English civil war* (Cambridge, 1974); Patricia Crawford, *Denzil Holles 1598-1680: a study of his political career* (Royal Historical Society Studies in History No. 16), (London, 1979).
5. Christopher Thompson, 'The origins of the politics of the parliamentary middle group, 1625-1629' in *R. Hist. Soc. Trans.*, 5th series, 22 (1972), p. 71.
6. Hexter, op. cit., p. 66.
7. Pearl, 'Oliver St John', pp 495, 514.
8. Underdown, op. cit., pp 45–6.
9. Clive Holmes, 'Colonel King and Lincolnshire politics, 1642-1646' in *Hist. Jn.* 16 (1973), p. 452.
10. David Underdown, 'Party management in the recruiter elections, 1645–1648' in *E.H.R.*, 83 (1968), p. 237.
11. Robert Ashton, *The English civil war: conservatism and revolution 1603–1649* (London, 1978), p. 194.
12. J. S. Morrill, *The revolt of the provinces: conservatives and radicals in the English civil war 1630-1650* (London, 1976), pp 117, 124.
13. Hexter, op. cit., p. 67.
14. Underdown, *Pride's purge*, pp 46–63; Hexter, op. cit., pp 66–7.
15. Morrill, op. cit., pp 117, 124.
16. Ashton, op. cit., p. 194.
17. Crawford, op. cit., pp 70–1, 83–4.
18. Ashton, op. cit., pp 194–5.
19. Pearl, 'Oliver St John', p. 514.
20. Underdown, 'Party management', p. 238.
21. Stephen Foster, 'Presbyterians, Independents and puritans' in *Past and Present*, 47 (1970), p. 146.

22. James E. Farnell, 'The aristocracy and leadership of parliament in the English civil war' in *Jn. Mod. Hist.*, 44 (1972).
23. G. F. Trevallyn Jones, *Saw-Pit Wharton: the political career from 1640 to 1691 of Philip, fourth Lord Wharton* (Sydney, 1967), pp 69–70, 78.
24. John R. Mac Cormack, *Revolutionary politics in the Long Parliament* (Cambridge, Mass., 1973), p. 6.
25. Mark A. Kishlansky, *The rise of the new model army* (Cambridge, 1979), pp 18–9, 24–5, 295–6; 'The emergence of adversary politics in the Long Parliament' in *Jn. Mod. Hist.*, 49 (1977), pp 617–8, 628–9.
26. Morrill, op. cit., p. 117; Ashton, op. cit., pp 194–5.
27. Patricia Crawford, 'The Savile affair' in *E.H.R.*, 90 (1975), p. 77.
28. Underdown, *Pride's purge*, pp 69–71.
29. Ashton, op. cit., pp 220, 231–2.
30. Underdown, *Pride's purge*, pp 64–5.
31. Ibid., pp 68–9.
32. MacCormack, op. cit., p. 7.
33. Crawford, *Denzil Holles*, pp 113, 123, 130, 135, 159–160, 168–9, 172; Ashton, op. cit., pp 239–241; Pearl, 'Royal Independents'.
34. Ashton, op. cit., p. 241.
35. Pearl, 'Royal Independents', p. 91.
36. Gardiner, op. cit., ii, 75–6; Ashton, op. cit., pp 216–8; Clive Holmes, *Seventeenth-century Lincolnshire* (History of Lincolnshire, Vol. VII), (Lincoln, 1980), pp 194, 196–7; 'Colonel King', pp 462–5; *The eastern association*, pp 189, 215; Anthony Fletcher, *A county community in peace and war: Sussex 1600–1660* (London, 1975), pp 116–120; Lawrence Kaplan, 'Presbyterians and Independents in 1643' in *E.H.R.*, 84 (1969), pp 253–5; George Yule, *The Independents in the English civil war* (Cambridge, 1958), pp 57–9, 61–2, 65, 78–9, 81; Crawford, *Denzil Holles* pp 121, 130, 159–160, 168–9, 172.
37. Murray Tolmie, *The triumph of the saints: the separate churches of London 1616–1649* (Cambridge, 1977), pp 89–95, 99–100, 101, 116–7, 119, 124–130, 130–138.
38. Pearl, *'Royal Independents'*, pp 91–5.
39. Kishlansky, *New model army*, pp 15–17.
40. Morrill, op. cit., p. 117.
41. Holmes, 'Colonel King', p. 452.
42. Alan Everitt, *The community of Kent and the great rebellion 1640–60* (Leicester, 1966), p. 13; *The local community and the great rebellion* (Historical Association Pamphlet G. 70) (London, 1969), pp 5–8.
43. Everitt, *Kent*, p. 20.
44. J. S. Morrill, *Cheshire 1630–1660: county government and society during the English revolution* (Oxford, 1974), pp 4–5.
45. Holmes, *Lincolnshire*, pp 83–4.
46. Morrill, *Cheshire*, p. 9.
47. Fletcher, op. cit., pp 48, 134–6, 241–3.
48. Everitt, *The local community*, pp 15–16.
49. Morrill, *Revolt of the provinces*, pp 43–4.
50. T. G. Barnes, *Somerset 1625–1640: a county's government during the 'personal rule'* (London, 1961), ch. 10.
51. A. H. Dodd, 'Caernarvonshire in the civil war' in *Transactions of Caernarvonshire Historical Society*, 14 (1953); *A history of Caernarvonshire 1284–1900* (Caernarvonshire Historical Society, 1968), chs 5 & 6.

52. Morrill, *Cheshire*, pp 16–17, 32–4.
53. Everitt, *The local community*, p. 18.
54. David Underdown, *Somerset in the civil war and interregnum* (Newton Abbot, 1973), pp 22, 117.
55. Fletcher, op. cit., pp 241–3, 255–6, 275–281.
56. Everitt, *Kent*, pp 34, 41–4, 207; Morrill, *Cheshire*, pp 15–16, 233–4.
57. Margaret Spufford, *Contrasting communities: English villagers in the sixteenth and seventeenth centuries* (Cambridge, 1974), p. 344; Peter Clark, *English provincial society from the reformation to the revolution: religion, politics and society in Kent 1500–1640* (Hassocks, Sussex, 1977), pp 121–5; Holmes, *Lincolnshire*, pp 1–12; Peter Laslett, *The world we have lost* (London, 1965), pp 53–80.
58. Holmes, *Lincolnshire*, pp 32–3; Perez Zagorin, *The court and the country: the beginning of the English revolution* (London, 1969), pp 130–1.
59. Wallace T. Mac Caffrey, *Exeter, 1540–1640* (Cambridge, Mass., 1958), pp 203–4, 279–282.
60. Ibid., pp 275–7.
61. Alan Macfarlane, *The origins of English individualism: the family, property and social transition* (Oxford, 1979), pp 4–5, 31–2, 55–6, 162–3; Keith Wrightson and David Levine, *Poverty and piety in an English village: Terling, 1525–1700* (New York, 1979), pp 73–141; Holmes, *Lincolnshire*, pp 13–28.
62. Kai T. Erikson, *Wayward puritans* (New York, 1966), ch. 1.
63. Derek Hirst, 'The defection of Sir Edward Dering, 1640–1641' in *Hist. Jn.*, 15 (1972), p. 193.
64. Everitt, *The local community*, p. 15.
65. Morrill, *Revolt of the provinces*, pp 43–4.
66. Everitt, *The local community*, p. 15.
67. Dodd, 'Caernarvonshire in the civil war', p. 1.
68. Dodd, *A history of Caernarvonshire*, p. 104.
69. Roger Howell, *Newcastle-upon-Tyne and the puritan revolution* (Oxford, 1967), pp 3, 23–4, 34, 35–62, 162–3, 171, 173–7, 214–5, 217, 333–343.
70. A. M. Johnson, 'Politics in Chester during the civil wars and the interregnum 1640–42', in Peter Clark and Paul Slack (eds), *Crisis and order in English towns 1500–1700* (London, 1972), pp 204–7, 208–214, 218–9.
71. Morrill, *Revolt of the provinces*, pp 13–4, 43–6.
72. Barnes, op. cit., pp 309–310; Underdown, *Somerset*, pp 38–41, 46–7, 67–70.
73. Dodd, 'Caernarvonshire in the civil war', pp 6–7, 23–5; *A history of Caernarvonshire*, pp 124–130.
74. Johnson, op. cit., pp 208–9.
75. Howell, op. cit., pp 61–2, 89, 122–4, 128, 144–5, 148–150, 163–4, 174–7, 214–5, 336–345.
76. Morrill, *Revolt of the provinces*, pp 13–14, 43–6; Derek Hirst, *The representative of the people? Voters and voting in England under the early Stuarts* (Cambridge, 1975), pp 147–184.
77. Mac Caffrey, op. cit., pp 118–125, 196–7, 200–202; Paul Slack, 'An election to the Short Parliament', in *I.H.R. Bull.*, 46 (1973), p. 109; David Underdown, 'A case concerning bishops' lands: Cornelius Burges and the corporation of Wells' in *E.H.R.*, 78 (1963), pp 21–2.
78. Fletcher, op. cit., pp 234–9, 258–263.
79. John T. Evans, *Seventeenth-century Norwich: politics, religion and government, 1620–1690* (Oxford, 1979), pp 85–98, 100–107, 122–3, 126–9, 131–149.

80. Slack, op. cit., pp 108, 110–112.
81. Zagorin, op. cit., p. 187.
82. Howell, op. cit., pp 71–2, 97, 107, 343–5.
83. I. M. Green, 'The persecution of "scandalous" and " malignant" parish clergy during the English civil war' in *E.H.R.*, 94 (1979).
84. Brian Manning, *The English people and the English revolution 1640–1649* (London, 1976), pp 30–45, 159–162; 'Puritanism and democracy 1640–1642' in Donald Pennington and Keith Thomas, *Puritans and revolutionaries* (Oxford, 1978), pp 139–160.
85. Ashton, op. cit., p. 70.
86. Christopher Hill, *Society and puritanism in pre-revolutionary England* (London, 1964), pp 429–430.
87. Ibid., p. 438.
88. Tolmie, op. cit., pp 89–95, 99–101, 116–7, 119, 124–138.
89. W. G. Hoskins, *The midland peasant: the economic and social history of a Leicestershire village* (London, 1957), pp 141–7, 195–204, 213–5; Spufford, op. cit., pp 66–90, 100–118, 165–6; Macfarlane, op. cit., pp 67–79.
90. Hoskins, op. cit., p. 208; Hill, op. cit., pp 432–4.
91. Clark, op. cit., pp 154–7, 157, 175–7; Hill, op. cit., pp 280–1, 293.
92. Wrightson and Levine, op. cit., pp 14–18, 103–6, 109, 140, 156–7, 158–162, 174–9.
93. Manning, *The English people and the English revolution*, pp 152–162; Hill, op. cit., pp 228–240.
94. Morrill, *Cheshire*, pp 225–246, 268–272, 331.
95. Clark, op. cit., pp 170, 177–8, 371; Holmes, *Lincolnshire*, pp 43–5.
96. Hill, op. cit., pp 440, 487.
97. Laslett, op. cit., pp 22–52.
98. J. W. Smit, 'The Netherlands revolution', in Robert Forster and Jack P. Greene (eds), *Preconditions of revolution in early modern Europe* (Baltimore, 1972), p. 40.
99. Wrightson and Levine, op. cit., pp 14–18, 103–6, 109, 140, 156–7, 158–162, 174–9.
100. Philip A. J. Pettit, *The royal forests of Northamptonshire: a study of their economy 1558–1714* (Northamptonshire Record Society, Vol. 23), (Gateshead, 1968), pp 174–5.
101. Hoskins, op. cit., pp 213–5.
102. Macfarlane, op. cit., pp 67–79.
103. Buchanan Sharp, *In contempt of all authority: rural artisans and riot in the west of England, 1586–1660* (Berkeley, 1980), pp 7–8, 36–40, 264.
104. Holmes, *Lincolnshire*, pp 22–8.

The Dublin convention, the protestant community and the emergence of an ecclesiastical settlement in 1660

J. I. McGuire

Prologue

On 27 January 1661 two archbishops and ten bishops were consecrated in St Patrick's Cathedral, Dublin. It was the first episcopal consecration in Ireland since 1645 and for the occasion the newly appointed dean of St Patrick's, William Fuller, who had suffered for his ecclesiastical loyalties during the interregnum, composed a triumphant anthem:

> Now that the Lord the mitre hath restored,
> which with the crown lay in the dust abhorred.[1]

Fuller's exuberance was understandable: twelve months earlier the king was in exile, episcopal jurisdiction was proscribed and the commonwealth ecclesiastical settlement was intact. All had now changed and this ceremony brought to completion the government's decision to restore episcopacy in Ireland.

That there would be a return to the old system of church government was clear within three weeks of the king's return to Whitehall, the names of the new Irish prelates being common knowledge before the end of June, quite some time before the identity of their English counterparts was known. Why did the government feel able to take this major step in its ecclesiastical policy at such a delicate stage in British political life, and more particularly for an Ireland dominated by the beneficiaries of the Cromwellian settlement?

Over the past thirty years or so a number of historians have dealt with the ecclesiastical situation in Ireland, but only in passing. The first of these was Robert S. Bosher, whose monograph, *The making of the restoration settlement. The influence of the Laudians*, itself a revealing title, was published in 1951. Dr Bosher, with his belief in a veritable Laudian conspiracy, dealt summarily with Ireland: 'there was no hesitation', he wrote, 'over ecclesiastical policy in Ireland, and action there anticipated the course of events in England. In a land where the tradition of autocratic rule prevailed and parliament was suspended, there was no need to temporize with the puritan party, and the government showed its hand plainly'.[2] More recently T. C. Barnard has argued that the Dublin convention favoured an Erastian presbyterian system but that the government's decision to restore episcopacy was accepted because the protestant gentry were more concerned with the preservation and extension of the protestant interest in Ireland than with the forms of church government.[3] Most recently Dr Ian Green has underlined the necessity of bearing in mind developments in all three kingdoms, 'for every move that the king made in one country was bound to be regarded as a foretaste of their own settlement by his subjects in the other two kingdoms'.[4] In his monograph Dr Green has shown that the Irish episcopal bench included a far higher proportion of 'sufferers', eleven out of fifteen nominees, than did the English, although he has not explored the potential significance of this fact for the situation in England. The episcopalian restoration in Ireland he attributes to the predictable support of Ormond at court, and the less predictable support of Lord Broghill and Sir Charles Coote, but he does not go into any detail since the English situation is his concern.[5] The purpose of this paper, therefore, is to examine the political context in which both the commonwealth religious settlement was overturned and presbyterian ambitions thwarted by the nomination of the Irish bishops in 1660. Central to this examination is the role of the convention which met in Dublin in the spring of 1660 and which was, in effect, the representative assembly of the Irish protestant community. But before this convention could meet the country had first to be secured.

Securing the country

Protestant Ireland felt keenly the effects of the political instability in England which followed the death of Oliver Cromwell in September 1658. The subsequent collapse of the protectorate, the failure of army and parliamentary leaders to establish a *modus vivendi*, the restoration of the 'rump' parliament in May 1659, its dissolution by the army in October and its rehabilitation in December, all seemed to presage a rapid drift towards either constitutional and social anarchy or some form of military dictatorship. The very foundations of government were in doubt.[6] In Ireland this constitutional uncertainty was all the more serious because of the need to secure the recently completed land settlement on an unchallengeable bedrock of law.[7] The fall of the protectorate, under which much of the settlement had been authorised and implemented, left the legal basis of that settlement in doubt.

The effects of this fundamental uncertainty were heightened in 1659 by the unpopular measures taken by Edmund Ludlow, who took command of the army in Ireland in July. Staunch republicans replaced officers associated with Henry Cromwell's government, and the displaced were quick to claim that Ludlow was favouring with promotion in the army extreme sectaries, particularly anabaptists. When Ludlow returned to England having remodelled the army to his own liking, he left behind him considerable discontent among the protestant gentry and many army officers.[8]

Against this background of disenchantment with Ludlow's activities, news in October of Lambert's expulsion of the 'rump' parliament must have appeared the last straw. Once again the foundations of government, with all that that implied for legal tenure, were being tampered with. So, on 13 December a group of army officers seized Dublin Castle in the name of the 'rump' parliament. They arrested the commissioners for government and issued a declaration which claimed that providence had thus prevented the ruin of religion and liberty.[9] Command of the army was taken from Ludlow's appointees and concentrated in the hands of the coup's main instigators. As a hostile republican pamphleteer put it,

> What means the self conferring of two regiments upon Sir H. Waller, two upon Sir Chas Coote and three upon his brother? So as upon the matter, two men have seven regiments.[10]

As for the rank and file, since Ludlow's officers had held 'a stricter hand upon the soldiers than others did, punishing them for swearing, drunkenness, absence from God's service or their duty', they naturally turned to their new commander, 'some upon promise of their arrears, some for a barrell of beer, and others for trifles'.[11]

Effective power following the coup of 13 December rested with Lord Broghill in Munster, Sir Charles Coote in Connaught and Colonel Cooper in Ulster. These three, together with Sir Theophilus Jones, ensured that army support for the coup was not confined to a handful of officers in Dublin. Broghill and Coote had considerable personal authority in Munster and Connaught respectively and their involvement ensured the goodwill of the landed English interest in the provinces, worried as they were by the apparent threat to the security of their estates and to the peace of the body politic which the continuance of disorder and the lack of a settled government clearly posed.

The attitude of those who had seized political power in Ireland was clearly going to be important for the success or failure of General Monck's plans for a general settlement in church and state in both islands. Substantial dissent in one country could have seriously endangered a settlement in all three. In November he had written from Scotland to Broghill urging him not to leave public life, and when news of the Irish officers' coup and declaration for parliament reached him towards the end of December he wrote to William Lenthall, speaker of the rehabilitated 'rump', telling him how he and his army had observed a day of thanksgiving for this Irish declaration.[12] Three days later he set out for England. Throughout January he was in touch with Coote, who assured him of support for his as yet ambiguous plans, thus amply justifying Ludlow's sour comment that Monck's dealings with Ireland were 'coloured with the name of Sir Charles Coote'.[13]

In the weeks immediately following the December coup, those who had taken power were content to seek relatively simple objectives, the legalising and protecting of what had been achieved under the protectorate. This can be seen in draft instructions prepared in late December or early January for Dr Henry Jones, Sir William Bury and Colonel Richard Lawrence to take with them on a mission to the council of state in London.[14] While it seems clear that this journey was never undertaken, the instructions merit attention as a statement of the protestant gentry's initially limited aims.

The draft instructions were divided into seventeen articles, most of which were concerned with regularising what had been made irregular by the fall of the protectorate and the subsequent uncertainty of the constitutional and legal position. The agents were to seek an act of oblivion for all who had acted under public authority after 19 April 1653, and an act to make good all laws and ordinances for Ireland made since that date and not repealed before 22 April 1659, as well as statutory confirmation of all grants of land, leases and contracts made since 19 April 1653. Other articles were concerned with the payment of army arrears and with trade, while three articles touched on ecclesiastical affairs, two of which concerned church lands.

The ecclesiastical settlement was covered in the fourth article of instructions, the agents being instructed to seek an act of parliament, presumably the Long Parliament, which would make provision for the settlement of 'Godly, faithful, orthodox, learned and gospel preaching ministers' in all parts of Ireland. They were also to seek measures for encouraging Dublin University and schools throughout Ireland in the education of the young in piety and learning. They were to ask that all impropriations and glebe lands at the commonwealth's disposal in Ireland should be used for the maintenance of schools, schoolmasters and preaching ministers of the gospel.[15]

Superficially these religious proposals did not amount to a radical departure from the commonwealth system as it had developed in the 1650s. Religion was to continue in the hands of ministers of the gospel who would be maintained where the government directed and by impropriations and glebes at the government's disposal. There was no suggestion that ecclesiastical organisation might revert to the pre-commonwealth system based on the parish as the ecclesiastical unit, although this was already happening in some areas as a result of local clerical initiatives.[16] This impression, which the instructions give, of a desire to perfect rather than to change the existing ecclesiastical system is confirmed in the eighth and tenth articles. Neither article is concerned with the religious settlement as such, although both of them imply a rejection of any return to a pre-commonwealth episcopalian church, concerned as they are with the revenues and rents to be had from lands formerly held by the late king, archbishops, bishops, deans, deans and chapters, and other such ecclesiastical persons.

But even if these instructions hint of no fundamental change in the commonwealth's ecclesiastical structure, the use of the word 'orthodox' in the fourth article certainly represents a departure from commonwealth practice. It implies a standard or norm against which the beliefs and practices of a preaching minister of the gospel might be tested, and such standards were not a feature of the commonwealth religious settlement, indeed the very nature of that settlement, based as it was on Cromwell's notion of toleration, seemed to preclude them. A religious settlement which included erstwhile episcopalians and presbyterians on the one hand and independents and sectaries on the other, among the officially licensed and salaried ministers, could not be said to have possessed a common ground of orthodox beliefs or standards.

The move towards orthodoxy is evident too in the first declaration of the council of officers after the seizing of Dublin Castle in December: the people were guilty of apostasy and of breaking the covenant; they were rapidly heading towards the Münster desolations and only God's providence would save them from this fate.[17] This reference to the Anabaptist disorders at Münster in 1534–5 suggests a close connection between religious and political anarchy in the officers' minds. While it can be argued, as did Godfrey Davies, that this reference to the Münster chaos shows presbyterian leanings, such an interpretative emphasis has the effect of missing the wider and more significant implications of this declaration: the goal was stability and stability in religion meant more than efficient organisation; it involved orthodoxy.[18] Furthermore, this association of orthodoxy and stability, seen in the context of a growing demand for a comprehensive settlement in church and state, offered opportunity only to those whose religious outlook could admit of orthodoxy, that is presbyterians and episcopalians.

When it became known in January that the instigators and supporters of the December coup were summoning a convention representative of the parliamentary constituencies to meet in Dublin, the news was greeted with dismay by commonwealthmen in both England and Ireland:

> What means the parliament-like convention to meet in Dublin the 24 of January, with other dismal news from thence? As if the interest of Jesus Christ and the good old cause of holiness and righteousness were taking leave of poor Ireland.[19]

General Ludlow hurried back to Ireland but was prevented from landing in Dublin and forced to sail south. His ship anchored off Waterford, from where he conducted a rather hopeless correspondence with the governor and mayor. The convention he regarded as the work of the Stuart interest and he was quite unconvinced by suggestions to the contrary.[20] In London the Council of State was similarly disturbed and suggested to General Monck that the Irish brigade should be sent to Chester in case it were needed in Ireland, advice which Monck chose not to heed.[21] Clearly external interference with the course events were taking in Ireland was not going to materialise.

Within Ireland, however, a further purge of the army was required before the convention could meet in safety. Broghill and Coote, as a near contemporary historian put it, 'projected to suspend the convention until they had modelled the army to their mind, and got rid of Sir Hardress Waller'.[22] It was Waller himself who provided them with their opportunity; supported by two companies of foot and a few officers he seized Dublin Castle on 15 February.[23] But within an hour of the take-over the citizens of

Dublin were besieging the conspirators.[24] When Waller and his associates tried to bargain with the mayor two days later, he sent them so 'resolute' an answer that the soldiers lost heart and surrendered their officers the following day.[25] In his memoirs General Ludlow (who was not of course in Dublin at the time) claimed that during Waller's occupation of the castle, Sir Charles Coote, accompanied by Sir Theophilus Jones and supported by his 'creatures', rode up and down the streets, declaring for a free parliament, 'which language was by that time sufficiently understood to be for the king'.[26]

Waller had always been an unlikely ally for those conservative members of the protestant gentry who had seized power in December. It is difficult to understand why he should have supported them in the first place, though having been snubbed by Ludlow in October it may not have been too difficult for him to find common cause with officers like Theophilus Jones, Charles Coote and Colonel Bridges, especially if his main concern was to preserve himself, as C. H. Firth suggested.[27] Self preservation must equally have been the motive behind his breaking with them in February, for as his fellow officers matured their plans to declare for the return of the excluded members of the Long Parliament, the problematic nature of this alliance must have appeared increasingly more dangerous. Waller, after all, had personally helped Colonel Pride in his purge of parliament in 1648 and had subsequently acted as one of the king's judges.[28] Since the restoration of the excluded members was soon to be the declared goal of his fellow army officers it was time for Waller to part company with them.

Waller's seizure of Dublin Castle on 15 February neither inhibited nor delayed the publication of two major declarations by army officers in Dublin and Munster. Sir Charles Coote and 54 officers stationed in Dublin issued their declaration for the readmission of the excluded members on 16 February, while Broghill and 43 Munster officers issued a longer and more detailed declaration two days later, the latter clearly drafted by the literary Broghill.[29] In both declarations the calamities of recent years were attributed to Pride's purge of parliament in 1648. Since then there had been chaos and without a return to a full and free parliament it would be impossible to restore conditions of legality and stability. Since 1648, in the well chosen words of Broghill's Munster declaration, 'we have been without foundation'. The dilemma of protestant Ireland was felicitously expressed in one key sentence:

Powers have made laws, and subsequent powers disowned and nulled what the preceding powers had acted; that now the questions are not so many, what is the meaning of the law as what is the law.[30]

The fundamental laws of the land were trampled on, arbitrary government was menacing their liberties, taxes were imposed which were excessive both in their manner of imposition and in the amounts demanded, and religion had suffered in several ways.

Both declarations deplored the increase in heresies and schisms, though they were not at one in identifying the symptoms of the disease. In the eyes of the Munster officers the legal maintenance of the ministry of the gospel had been conferred on men 'unable, unwilling or unfit to dispense it, who had less ill deserved a maintenance for their silence than their speaking'. For their part the Dublin officers commented simply that 'the Godly ministers of the gospel' were despised and the ministry itself vilified; tithes and other means of maintaining the clergy were being misapplied, while anabaptists, quakers and other sectaries had been countenanced.[31]

Broghill's lengthy prologue to the Munster declaration, making it a much longer statement of grievances than its Dublin counterpart, should not disguise the fact that both declarations were part of a carefully concerted drive towards a general settlement in church and state. Both documents bore the same formula of words in their statements of aim. They sought a full and free parliament in England which would include those excluded in 1648; they trusted that the fully restored parliament would see to the establishment of the true protestant religion, the maintenance of 'Godly, learned and orthodox ministers of the gospel' by tithes 'and other their accustomed rights', together with the suppression of heresies and schisms. More generally the declarations called for the removal of needless taxes and impositions, a guarantee that there would be no taxation in any one of the three nations without the authority of its own parliament, and the security of the Irish plantation in the hands of adventurers and soldiers.

Implied in both declarations was the abandonment of the commonwealth system, i.e. autonomous congregations served by licensed ministers of varying theological positions; instead they sought some form of national church where orthodoxy would be maintained and heresy suppressed. The prologue to the Dublin declaration went even further, pointing to the vestiges of the old order in church and state as providing the foundations on which parliament might build a settlement:

And considering also that the marks of the true reformed religion according to the word of God and of the fundamental laws of the land,

and of our now dying liberties and freedom, are not yet so utterly razed and defaced but that some footsteps of them do remain, so as (by the wisdom of a full and free parliament) they may be again renewed and firmly established...[33]

Taken in a purely Irish context, the implications of this rhetoric are considerable: a legal Irish parliament had remained in existence until 1646, meeting spasmodically, with bishops taking their seats in the upper house.[34] There had been no legal prohibition within the kingdom of Ireland on the exercise of episcopal jurisdiction or the use of the prayer book and the ecclesiastical statutes and ordinances of the Long Parliament only began to be applied in Dublin in the summer of 1647. Of course in February 1660 no one was suggesting a restoration of monarchy and episcopacy, in print at least. In that sense these words of the Dublin officers' declaration were not so much a statement of aims as a straw in the wind.

Radical ministers of religion soon began to experience the effects of the new religious climate. The republican author of the *Sober vindication* described the persecution of Godly ministers: Mr Rogers, imprisoned on his landing in Dublin though sent over to preach by parliament; Enoch Grey, prevented from preaching and threatened by porters and watermen with being stoned or thrown into the water; Mr Wotten, kept out of his pulpit and confined to his house; Dr Harding and his friends driven from their meeting place; Mr Blackwood, warned that if he preached any more at Chichester House 'his throat should be cut'. All this had happened since the December *coup d'état* and 'was done by the instigation and incitement of such of the clergy as are implacable enemies to the sectarians'. The prospects were dire:

> the light of the gospel will be extinct at Dublin and what remains but gross Egyptian darkness.[35]

With the convention under way from early March the sectaries' position went from bad to worse.

The convention

In March 1660 the Londoner, Thomas Rugg, recorded in his diary a report from Ireland that there was 'a convention sitting at Dublin, the Lord Broghill and Sir Charles Coote and other principal persons being among them, and also they [have] the formality of a speaker and seemed to proceed after a parliamentary manner'.[36] The convention was in effect the political mouthpiece of the protestant gentry. Unicameral in structure, parliamentary in procedure, it was elected on the basis of the traditional parliamentary constituencies, although in most cases only one member was returned for each constituency; in all it had 137 members.[37] Contemporary and near contemporary opinion attributed the decision to summon it to the army officers and certain influential civilians, including the mayor and aldermen of Dublin, and especially Dudley Loftus, the orientalist and member of a long established protestant family.[38]

The convention's first regular session to transact business was on 2 March at the Four Courts.[39] Apart from its declarations which were printed in newsletters and sermons, there are no surviving official sources for the convention, no journals or proceedings. But if the records are non-existent and the doings of the convention must be pieced together from a variety of sources, memoirs, correspondence and newsletters, the general drift of the convention is unmistakable. From the start it was intended to pave the way for a general settlement in church and state, a settlement which would end the chaos and uncertainty of the preceding eighteen months and accord with the interests and aspirations of the protestant gentry. In this respect the convention's attitude to religious matters was particularly important, revealing as it did the essentially conservative character of protestant politics and, subsequently, enabling the king's government to proceed with laying the foundations of an ecclesiastical settlement for Ireland within weeks of the restoration.

The desire for a settled and established church, apparent in the army officers' declarations in February, found definitive expression in a convention declaration passed on 8 March. This committed the convention, in words reminiscent of the army declarations, to work for 'a learned and orthodox preaching ministry of the gospel', adding the important qualification 'and no other'. It called for ministers to be supported by tithes and 'other legal maintenance' and settled in parishes, just as the army declarations had done, but it prefixed 'only' to this stipulation about parochial organisation.[40] This addition went beyond fixing standards for the ministry and the form of church government to be encouraged; it effectively precluded from recognition those who might dissent from a general ecclesiastical settlement and made no allowance for a toleration of religious practices out of line with a newly established order. From now on the question was to be one of determining what orthodoxy and what system of church government would be adopted; the principle of a state church itself was no longer in question. Five days after issuing this declaration the convention appointed a committee to draft an order for the suppression of unlawful assemblies.[41]

Initially, developments both within and outside the convention seemed to augur well for the establishment of a presbyterian system. Samuel Cox, 'a man reputed the soundest presbyterian in Dublin', was appointed as chaplain to the convention and Patrick Adair, a leading presbyterian minister from Ulster, was elected to a committee of eight ministers whose function was to advise the convention's committee of religion.[42] Membership of this advisory committee encouraged Adair to believe that he was well placed to press for the implementation of the instructions his Ulster brethern had given him on his setting out for Dublin: to promote the work of reformation and to guard against episcopal and sectarian courses.[43] When the convention ordered a general fast, one of the reasons being the breach of the covenant, it must have seemed to Adair that the wishes of his Belfast brethern might well be realised. A similarly encouraging development outside the convention was the English council of state's choice of four commissioners for the management of the affairs of Ireland, a *de facto* Dublin government.[44] Three of those chosen, Sir John Clotworthy, William Bury and Lord Broghill, were known or reputed presbyterians. The ambiguous Broghill, along with two prominent Ulster landowners, went so far as to write to a leading presbyterian minister in Scotland urging a close correspondence and expressing concern for the settlement of religion, liberty and uniformity in all three countries.[45]

Responsibility for religious and ecclesiastical policy in the convention was the function of the committee of religion, or the committee for the maintenance of ministers, to give it its full title.[46] The chairman of this committee appears to have been Dudley Loftus, since it was he who reported to the convention the committee of religion's recommendation that an advisory committee of ministers be appointed to assist them.[47] For its part the advisory committee of ministers consisted of eight clergy, two for each province: Samuel Cox and Stephen Charnock from Leinster, Mr Burston and Mr Burdet from Munster, Thomas Vesey and Patrick Adair from Ulster and John Wilkinson and William Portman from Connaught.[48] Adair and Cox were known presbyterians, Vesey and Charnock episcopalian and independent respectively, while the affiliations of the other four in 1660 are not clear.[49] According to Adair, their advisory duties required them 'to consult among themselves anent what overtures might tend to the good of the church' and 'withal to give their advice to that committee', i.e. of the convention, 'anent such offers as they should be asked of by it'.[50]

This clerical committee of eight performed its advisory functions with considerable thoroughness. It presented two lists to the convention, one containing the names of 160 ministers deemed suitable for maintenance (it is likely that most of these were already settled and so their inclusion was no more than official recognition of their general acceptability).[51] The second list named the known anabaptists 'who a little before had ruled all', and from these the convention withheld both salary and authority to preach.[52] This was a further blow to the sectaries and the effect was to leave those ministers who favoured a settled form of church discipline, mostly presbyterians and episcopalians together with pliable independents, with the field largely to themselves.

With the sectaries no longer a major threat to the restoration of ecclesiastical order, the rivalry between presbyterian and episcopalian became increasingly apparent among both clergy and politicians. Patrick Adair's narrative of events, though written many years later, provides an invaluable account of these developments from a presbyterian viewpoint. According to Adair it was not long before the committee of eight were forced to alter course because of episcopalian pressures from the convention's committee of religion. When they refused to recommend 'divers old prelatical men who were corrupt in their doctrine and immoral in their lives, and were generally known to be unworthy of all place in the church', the committee of religion not only pleaded for them but threatened to recommend them unlilaterally for approval to the convention. As a result of this threat some of the eight ministers, clearly a majority though Adair did not say so, succumbed and endorsed the unworthy candidates.[53] It is likely that Adair had in mind the case of Heritage Badcock, an outspoken episcopalian suspended in 1659, who was restored to his post about this time. It is possible too that he was referring to Essex Digby, the rector of Geashill until the rebellion and subsequently an official minister of the gospel at Belfast. In April 1660 he successfully petitioned for restoration to his old rectory, thus becoming the first clergyman to be restored to his old living.[54] Both cases were signs of the times.

Political opinion, too, was growing increasingly hostile to a presbyterian settlement. When Adair, acting on instructions from his Ulster brethren and supported by sympathetic ministers on the committee of eight, attempted to persuade the convention to acknowledge the covenant, he suffered a serious rebuff.[55] According to Adair's own account of the affair, Thomas Vesey, one of the committee of eight but 'highly prelatical in his heart and not sound in his principles', kept the 'prelatical' party in the convention informed of these plans.[56] Sir James Barry, chairman of the convention, was consulted and tactics were agreed upon. Barry, one of Strafford's small circle of supporters in 1640, let it be known that he would leave the chair and personally oppose any vote being taken on the covenant.[57] This warning, according to Adair, was applauded by Barry's episcopalian supporters while other convention members remained indifferent, with the result that the pro-covenant party was in a minority and their 'design was crushed in the bud'.[58] Clearly there was to be no slavish imitation of what was happening in England contemporaneously, where the Long Parliament, soon after the restoration of the excluded members, adopted the Westminster confession and ordered the displaying in all churches of the solemn league and covenant.[59] Irish presbyterians had to be satisfied with a passing and ambiguous reference to the covenant in the convention's declaration of 1 May which expressed detestation of the king's trial and execution, a crime perpetrated by certain persons 'contrary to that solemn league and covenant which they themselves had taken'.[60]

As the restoration of the monarchy seemed more certain episcopalian fortunes continued to revive. A report sent from Dublin to Secretary Thurloe on 25 April brought the news that five surviving bishops, including the bishops of Raphoe and Kilmore, had been 'put in' and each given two hundred pounds a year.[61] Three weeks later an order was made that the episcopal brothers, Henry and John Leslie, were to receive a grant of money and a lump sum.[62] Of course this recognition of the bishops did not go beyond their rank and title; their jurisdiction was not being restored. Indeed for all practical purposes these bishops were now being treated like salaried ministers of the gospel. It was purely an interim arrangement 'till things should be otherwise ordered'.[63] But this restoration to favour was very important for what it promised for the future. For presbyterians it was an ominous development and one which Adair explained with the hindsight of many years:

> But when our grandees had intelligence of the pulse of the court at Breda, and especially of the king's arrival in London, they altered their course. Then they began to court the few old bishops who were in Ireland and who then had repaired to Dublin. They allowed them considerable salaries in the meantime, and began to give them their titles... All things then turned just as the king's inclination was observed to be.[64]

Others, too, noticed the care with which developments at court were being watched in Dublin. On 18 April Colonel Marcus Trevor wrote to Colonel Cromwell, a royalist officer serving with the king at

Breda, that 'our two great ministers of state', clearly Coote and Broghill, 'are tracking of you there very closely'.[65]

Sometime in late February or early March contact had been made with the exiled court. Sir Charles Coote was chiefly involved, though Lord Broghill subsequently claimed that he too had been in touch with the king.[66] Coote's contact was Sir Arthur Forbes whom he despatched to Breda with an unconditional offer of loyalty.[67] While this was clearly Coote's own initiative, taken in secret, it is doubtful whether he would have made overtures to the king had he not felt that they were in accord with the sentiments of the protestant gentry, anxious for a return to stability and order. Powerful though he was, he could hardly have taken the risks which his overtures to the exiled court involved had opinion in the convention or among his fellow officers been anti-monarchical or strongly in favour of a restoration with specified conditions.

Adair's allegation, that the increasingly favourable attitude to the bishops was the result of these contacts with the court, seems well founded. The presence at Breda of Ormond and Hyde, both firm advocates of church government by bishops, was most probably crucial in any discussions with Sir Arthur Forbes about an ecclesiastical settlement, despite the latter's presbyterian sympathies.[68] In any case for the court the main problem was support for the restoration of the monarchy and for the protestant Irish the overriding consideration was the preservation of the land settlement; to both sides religion can only have been one element, however important, of a wider problem. From the court's point of view Forbes's mission was clearly very encouraging. On 13 March the king wrote to Coote (*via* Forbes) commending him for his loyalty, promising an earldom and enclosing two blank commissions one or other to be used as Coote saw fit.[69] No mention was made of a church settlement but it is highly probable that Forbes left Breda well versed in all aspects of court policy, including ecclesiastical policy as outlined by Ormond and Hyde, all of which he would then have intimated to Coote on his return to Dublin (however much Forbes might personally have deplored it), hence Coote's increasingly favourable attitude towards the surviving bishops.

For their part the leading presbyterian politicians, Sir John Clotworthy and William Bury, both of them commissiners for the government of Ireland, did what they could to thwart the revival of episcopal fortunes. Clotworthy, described approvingly by Adair as 'that true worthy person', decided to set out for Breda to undo any impression at court that protestant Ireland was well disposed to bishops and at the same time to dispose the king to favour a presbyterian settlement. But he got no further than London since 'Monck's actings', as Adair put it, 'prevented his further journey'.[70] The general was obviously anxious to avoid any initiative likely to endanger his careful progress towards the king's restoration.

William Bury's presbyterian sympathies are clearly discernible in the instructions for the guidance of the eight advisory ministers which the governmental commissioners, not the convention, issued in April or early May.[71] They were not entered in commonwealth book A/25 until 7 May, possibly because Bury, 'a religious prudent gentleman', could not persuade Coote to agree to them.[72] In retrospect they appear as a last ditch attempt to assert presbyterian values at a time when the episcopalian momentum appeared to be getting out of hand. Parishes, it was stated, should be given to 'pious, orthodox, sober and ordained' ministers, who should baptise children and administer the Lord's supper to those not ignorant or scandalous, in accordance with the rules 'advised by the late reverend assembly of divines at Westminster'; no minister was to be presented to a parish if he were scandalous, an anabaptist or refused ordination by orthodox ministers.

Too much significance, however, need not be read into these 'rules'. Their importance lay more in their reaffirmation of anti-sectarian policy than in the reference to the Westminster assembly.[73] In fact there was an obvious division over religious policy among the commissioners: Clotworthy and Bury were consistently loyal to presbyterianism, Coote was increasingly sympathetic to episcopacy and Broghill, always an opportunist, remained ambiguous until it was time for him to be episcopalian as well.[74] In any event both Clotworthy and Broghill were in England from the spring of 1660 and so it was left to Coote and Bury to provide *de facto* government from Dublin Castle over the succeeding months.[75] Their main responsibility was to operate a holding policy, taking whatever interim decisions seemed appropriate until authoritative instructions should come from London. Both found it hard to agree on ecclesiastical policy, Bury doing what he could for the presbyterian cause, while Coote cautiously pressed for a return to the old order:

> I have with much difficulty prevailed upon Mr Bury for the adding of four ministers at Christ Church by means whereof I do undertake the common prayer book will be sufficiently used there, but what the consequences of it will be I know not, but I am sure if it had not been done gradually by such a way as this, it would have had great disturbance.[76]

In the convention, meanwhile, episcopal fortunes continued to rise.

On 14 May, the day that Charles II was proclaimed king in Dublin on the authority of an impressive array of public figures and institutions, Henry Jones was asked by the convention to preach a thanksgiving sermon ten days later in Christ Church. In the convention's order he was referred to as 'Dr Henry Jones, lord bishop of Clogher, one of the members of this convention'.[77] Even if the style accorded him was not strictly correct, the use of the term 'lord bishop' was significant for two reasons: it was a further endorsement of the growing practice of referring, however clumsily, to the surviving bishops by their titles, and it was the first indication that Jones, perhaps the key figure in the convention, had rediscovered his episcopal vocation.

Jones's homily was as much a justification for the king's restoration as a sermon of thanksgiving. Monarchy would restore order and legality. As for the church Jones chose his words carefully:

> We see already in the work of the day the happiness of the state, and we have hope of the happiness of our church also under his majesty, whose piety hath been so eminently evidenced to the comfort and satisfaction of his people. We well know much of the evil in the state hath broken in upon and proceeded from sad divisions and factions in the church. Our happiness in the state will be in union with the church.[78]

Jones was reiterating here the calls for orthodoxy and the suppression of heresy which had been a feature of various declarations since the December *coup d'état*, only this time in the context of the restored monarchy. Order in the state required order in the church, the restoration of that bond would end upheaval and uncertainty. Though Jones was careful not to anticipate the forms of church government to be enjoined in the coming ecclesiastical settlement, the very fact that he himself had reverted to his episcopal title was sign enough that the church settlement he anticipated would indeed have a place for bishops.[79]

By the time the convention adjourned, three days after Jones's sermon, 'commissioners' or agents had been appointed to represent the interests of protestant Ireland in London.[80] They travelled over well prepared, the convention's instructions covering the essential requirements for a settlement (as perceived by the political nation). They were to seek a return to traditional constitutional practices and institutions; in particular, bills for securing adventurers' and soldiers' estates and for pardoning those who had served under the commonwealth should be laid before a restored Irish parliament. As for religion, the agents' instructions were confined to church land and finances, there was no reference to church government.

This was very likely a deliberate omission, enabling the agents to accommodate the court on the details of the ecclesiastical settlement at a time when it would be expected to accommodate protestant Ireland on the land question. Certainly the final clause of the instructions made the agents veritable plenipotentiaries, specifically granting them 'latitude' in 'managing or ordering the present instructions committed to their charges'.[81]

Considerable use was made of this 'latitude' over the succeeding weeks. When the delegation from Ireland met the king on 18 June they raised the question of church government despite its absence from their instructions. As the Scottish divine James Sharp reported back to his presbyterian brethren in Edinburgh:

> Yesterday his majesty gave audience to the commissioners for Ireland, who, among other desires, moved that religion might be settled there as it was in the days of the king's grandfather and father, that establishment being the only fence against schism and confusion. From this we may guess what our presbyterian brethren may meet with . . .[82]

Following their audience with the king the agents redrafted the proposals outlined in their original instructions and made some additions as well. These were presented in writing on 21 June to the privy council (which had appointed a special committee 'to consider the present affairs of Ireland' the day before).[83] The ninth clause in this enlarged set of proposals dealt with church government, requesting

> that the church of Ireland be resettled in doctrine, discipline and worship, as it was in the time of your most royal father of blessed memory, according to the laws then and now in force in that kingdom, with such liberty to tender consciences as your majesty in your declaration dated at Breda . . . hath been graciously pleased to declare, and that Godly, learned, orthodox and ordained preaching ministers of the gospel be settled there as speedily as may be in a parochial way and supported by tithes, glebes and other legal maintenance.[84]

Juxtaposed in this submission are two quite distinct positions, anglican and presbyterian, linked together by a reference to the declaration of Breda. The phrase, 'Godly, learned orthodox and ordained preaching ministers', was not one with which most episcopalians would feel comfortable, just as few presbyterians would support a return to doctrine, discipline and worship 'according to the laws then and now in force', since these were enshrined in the 1560 act of uniformity and, more recently, in the articles approved by the convocation of 1634–5 when Wentworth was viceroy.[85] This submission was therefore no more than an artificially contrived attempt at compromise and its latter half was more than likely tacked on at the insistence of the non-anglican commissioners, a minority among the convention's delegation. While the sympathies of Barry, Davies, Rawdon and Eustace were undoubtedly episcopalian, it is certain that Clotworthy and it is likely that Mervyn and one or two others were not so enthusiastic about giving the court *carte blanche* for a full scale restoration of the pre-revolutionary church. While they had clearly remained silent at the audience with the king on 18 June the subsequent preparation of written submissions offered an opportunity to the non-episcopalians to water down the impact of what had then been said.

Not that it made much difference. The first part of this written submission, taken with the earlier oral request, was sufficient to enable the government to follow whatever course of action it favoured; within a matter of days clerical appointments were being made. On 22 June Samuel Pepys dined with William Fuller who told him how 'he hath the grant of being dean of St Patrick's in Ireland'.[86] The following day James Sharp reported back to Edinburgh, 'all the bishops in Ireland are nominate. Dr Bramble [sic] is archbishop of Armagh'.[87] The granting of letters patent came later and the consecrations were delayed for seven months but no great significance need be attached to these delays. It was not so much that the government was having second thoughts in the light of the delicate ecclesiastical situation in England, it was rather that the restoration of legal and administrative normality in Ireland took close on six months to achieve, hence the delay in consecrating the bishops and restoring their legal jurisdiction.[88] The important fact was that the vacant sees had been filled in June. When a two man presbyterian delegation from Ulster arrived in London it took them the best part of a month to gain an audience with the king. Charles promised them royal protection and 'gave them good words', but little else. They were too late to prevent an episcopalian settlement.[89]

These early appointments to the episcopate were possible once the convention's commissioners had submitted their proposals. Coming from the representatives of the protestant political nation the request to restore the church in its doctrine, discipline and worship removed all inhibitions from the government, a number of whose leading members were more than anxious to see a return to the old order. In this respect Ormond was the key figure. No longer lord lieutenant he was nonetheless the dominant influence in the making of Irish policy.[90] He was too a particular friend and ally of the church and was soon to play a decisive role in recommending clergy for appointment and promotion.[91] It was to him that Dudley Loftus wrote on 1 June, a few days after the convention had risen, soliciting for the church's welfare and the restoration of episcopacy:

> our ecclesiastical government is episcopal by the laws and constitutions of the land which have not yet received any alteration.[92]

He told Ormond that he was

> stirred up in the behalf of the orthodox protestant clergy to solicit your lordship's watchfulness over them for the preservation of the sacred order of bishops and the use of the liturgy,

and he helpfully enclosed a list of vacant preferments.[93]

That this advice should have come from Loftus, the leading member of the convention's committee of religion and within days of its adjournment, is an indication of the quality of support enjoyed by the episcopal cause. Indeed it is clear that the early nomination of the Irish episcopate owed much to the climate created in the convention by certain leading members. They had managed to forestall the adoption of the covenant while at the same time gently pushing the surviving bishops back into prominence. When the commissioners in London sought the restoration of the old order they were doing no more than reflecting the consensus of opinion in the convention.

Apart from Loftus three convention members stand out as special friends of the episcopalian cause: Sir James Barry, Sir Charles Coote and Dr Henry Jones. It was Barry who prevented the adoption of the covenant and it is likely, to put it no stronger, that this survivor from Wentworth's regime used his influence as convention chairman to similar effect on other occasions. Coote's unobtrusive support for the adherents of the prayer book (already mentioned) showed where his sympathies lay. The varied nature of his power base was indeed impressive: his army command, his appointment as a government commissioner by a Whitehall under Monck's domination, his contacts with the exiled court, his authority to act in the king's name, his membership of the convention. He was a formidable friend for any cause. But the most significant ally that episcopacy possessed turned out to be the erstwhile bishop of Clogher, Henry Jones.

Bishop Jones participated to a greater or less extent in virtually every aspect of political life between December and May. Involved in the army coup of 13 December, he was subsequently chosen to represent the council of officers as one of its agents in England.[94]

Credited by a contemporary historian with giving 'much help' to Dudley Loftus in the summoning of the convention, Jones was singled out, along with Broghill and Coote, as being entitled to special and specific confirmation of his land grants.[95] He was also one of the seven signatories of the army declaration of 13 April, as were Broghill, Coote and Bury.[96] Perhaps the most telling witness to his significance was Jeremy Taylor who told a correspondent that though Broghill and Coote were greater in name, it was Colonel Arthur Hill, Sir Theophilus Jones and 'his brother the bishop', who had command of the army and were prepared to declare for the king.[97]

Jones's preparedness to accept a return to episcopacy, evidenced in the resumption of his episcopal title, must have done much to reassure protestant landowners and to dispose them to accept church government by bishops. An established and episcopal church which could include Cromwell's scoutmaster-general among its bishops could also embrace Cromwellian planters more interested in the security of their estates than in the forms of religious practice or the manner of church government. Not that the politics of protestant Ireland in 1660 was exclusively dominated by Cromwellian soldiers and adventurers; it was rather the preserve of longer established, more conservative protestant settlers, those who sometimes referred to themselves as the 'old English' or 'ancient protestants of Ireland', thereby distancing themselves from the parvenu settlers of the 1650s.[98] The older settlers, of course, had benefited either directly or indirectly from the Cromwellian settlement since it created protestant hegemony in landownership and politics. But these recent gains had to be protected from the threats of radical innovation or Irish revival; this could only be achieved in conditions of enduring stability and unimpeachable legality, conditions in which the land settlement remained intact and society itself was secure. In England the mood of the protestant gentry was conservative, tired of experiment and favoured the return of the old constitution in church and state.[99] In Ireland this constitution, grafted on to the new political reality of protestant landed dominance, seemed to offer the best guarantee of security, permanence and stable social order, grounded as it was on the concept of hierarchy in state and church. The traditional hierarchical structure of the anglican church well suited the mood of the protestant gentry. They too might appreciate Dean Fuller's celebratory anthem:

> Angels look down, rejoice to see
> like heaven above, a hierarchy.[100]

Notes

1. Henry B. Swanzy, *Succession lists of the diocese of Dromore* (Belfast, 1933), pp 49–50; James B. Leslie, *Ardfert and Aghadoe clergy and parishes* (Dublin, 1940), p. 4; *D.N.B.*, vii, 762–3; Bodl., Carte MSS 45, f. 55; F. R. Bolton, *The Caroline tradition of the Church of Ireland* (London, 1958), p. 32.
2. Robert S. Bosher, *The making of the restoration settlement. The influence of the Laudians* (London, 1951), p. 157.
3. T. C. Barnard, *Cromwellian Ireland. English government and reform in Ireland, 1649–60* (London, 1975), pp 130–4.
4. I. M. Green, *The re-establishment of the church of England 1660–1663* (Oxford, 1978), pp 16–18, p. 32.
5. Ibid., p. 18.
6. G. Davies, *The restoration of Charles II* (San Marino, 1955), pp 162–89; J. R. Jones, *Country and court. England 1658–1714* (London, 1978), pp 118–26.
7. Beckett, *Mod. Ire.*, pp 115–17; Bagwell, *Stuarts*, ii, 350–68.
8. C. H. Firth, *Memoirs of Edmund Ludlow* (Oxford, 1894), vol. i, introduction, p. xxxviii.
9. Davies, *Restoration*, p. 249.
10. *A sober vindication of Lt Gen. Ludlow* (London, 1660), p. 2; an examination of this pamphlet's contents makes it clear that it was written not later than mid-February, although the date on the title page suggests that it was not printed until after 25 March.
11. Ibid., pp 14–15.
12. *A letter sent from General Monck, Dated at Coldstream Dec. 29, 1659* (London, 1659, i.e. 1660 new style); Monck's letter was read in parliament on 6 January and ordered to be printed. His earlier letter to Broghill is quoted in Kathleen Lynch, *Roger Boyle first earl of Orrery* (Knoxville, 1965), p. 100.
13. This is quoted in Davies, *Restoration*, p. 267.
14. 'Instructions for Sir William Bury knt, Col. Richard Lawrence and Dr Henry Jones'? (T.C.D., MS 808, ff 160–2); Jones's surname is barely discernible having been partly obliterated.
15. Ibid.
16. *The agreement and resolution of several associated ministers in the county of Cork for the ordaining of ministers* (Cork, 1657); *The agreement and resolution of the ministers of Christ associated within the city of Dublin* (Dublin, 1659).
17. White Kennet. *A register and chronicle ecclesiastical and civil* (1728), pp 24–5.
18. Davies, *Restoration*, p. 250.
19. *Sober vindication*, p. 3.
20. *Cal. S. P. Ire., 1647–60*, pp 706, 708, 715. The governor and mayor of Waterford tried to reassure Ludlow by telling him that the assembly summoned to meet in Dublin was no more than a convention of the kind formerly called to determine the equal distribution of financial contributions from among the counties and the towns. Ludlow, never having heard of such a constitutional device, was not mollified by their reassurance and he continued to reiterate his view that the Stuart interest was at work in Ireland.
21. Council of state to General Monck, 14 Jan. 1660 (*Cal. S. P. dom., commonwealth*, xiii, 310).
22. H. R., 'A letter to the author of the history of Ireland', p. 2, which is separately paginated at the end of Richard Cox, *Hibernia Anglicana* (London, 1689),

part ii; the passage quoted was used almost verbatim by Thomas Carte, *Life of the duke of Ormond* (London, 1851 ed.), iv, 5.

23. *The declaration of the army in Ireland... together with a letter concerning the present transactions there, directed to a friend in London* (London, 1659, i.e. 1660); the letter, which contains a brief account of Waller's seizure of the castle, is dated 18 February, initialed 'W. G.' and printed facing page one of the declaration.

24. *A letter sent from a merchant in Dublin... February 22, 1659*, broadsheet.

25. Ibid.

26. Ludlow, *Memoirs* (1894 ed.), ii, 230.

27. *D. N. B.*; on being recalled to England in October, Ludlow had passed over Waller and appointed Colonel John Jones to act in his place.

28. Ibid.

29. *The declaration of Sir Charles Coote... lord president of the province of Connaught, and the rest of the council of officers of the army in Ireland present at Dublin, concerning the readmission of the secluded members* (reprinted at London, 1659, i.e. 1660 new style); 'A declaration of the Lord Broghill and the officers of the army in Ireland, in the province of Munster', printed in *Thurloe state papers* (1742), vii, 817–20; Lynch, *Orrery*, p. 101; Davies, *Restoration*, p. 251n.

30. *Thurloe state papers*, vii, 817.

31. *Thurloe state papers*, vii, 817; *Declaration of Sir Charles Coote*, p. 2.

32. *Thurloe state papers*, vii, 819–20; *Declaration of Sir Charles Coote*, pp 7–8.

33. *Declaration of Sir Charles Coote*, pp 5–6.

34. When the Irish house of lords met on 2 May 1646 six bishops and two temporal peers were present (*Lords' jn. Ire.*, 1783 ed., i, 227).

35. *Sober vindication*, pp 2–3.

36. William L. Sachse (ed.), *The diurnal of Thomas Rugg 1659–1661* (Camden third series, xci, London, 1961), p. 64.

37. The Dublin newsletter, *Account of the chief occurrences*, which carried brief accounts of the convention's sittings, printed a list of the convention's members in its edition of 12–19 March 1660; there is a useful account of the convention in Fergus O'Donoghue, 'Parliament in Ireland under Charles II' (Nat. Univ. Ire., Univ. Coll. Dubl., M.A. dissertation, 1970), pp 1–32.

38. It is hard to get a clear picture of Loftus's role, though Edmund Borlase, writing within twenty years of these events, stated categorically that the convention was 'summoned by the vigilance and excellent contrivance and industry of Doctor Dudley Loftus', *History of the execrable Irish rebellion* (London, 1680), p. 316; the following entry occurs in the short account initialled 'H. R.' which is printed at the end of Cox's *Hibernia Anglicana* (see n. 22): 'the government being thus in the hands of the army was managed by a committee or council of officers, who, upon the petition of the mayor and aldermen of Dublin did (as they had before designed) summon a convention'. Patrick Adair, the presbyterian historian and a participant in the events he described, wrote many years later that Broghill, Coote and Bury 'were the chief instruments for gathering it' (Adair, *True narrative of the rise and progress of the presbyterian church in Ireland*, ed. W. D. Killen, Belfast, 1866, p. 236). Carte stated that the council of officers summoned the convention on the advice of Dudley Loftus and having been petitioned by the city of Dublin (Carte, *Ormond*, iv, 5).

39. There is some confusion over the date of the convention's first meeting. It was originally intended to have it assemble on 24 January but it is widely stated that it first met on 7 February. It seems certain that it did not meet in January and unlikely that it met, if at all, for other than purely formal reasons in February. There are no surviving references to convention deliberations or proceedings for February and it must be remembered that on 7 February neither Waller's attempted coup nor Coote's subsequent purge had yet taken place. A meeting planned for 27 February had to be postponed because of the failure of a sufficient number of members to turn up, for which see *A declaration of the general convention of Ireland, with the late proceedings there* (London, 1660), p. 8; pp 6–8 of this pamphlet are extracted from the newsletter *An account of the chief occurrences*, the declaration itself being printed on pp 3–6. See also Borlase, *History*, p. 316; H.R., 'A letter', p. 3 in R. Cox, *Hib. Angl.*; Carte, *Ormond*, iv, 5; Davies, *Restoration*, p. 250; Beckett, *Mod. Ire.*, p. 116.
40. *A declaration of the general convention of Ireland with the late proceedings there, newly brought over by a gentleman to the council of state in England* (London, 1660), pp 3–6.
41. *Chief occurrences* (13 Mar. 1660), pp 35–6.
42. Adair, *True narrative*, p. 233.
43. Ibid., p. 234.
44. *Chief occurrences* (13 Mar. 1660), p. 40.
45. The contents of the letter are summarised in Robert Wodrow, *The history of the sufferings of the church of Scotland* (later ed., 4 vols, Glasgow), i, 12. The other two signatories were Colonel Gorges and Mr John Greig.
46. *Chief occurrences* (13 Mar. 1660), pp 35–6.
47. Ibid., p. 36.
48. Presumably Mr Burston and Mr Burdet were Daniel Burston and George Burdett (or Burdet) respectively, both of whom are listed in Seymour's 'list of the ministers of the gospel', St John D. Seymour, *The puritans in Ireland 1647–1661* (Oxford, 1921), p. 208. The names of the eight ministers together with the provinces they represented were printed in *Chief occurrences* (see previous footnote), a point which Seymour did not seem to be aware of (p. 178), though from his own meticulous study of the commonwealth books (in P.R.O.I. he rightly deduced that Vesey, Cox and Charnock were members. The commonwealth books were subsequently lost in the destruction of the P.R.O.I. in 1922. Seymour's extensive notes, however, are housed in the library of the Representative Church Body in Dublin (Lib./20).
49. Seymour, *Puritans*, pp 178, 208, 209, 219 and 223.
50. Adair, *True narrative*, pp 233–4.
51. Ibid., p. 235. According to Adair sixty of these ministers belonged to the presbytery in Ulster.
52. Ibid., p. 235.
53. Ibid., p. 240.
54. Seymour, *Puritans*, pp 181, 182.
55. Adair, *True narrative*, p. 234.
56. Vesey was appointed bishop of Limerick in 1673 and promoted to Tuam in 1679.
57. After the restoration Barry was created Viscount Santry; see *D.N.B.* for details of his career.
58. Adair, *True narrative*, p. 234.

59. Bosher, *Restoration settlement*, p. 102.
60. *A declaration of the general convention of Ireland expressing their detestation of the unjust proceedings against the late king in a pretended high court of justice in England* (Dublin, 1660), broadsheet.
61. *Thurloe state papers*, vii, 909.
62. Seymour, *Puritans*, p. 183; see also note 48.
63. Adair, *True narrative*, p. 231; the bishops, he wrote, were given 'considerable salaries in the meantime' (p. 240).
64. Ibid., pp 239–40.
65. Col. Marcus Trevor to Col. Cromwell, 18 April 1660 (Bodl., Carte MSS 30, f. 572). In Lynch, *Orrery*, p. 106 this has been described as an intercepted letter which Ormond opened and subsequently preserved among his papers; in fact it was a letter from one royalist to another and was clearly passed on to Ormond. In a report to Hyde Col. Trevor was referred to as being 'of the king's party' in Ireland (Jeremie Baker, i.e. Dr George Morley, to Hyde, 18 Apr. 1660, *Cal. Clar. S.P.*, iv, 664).
66. In her biography of Broghill, created earl of Orrery after the restoration, Kathleen M. Lynch relied on Orrery's speech at the impeachment proceedings against him in 1669 and on the testimony of his chaplain, Thomas Morrice, as sources for his contacts with the exiled court (*Orrery*, pp 101–2). Broghill may indeed have been in touch with the court but he was still expressing anti-monarchical sentiments to Thurloe as late as 24 April (*Thurloe state papers*, vii, 908).
67. Carte, *Ormond*, iv, 6.
68. J. C. Beckett, *Protestant dissent in Ireland 1687–1780* (London, 1948), p. 139, n. 2; J. G. Simms, 'The restoration, 1660–85' in T. W. Moody *et al.* (eds), *A new history of Ireland* (Oxford, 1976), iii, 437.
69. Bodl., Carte MSS 30, f. 551.
70. Adair, *True narrative*, p. 232; Adair gave a purely ecclesiastical motive to Clotworthy's travels. In fact he had been sent to England at the end of March, along with William Aston, to look after Irish protestant interests in general and the future of the land settlement in particular (H.M.C., *Eighth report*, app. 1, p. 90).
71. Seymour, *Puritans*, pp 179–80.
72. The description of Bury is Adair's.
73. Insistence on ordination would be a sure guarantee that sectaries could not receive official approval as ministers of the gospel. Some clergy had tried to implement a similar qualification as far back as 1657, though without official encouragement (*The agreement and resolution of several associated ministers in . . . Cork*, 1657).
74. As Clarendon in his last exile wrote of Broghill's role in 1660: 'he appeared very generous, and to be without the least pretence to any advantage for himself, and to be so wholly devoted to the king's interest and to the establishing of the government of the church, that he quickly got himself believed' (*The life of Edward, earl of Clarendon*, later ed., Oxford 1857, i, 379).
75. Clotworthy appears to have left Ireland in March (see n. 70 above), while Broghill travelled to London sometime in April or early May to sit as member for Arundel in the convention parliament.
76. Bodl., Carte MSS 31, f. 3. This undated letter from Coote to his brother was probably written after the restoration but certainly well before the return of legal formalities.

77. *A proclamation, 14 May 1660* (Dublin, 1660); the convention's order was printed facing the title page of *A sermon preached at Christ Church, Dublin before the general convention of Ireland May 24, 1660* (London, 1660).
78. Jones, *Sermon, p. 27.*
79. In the traditional parliamentary manner the convention ordered its chairman to return hearty thanks to 'his lordship' and voted that the bishop he asked to have his sermon printed at the convention's expense; this order and vote are printed facing the title page of Jones's *Sermon* without page number.
80. To avoid confusion with the *de facto* administration, the commissioners for the government of Ireland, I have frequently referred to the convention's representatives as 'agents', although their official title was 'commissioners employed by the general convention of Ireland'. Those appointed were Lord Broghill, Sir Charles Coote, Sir James Barry, Sir Paul Davies, Sir John Clotworthy, Sir Theophilus Jones, Sir John King, Arthur Hill, Richard Kennedy, Audley Mervyn, William Aston, George Rawdon and Sir Maurice Eustace.
81. P.R.O.I., Carte transcripts 30, p. 470.
82. Sharp to Douglas, 19 June 1660 (Woodrow, *Sufferings of the church of Scotland*, i, 43-4).
83. P.R.O., P.C. reg., 1648-60, pp 34-6; P.C. 2/55/ii; *Cal. S. P. Ire., 1660-62*, p. 1.
84. 'The further humble desires of the commissioners of the general convention of Ireland appointed to attend your majesty' (T.C.D., MS 808, ff 156-8).
85. Bagwell, *Tudors*, ii, 6-7; *Stuarts*, i, 227-9; H. F. Kearney, *Strafford in Ireland 1633-41* (Manchester, 1959), pp 115-16.
86. *The diary of Samuel Pepys*, ed. Robert Latham and William Matthews (London, 1970), i, 181.
87. Sharp to Douglas, 23 June 1660 (Woodrow, *Sufferings of the church of Scotland*, i, 44).
88. The Dublin Castle administration was continued on an *ad hoc* basis under the commissioners appointed by the Long Parliament until December 1660, when the duly appointed lords justices took up office.
89. Sharp to Douglas, 7, 26, 28 July, 4 Aug. 1660 (Woodrow, *Sufferings of the church of Scotland*, i, 50-3); Adair, *True narrative*, pp 241-4.
90. Throughout the 1650s Ormond was treated as lord lieutenant of Ireland by the exiled court and at the very first meeting of the privy council at Whitehall after the king's return to London he was still referred to by that title. He was, however, soon replaced by the nominal appointment of General Monck, now duke of Albemarle, to the lord lieutenancy. (P.R.O., P.C. reg., 1648-60, pp 1-2, 5-6).
91. *Cal. S. P. Ire., 1660-62*, pp 94-5.
92. Bodl., Carte MSS 30, f. 685.
93. Ibid., f. 689.
94. Borlase, *History*, p. 316; T.C.D., MS 808, ff 160-2.
95. H.M.C., *Eighth report*, app. i, 99; see also F. O'Donoghue, 'Parliament in Ireland under Charles II', p. 10, n. 1 (see n. 37).
96. *A new declaration and engagement of the army and forces in Ireland* (reprinted at London, 1660), broadsheet.
97. Jeremie Baker, i.e. George Morley, to E. Hyde, 18 Apr. 1660 (*Cal. Clar. s.p.*, iv, 664), in which Morley told Hyde about the news Taylor had just brought from Ireland.

98. See Karl S. Bottigheimer, 'The restoration land settlement: a structural view', in *I.H.S.*, xviii, no. 69 (Mar. 1972), pp 1–21 and especially pp 3–5; see also T. C. Barnard, 'Planters and policies in Cromwellian Ireland', in *Past and Present*, no. 61 (1973), pp 31–69.

99. Green, *Re-establishment of the church of England*, p. 180. In his autobiography Clarendon wrote that the commissioners from Ireland 'all pretended to be well wishers to the old government of the church, and the more by the experience they had of the distractions which were introduced by that which had succeeded it, and by the confusion they were now in without any'. (*The life of Edward earl of Clarendon*, i. 380).

100. Bodl., Carte MSS 45, f. 55^v.

Tory democracy and political elitism: provincial conservatism and parliamentary tories in the early 1880s

R. F. Foster

One of the most intriguing questions regarding parliament and its relation to the people, in terms of British politics, is surely the way that parliament conditions the representatives of 'the people' into its own mould—alterations in society, the electoral system and the world at large notwithstanding. From the Birmingham Reform League to the Clydesiders, those who enter Westminster with a mandate for changing it rapidly discover the old truth that any two politicians have more in common with each other than with any third person outside politics. (The conspicuous exceptions are all Irish, who entered parliament with no thought of, or interest in, changing it—and often, indeed, with the express object of not attending it.) Of the attempts to inject into the world of parliamentary parties an infusion of ideas from outside, the tory democratic movement of the early 1880s comes to mind as both bizarre and hopeless, though no less interesting for that. But first it requires some background definition.

For tory democracy has in fact received close attention, in its widest sense: the recurring attempt of nineteenth-century Conservatives to link their party in parliament with the 'working classes' (as they put it) and to shunt both whiggery and radicalism on to mutually exclusive branch lines of politics, by claiming that the tory party in parliament represented an articulation of the real identity of the England of outdoors. This began after the First Reform Bill with the Operative Conservative societies and the manful efforts of Richard Oastler to square a number of circles. It was largely limited to the north–west, where a similar initiative revived in the 1860s, when, under the rather vague tutelage of Disraeli, and with the committed organisational ability of John Gorst, the Conservative Workingmens' Associations were begun to try and capitalise upon the new electorate.[1] Thus three recurring components are isolated: Gorst, Lancashire, and the appeasement of democracy. Not to mention, in the background, a more troubling issue, providing illimitable mileage for sociologists and political scientists as well as historians; what constitutes a class, politically as well as socially, and how you identify it (let alone how it identifies itself).[2]

Remaining, however, with the Disraelian notion of what was later to be called 'tory democracy': obviously this had little to do with 'democracy' in the sense of co-opting the working class into the party. Recent views of Disraeli as attempting in the 1870s (like everyone else) to be Palmerston *redivivus* are more relevant than memories of Young England (though Lord John Manners was always obligingly ready to be wheeled on as the living proof of the spiritual regeneration of aristocracy[3]). Far more immediate to tory fortunes, however, was the looming figure of W. H. Smith, self-consciously humble bookstall magnate and refugee from Liberalism; for where the Conservative party was to score most heavily from now on was in its recruits from the suburban middle class.[4] Recruits to its legions of *voters*, that is; innumerable careful studies have shown how slowly this percolated into the party's representation at Westminster, much less into the circle round the cabinet table. Both Disraeli and his disgruntled lieutenants tried to use 'democracy' after 1868; social reform, however, was accommodated in the limiting framework of Conservative defensiveness.[5] While the party at grass roots seemed revived by Gorst's determined attempts to reorganise it into a coherent structure of local organisations (the 'National Union'), this effort was superficial (and personalised) enough for its effect to be nullified ten years later in the great defeat of 1880. This was partly due to misapprehensions—especially regarding Lancashire, one of the joker cards which will continually turn up, and which Disraeli seems to have seen as the trump in a winning hand. In fact, he betted too heavily on a popular tory alliance in Manchester; just like Engels, he made the mistake of reading too much from that one idiosyncratic cockpit of change (though unlike Engels he did not have the excuse of youth and moral fervour).[6] Disraeli's appeal outside the traditional tory limits was also dictated by the insecurity of his own position within the party until (at least) 1872; the county, the land, the family remained the kernel of the party, with borough members in the background (except once again Smith, who nonetheless did his best to efface himself from his colleagues, agonising over whether his daughters were good enough to marry peers). And yet outside opinion—like the *New York Herald Tribune*, or John Morley—could see that by the mid-1870s Conservatism's vital support was coming not from broad acres but—in Lord Randolph Churchill's vivid phrase, applied as it happened to Smith himself—the 'lords of pineries and vineries'.

And this, in fact, had little to do with the occasional obeisances made by the parliamentary party towards a working-class audience, such as the New Social Movement of 1871. Lancashire businessmen were uninterested in co-opting the working-classes; they knew them too well. The bizarre thing is the way that the 'tory democratic' flag could be made rhetorically to wave over both middle *and* working-class; it shows, if anything, how far the decision-making centre of the Conservative party was divorced from both. (One might also instance here the way in which tory labour legislation of 1875, instead of 'gaining and retaining for the Tories the affection of the working-classes' as Disraeli affected to imagine, merely aided the rapprochement of Liberals and labour by removing a contentious issue.[7]) Nevertheless, the phrase 'tory democracy'—and the concept—gained currency in the late 1870s; and for all the private admission of Churchill, playing the part of honest rogue, that it was 'chiefly opportunism', it remained an elastic, and for some a potent, idea. 'Am I a Tory Democrat?' asked Wilfred Scawen Blunt grandiloquently in a manifesto drawn up for the bemused Camberwell electorate in 1885; and, on his way to replying in the affirmative, he listed a number of essential beliefs and commitments, climaxing with home rule, which can be declared with assurance the one thing tory democracy never stood for.[8] By that election, in fact, tory democracy was effectively ended as a rhetorical card.

And yet the concept recurrently emerged for discussion: increasingly academic, gaining interest with the class polarisation of British politics in the 20th century, and usually prompted by the political events of the day. Thus discussion of the issue in the journals during the early 1900s[9] was prompted not only by works like Ostrogorski's *Democracy and the organisation of political parties* (1902) and Lowell's *The government of England* (1900), both of which cast a more ambivalent eye on the processes of nineteenth-century parliamentary politics than had been customary; nor was it merely the result of Winston Churchill's dazzlingly whitewashed

Life of Lord Randolph Churchill (1906) or Harold Gorst's riposte on behalf of his embittered father and the 'real' Tory democracy (*The fourth party*, 1906). The interest was also awakened by the spectacle of Lib–Lab'ism at work, and the crumbling of tory bastions in the north–west; and, as the momentum of progressivism gathered, by ideas of class reconciliation through an amalgam of socialist nostrums and Conservative value-systems. (Both are reflected, in their different ways, by H. G. Wells's *The new Machiavelli* (1911) and Goldwin Lowes Dickinson's *A modern symposium* (1905); and in both works Tory democracy gets an airing, if somewhat satirically.) Similarly, the next rash of commentaries appeared immediately after the first world war, with another shake-up of party lines.[10] (Why the mid-1960s saw such a concentration of monographs on the survival of nineteenth-century Conservativism is a question which historical perspective does not yet allow us to judge[11]; but, besides the purely academic stimulation of Hanham's trailblazing work at the beginning of the decade, it must have been related to the experience of a Labour government in power for the first time since 1951, and the popular conception that Macmillanism had finally come to an end. And it may be no accident that the gospel of tory democracy has most recently been heard in the land from Lord Randolph Churchill's last biographer, Mr Rhodes James, in a speech at Edinburgh in 1980: a hundred years after Churchill preached the same message in the same place, and about a hundred and fifty years too late.)

Certainly, interest in tory democracy has been fuelled by the anti-Whig view of nineteenth-century politics—which are now more often seen as a holding operation by the aristocracy than the march of Everyman towards the democratic light. The successful survival of the Conservative party, and the establishment of a Cecil hegemony in parliament during the 1880s and 1890s, can no longer be seen as simple functions of Liberal disunion or political exhaustion. New preoccupations have also been encouraged by borrowings on the part of historiography from sociology and political science. The mechanisms of reaching a voting decision, in the oracular language of Talcott Parsons, are seen as 'typically non-rational . . . it may be said that the question is not so much . . . for *whom* [the voter] is voting as it is *with whom* he is associating himself in voting'.[12] Applied to tory democracy, past and present, this opened a merry intellectual amusement ground: comparative critiques of deferential behaviour patterns, explorations of false consciousness, definitions of political culture and social control, whose swings and roundabouts are innocently being played upon still.[13] All the more so, as—with the working-class historiographically exhausted, and the aristocracy not yet academically respectable—the middle and lower-middle class culture of nineteenth-century England is just beginning to be breached.[14]

II

It may be time, then, for the historian to look at tory democracy again, and to return to the early 1880s and the context within which Churchill, Gorst and Wolff attempted to reorientate their party in the country—and the structure of parliamentary leadership within the party. For the two issues were closely intertwined. As in 1868, the rediscovery of 'the people' came about after a disillusioning political defeat, and after an election campaign in which the tories had resolutely ignored both domestic social issues and the very idea that it might have a working-class political constituency. The result was that they were, effectively, blamed for the economic depression. Lancashire alone demonstrated popular support and here, as elsewhere, this was concealed by the electoral system—though a pioneer psephologist, writing in the *Fortnightly Review* in 1881, effectively demonstrated that the Conservative total vote in the largest constituencies had increased dramatically.[15] London alone— and this effectively a business vote—had rallied. Paul Smith has argued that the result at the polls 'tended to discredit the idea of a tory democracy' and to turn the conservative party back into the paths of 'a stolid resistance to change';[16] and so it did, looked at from the Carlton Club perspective. But this is to beg the question of what tory democracy meant, and to whom it appealed. There is evidence that, almost at once, among politicians as cautious as Northcote and Smith, the reaction was a realisation that the middle classes must be organised; and an answering initiative was not long in coming from the other side either.[17] But this did not come from the working classes themselves: it came from the aspiring middle classes, in whose interests were the policies and organisational initiatives which made up the 'Democracy' to which toryism appealed.

The conditions of post-1867 politics of course imposed the necessity of a formal appeal to all elements of the middle and lower-middle class; but the restrictions of the registration system, and the inadequacy of the redistribution measures, in reality kept their influence at a minimum. In terms of the Conservative party militant, they were foot-soldiers with little hope of rising to officer class. And if the provincial support for Conservatism came from the aspiring middle classes, the parliamentary membership even after 1880 was still overwhelmingly landed (37 of the 50 new M.P.s of that year being of that identification, and only 13 commercial or professional[18]). This was a bias that, in terms of decision-making, would remain (even when, after 1885, the organisation of the party settled into a more or less efficient mould, it did so under the auspices of a Mafia known as 'the Kentish Gang' because of their landed associations with that county). The question of how the Conservatives survived democracy becomes more pointed. They did not do so by a naked appeal to resistance values. But nor did they follow the ideas of social reconciliation which Disraeli used in his novels and ignored in his politics. Neither can Ensor's comfortable idea that the Irish question saved the Conservatives by sending over the moderate Liberals to them be seen as an adequate answer.[19] Winston Churchill's epic vision of his father as a doomed Prometheus reviving his party through the fire of democracy and being cast out for it can also be discounted. But elements of all these theories cannot be eliminated: even if one returns in the end to Cornford's emphasis on the importance of redistribution in 1885, creating a kind of constituency which isolated and capitalised upon the middle-class and suburban support becoming slowly evident over the previous twenty years. And where this leaves the tory democracy, as usually defined, is a rather doubtful question.

For the story became confused in its beginnings, in 1880, and was further obscured by the rationalisations of the principal actors at the time, in speeches, articles, and even private letters; and the even more disingenuous versions of their sons and disciples long after the event. Immediate political preoccupations counted at the time for far more than could later be admitted. For one thing, the contest for the leadership succession began as soon as the Conservatives lost the election; well before Disraeli's death, Northcote (of all people) was decisively declaring that the leader's political career was finished and he must be replaced. Just as Northcote was a tougher (and more ambitious) customer than the later version of events (which was essentially the Fourth Party version) could allow, so his rivalry with Salisbury for the succession was less covert and less gentlemanly (especially on Salisbury's side) than one might gather. And this has its importance in the tory-democratic initiative: since it was very often part of a Salisburian ploy, headed by the Fourth Party.

Moreover, the strident and populist line taken by many parliamentary tories after 1882 should also be related both to the marked if temporary economic upswing from that year, which helped Gladstone by removing the Conservatives' opportunity to take a class line in politics; and to the fact that Gladstonian policy in Ireland and Egypt during the early 1880s, however decried by hindsight, at the time helped Gladstone present the Liberals as a national—even a Palmerstonian—party once more. The fact that Churchill, Gorst and Wolff opposed Liberal policy in both these areas should not obscure the fact that it was extremely difficult for Conservatives to follow them in such a line. Immediate political conditions in his personal life carried Churchill still further into his tory democrat initiative. He had just been absent from politics for six months with a mysterious illness; and on his return in late 1882 the talk was all of coalition,[20] a development which would strengthen Northcote (who wanted it) and weaken Salisbury (already badly shaken by his failure to carry a majority of peers with him in his intention to oppose the Arrears Act in the lords). This was the background to Churchill's first public appeal to 'the great tory democracy' in October 1882, on the occasion of his attacking Gibson and his own party over limiting the freedom of parliamentary procedure. It was a declaration of restored initiative from the Conservative opposition, a forecast of the restoration of sharp party lines, and an indication of an Irish alliance: which was how it was interpreted. Tory democracy, in fact, only came in as a flourish at the end.[21]

And to whom, by this stage, was such an appeal in reality addressed? It seems clear that the provincial constituency of toryism was by now recognizably the disgruntled business classes rather than the disillusioned workers: the sort of people who were already inviting Churchill to Lancashire and complaining about their cavalier treatment by 'ornamental nobodies'. 'No man professes Conservatism', admitted a Conservative writer in the journals debate of 1882–3, 'who has not got something to lose'.[22] In fact, the process was already under way whereby the middle-class champions of 'tory democracy' were disliked by the old guard of county members for the openness (and realism) with which they used the accents of class warfare in relation to the real 'democracy'.[23] This reflected a distinction between aspiring middle-class tories and the old guard—a characteristically English manifestation of arcane class distinctions preserved between those whose objective interests were actually identical. It is best symbolised in an anecdote in the memoirs of Sir Henry Drummond Wolff—genial, *bon viveur*, and aristocratic. At the theatre one night in the company of the equally jovial and noisy Sir William Edmonton, they were shushed by the attendant. Billy Dyke, also in the party, was overcome by laughter but their two other companions, Smith and Cross, were mortified and 'affected to ignore our existence, turning their backs upon us morally as well as physically'.[24] Such snobbery created the kind of political anomaly expressed by Churchill in his wilderness days, when he spoke of the English aristocrat and workman being united against the middle classes by their 'common bond of sport and immorality'. But this was by now no more than the sentimental memory of a liaison long made impossible by events.

What was at issue in the tory democratic initiative of 1882 was parliamentary influence for local notables, not the adoption of policies to woo the masses. From early on, in fact, clever tories had seen the provincial manufacturing classes as 'material for Conservative principles to work upon, though the idiot squires treat them as levellers, democrats, etc'.[25] And from the 1860s writers in the reviews were noting the movement of Liberal capitalists into the Conservative ranks.[26] The 1874 election confirmed it, and much Conservative legislation in the following administration had been carefully gauged not to jeopardise the process. There was, however, by the early 1880s a feeling among the local notables who had embraced Conservatism that they had not received their due in parliamentary influence. It is expressed by a letter from Thomas Freston, an influential Manchester businessman and Conservative, to Arthur Balfour:

> The future of English politics will be found to rest very much in these northern constituencies—now, these masses must be led by cultivated, self-denying noble-minded men of power and position... For my part, if I had not gone amongst the workingmen in the wards I should have thrown up politics in very disgust of all I saw and heard in the clubs.[27]

Balfour himself was led to notice that social conditions rather than political constitutions now formed the main issue of contemporary political speculation; 'in the west, where, under whatever variety of external form, the supremacy of democracy is thought to be assured, discussions on the distribution of power are slowly being replaced by discussions on the distribution of wealth'. His uncle, Lord Salisbury, had seen this twenty years before in his trenchant articles for the *Quarterly Review*: reform being 'a battle not of parties but of classes', and the 'great political struggle of our century' being 'the struggle between property, be its amount small or great, and mere numbers'.[28] How could this be reconciled with an appeal to the desideratum of the tory working-man, who had no property at all? It could not; not, at least, without some sleight of hand. One subterfuge involved the kind of demotic, jingoist, chauvinist Orange-and-Primrose-coloured rhetoric which populist toryism (and Lord Randolph Churchill) invented in the 1880s: this was intended to identify the working-man with Tory stances in parliament. Another feint meant using the phrase 'tory democracy' to embrace the business classes, and on occasion the superior artisans, while ostensibly appealing to the class beneath them. And it was these businessmen, the local notables, who figured prominently in the attempt to revitalize the national organization of Conservatism, spearheaded by Churchill and Gorst in 1882–4. Moreover, this attempt was closely linked with the impatience felt by energetic Conservative M.P.s about their party's weakness in the 1880 parliament. The interesting thing is that the recognition that parliamentary weakness was linked with national disorganization was *not* always followed by what one might think would be the necessary corollary argument: the idea that local notables should be advanced to positions of critical importance in the metropolitan circles of party organization and decision-making at Westminster. These ideas were tentatively floated in the article Gorst and Churchill published in the *Fortnightly Review* in November 1882, entitled 'The state of the opposition', but they were essentially restricted to immediate political circumstances.[29] From Gorst's side the article presented ideas which he had nurtured since the 1860s. It should, he wrote to Churchill, be about 'the feebleness of the conservative party as a political organization, pointing out that it is led by and in the interests of a narrow, oligarchic and landowning class, and that the people in whom the real Conservatism of the nation resides have no interest in the matter, nor are their interests ever consulted'. But he also told Churchill that the time was ripe for 'a democratic tory party, which was always Dizzy's dream, at the head of which you might easily place yourself'.[30] These two priorities were not easily compatible; and this was evident in the campaign mounted by Gorst and Churchill through review articles, public meetings, and private intrigue. Revitalization of the party, it was indicated, would come, Antaeus-like, from contact with the 'people', who would provide a new kind of representative M.P.—though the 'people' designated seem to have been the middle-class businessman whom Gorst wanted to see represented in Westminster as well as in the local Conservative associations. Churchill's manifestoes, however, restricted themselves largely to attacks on his own front bench.

The Gorst–Churchill initiative, different though the partners' preoccupations implicitly were, launched a general discussion of the nature and direction of Conservatism which dominated the reviews in the winter of 1882–3.[31] Much of this was restricted to parliamentary and leadership questions. But at the same time Balfour, Carnarvon, Lytton, Stanhope, Raikes and Austin—no tory democrats they—were circularising leading Conservatives in an effort to call into play the literary and political talent of the Conservatives and place a 'truly national' policy before the country, while the most staid Conservative newspapers carried inspired articles calling for new initiatives. All this reflected subterranean upheavals in the question of who would lead the party, still lurching on under Salisbury in the lords and Northcote in the commons. And it meant that Churchill and his allies, bent on cutting out Northcote and asserting a positive, non-fusionist Conservatism, had to play to a constituency far removed from their rivals and colleagues at Westminster—who, as regards the inefficiency of the parliamentary leadership and the necessity to organize the party nationally, in fact agreed with them too closely for comfort.

Thus the rebellious Conservatives already known as the Fourth Party (Churchill, Gorst and Wolff, no longer including Balfour) rediscovered tory democracy in 1882–3, and emphasised the unrepresentativeness of parties in parliament, along with an admiration for Disraeli which they had often been very far from feeling when he was alive. It was a link which relied heavily upon Gorst's useful history as the organizer of victory in the 1860s; but in their *frondeur* activity during the past years there were pointers which seemed to argue that such a departure had always been on the cards. They had come to prominence as attackers of Bradlaugh and of the right of an atheist to affirm, which was an issue popular in the provinces—as Churchill well knew.[32] They had taken up issues like the Employers' Liability Bill, in which Harold Gorst and Winston Churchill later fondly discerned their fathers' commitment to social measures. But it should be noted that the struggle over the Employers' Liability Bill was waged by Churchill in the interests of the *employers*; he claimed it denied them 'the protection to which they were entitled' and he proposed an insurance scheme whose premiums would be deducted from workmen's wages 'to make them more careful'. This may well have been welcome to the 'Tory Democracy' which ran Lancashire factories, but was hardly aimed at 'the people'.

The important groundwork laid in their Fourth Party days for Churchill's and Gorst's appeal to the provinces had to do with other issues. There was the exposure of Northcote's inadequacy, the appeal to a demotic audience, and, most importantly, the capturing of publicity. As early as 1880 not only Borthwick's *Morning Post* but also Gibson Bowles's *Vanity Fair* were effectively Fourth Party organs. Both Churchill and Gorst produced anonymous contributions to the latter, attacking Conservative organization and its 'superannuated oligarchy', paternalist electoral machinery, indolence and aristocratic bias. Along with this, there was articulated in *Vanity Fair* sooner than anywhere else an accompanying refrain which, while making the appeal to 'democracy' all the more potent, held within it the seeds of future strife: the as yet extraordinary vision of Churchill as leader of the future.[33]

III

And that is what gave the revolt of the constituency associations against the parliamentary tory powers much of its motive force; and what sabotaged it in the end. From the beginning there were three interlinked factors. First, the weakness of the Conservative party in parliament, highlighted by the Fourth Party. Second, the weakness and incoherence of the organization in the provinces, again spotlit by Churchill's brilliant touring performances from 1881, which deliberately set various cats among pigeons, and further defined the split between provincial Conservatism and the articulation of the party at Westminster. And third, there was the issue of the leadership struggle. Later events, and Winston Churchill's brilliant obfuscations, concealed the degree to which the Fourth Party, and by extension a great deal of tory democratic rhetoric, was pro-Salisbury as well as anti-Northcote. And this was more easily obscured by the assiduity with which Churchill worked up his own, threatening provincial contact-system. Overtures from Manchester began in August 1881; he visited W. H. Houldsworth, the pillar of Lancashire toryism, in December and shortly afterwards was asked to stand for the city. His readiness to 'star' on platforms and indulge in superb vulgarities looked like the playing of a single hand; 'the "I" is driving the "We" to the wall', remarked contemporary observers.[34] But this should not hide the fact that his ambition was becoming centred on the commons leadership, as Salisbury's lieutenant.[35] This ambition, and Churchill's own tactics, were speeded up by his long illness and withdrawal in the summer of 1882, and again by other personal crises in 1883. The campaign which began with the composite article in the *Fortnightly* and continued with Churchill's

'Elijah's mantle' salvo the following spring, attempted to relate the leadership struggle to an appeal to 'the people'; thus it involved presenting Salisbury as 'a statesman who fears not to meet and who knows how to sway immense masses of the working classes, and who either by his genius or his eloquence, or by all the varied influences of an ancient name, can "move the hearts of households"'.

This is an appropriate point to turn to a larger issue and try to define, ideologically, the tory democratic constituency. In terms of an actual platform of issues, this is no easier for us that it was for Churchill. One can instance review articles by Lord Dunraven and Arthur Forwood, and isolate issues like protectionism, imperialism, local government reform, housing reform, and redistribution of church endowments; but Churchill often unequivocally repudiated such programmes. This was in a sense inevitable, because those who traded under 'tory democracy' appealed to a set of attitudes rather than an agenda. Indeed, the attitudes could be highly specific, even local: London cabmen's irritation at the law restricting the use of cabs at elections; the favouring of protection by Coventry ribboners, Nottingham lace-makers, Boston fishermen, or Sheffield metal-workers; the personal influence of a candidate like Howard Vincent or James Lowther; anti-semitism in the East End or anti-Irishism in Liverpool; all these special attitudes helped the tories among a working-class electorate on one occasion or another.[36] The broader spread of the roots of working-class toryism may be partly traced in what Geoffrey Best has called in another context 'that flag-saluting, foreigner-hating, peer-respecting side of the plebeian mind'.[37] The Conservative workingmen's club, the traditions of the church defence movement, and the complex of attitudes which made up Lancashire politics add to the picture.[38] In this last arena, special yet again, 'deferential behaviour' counts for less than peculiar traditions of tory families' involvement in trade, the connexions of the tory gentry with municipal politics, and the precocious development of 'modern business toryism' in figures like Churchill's friend and mentor, Houldsworth (himself a convert from Liberalism). In Lancashire, too, local divisions which broke along religious lines were exceptionally influential (catholics as well as dissenters were Liberal supporters). In the Conservative workingmen's club, the tory managerial class was represented along with the upper-level spinners; the paternalist factory style survived suburbanisation. There was also an overlap with popular anglicanism (often in the form of savage evangelicalism) and the cause of the Englishman's right to his alcohol.

158

Further cementing factors, much remarked upon, included anti-Irishism (which transcended the gap between skilled and unskilled working-class). Also, more positively, there was the Orange movement—whose lodges were, however, the preserve of the skilled artisans.[39] In Blackburn, Orangeism was closely identified with progressive toryism and fair trade; in Liverpool, Forwood addressed Orange lodges in the name of tory democracy. The iconography of the movement in Lancashire composed a curious collage made up of bits of the bible, the constitution, the Stanley family, and the history of Ulster. Orange street theatre, featuring escaped nuns and protestant Red Indians, persisted until the mid-1880s.[40] Though the tory leadership privately had little patience with the conspiracy theories and paranoia of this grass-roots movement, they had no objection to integrating it into Conservative party organisation. (Even Murphy, the great Orange demagogue, could speak out dangerously against the tory elite and had to be conciliated.) Much of the same impulse was channelled after 1883 into the Primrose League—surely one of the most bizarre manifestations of the occult depths of the English class system. Started by Churchill and Wolff (and keyed closely into Churchill's campaigns for Birmingham), it was rapidly taken over by the established grandees of the party, and adopted enthusiastically in the provinces. Possibly its 'sham titles and gimcrack rhetoric partially filled the need felt by local notables for some evidence of ennoblement as political reward (tory administrations being notoriously less generous than the Liberals with honours for their provincial supporters).[41] But it also met the political and social needs at a certain electoral level which are best summed up in the awkward concept of deference. At its simplest this was indicated by the nature of Hicks Beach's 20-year majority at Clifton, described at the time as 'the two classes of the luxurious rich and the obsequious poor';[42] at its most complex it can be interpreted as a political behaviour-pattern which transcends class as well as party (though recent work has related deferential political behaviour much more closely to parental political loyalties and local work-patterns). 'Deference' has fallen among the political scientists, becoming a theory in search of data; but to contemporaries it was a simpler reality. 'The love of caste that in England as in Hindostan devours all hearts is confined to no walks of society', wrote Cobden, 'but pervades every degree'.[43]

And deference found its natural 'habitation' in the Primrose League, which focussed its activities on bazaars and fairs where humble party workers could meet the grand and influential; as well as enjoying 'a rich profusion of punchinellos, pierrots, jugglers, ventriloquists, vying for favour with oriental illusionists, equilibrisms, waxworks, conjuring tricks, marionettes, and exhibitions of microscopic objects or of Egyptian antiquities'.[44] It also involved political women in a demeaning and frivolous way, as Liberal feminists pointed out; and overall it was calculated to preserve the self-esteem of local notables not only by allowing them to rub shoulders with countesses but also by its very subscription-structure. (One guinea to full members, who sat on committees; one shilling to 'associate members', cynically defined by political opponents as 'agricultural labourers and servant-girls',[45] who provided audiences.) Though at the time of its foundation it was intended as a publicity-machine for Churchill, it rapidly reverted to an aboriginal toryism which later set it against him. And in this development too was an indication of the latent tensions between the various interpretations put upon 'tory democracy'.

Other elements in the tory democratic constituency comprised imperialism, protectionism and a raucous devotion to the monarchy. (Gorst noticed in 1870, with vague surprise, that Lancashire operatives were addicted to 'old-fashioned ways with guilds and strange customs and medieval ceremonies'). All this provided highly-coloured, vivid and fairly well defined rhetorical effect.[46] What was usually left vague, however, was the nostrum of social reform. Nowhere was this more true than in the seminal article in which Churchill challenged the Conservative old guard in May 1883, 'Elijah's mantle'.[47] By judicious and selective quotation, Winston Churchill made this appear an appeal to social reform in the name of tory democracy; in fact, this theme merely provided a coda at the end. The dominant refrain was self-consciously Disraelian, violently anti-Whig and extremely diehard in its appeal to the lords for a bold lead against subversive policies originated in the commons. In fact, tory democratic ideology, in Gorst's sense, was strictly subordinated to political tactics. As the manifesto of a creed, it deserved the accurate judgement given by Labouchere: '"Tory" it no doubt is, but why in the name of reason does Lord Randolph also call it "democracy"?'[48] The real point of 'Elijah' was, that the idea of tory democracy, if it had ever stood a chance of coherent exposition, was rapidly being scrambled into the quicksilver mould of Churchill's drive to remodel the party leadership. His strategy depended on moving the arena of conflict to the provinces: first, by coming forward as candidate for Birmingham, then by mounting his celebrated campaign to infiltrate the National Union of Conservative

Associations, on the grounds that the parliamentary membership no longer represented the Conservative community. In both initiatives, the rhetoric of tory democracy was used, aimed at the audience of provincial notables who formed its natural cohorts. But central to the rules of the game, and never far from Churchill's mind, was their essential dispensability in terms of the real political world, to which they traditionally had been nervous about claiming entry. And though some of his tory democratic supporters were carried away enough to forget this, they would receive an abrupt reminder of it in the end.[49]

IV

Churchill's appearance in January 1884 as future candidate for Birmingham was an important opening gambit in the campaign to use provincial toryism against the charmed metropolitan circle. It provided the possibility of an urban base for Churchill's own career, necessary for private reasons. But it was also the home of the Liberal Caucus against which the National Union crusade was supposed to define itself. Churchill's public stance from Christmas 1883 involved obeisances to Birmingham opinion. He similarly took up an Orange stance on the Rossmore affair at this very time, greatly appreciated by the church, the anti-Irish, and the Conservative workingmen's clubs.[50] But at the same time as consolidating a tory democratic base at Birmingham he was making diehard pronouncements on all issues except protection. In mid-April 1884, when the struggle with the leaders over the National Union was at its height, Churchill canvassed Birmingham indefatigably and represented himself publicly as cast out by the old guard of the party, and cultivating 'the intelligent independent and instructed masses'. But he also added that 'politics were the ruin of trade unions'; and that toryism should become a 'self-governed party' by the exertions of influential businessmen like those in his audiences, who must set up clubs for their grateful artisans. (The celebrated phrases 'trust the people' and 'I have no fear of democracy', made so much of by Winston Churchill, appeared in the context of Lord Randolph's defence of his record on reform and the agricultural labourers[51]). The entire Birmingham venture was dominated by Churchill's attempt to state his personal position, not to define a new Conservatism; he conspicuously did not take Gorst's advice, which was to try and cut out Salisbury by a general appeal to democracy.[52] And this may have shown that his grasp of the strengths of 'tory democratic' support in Birmingham was more realistic than his colleague's: though the organisation of Conservative clubs in Birmingham was formally representative, it was dominated by a few influential businessmen.[53] And this in turn reflected Churchill's different apprehension of their power-base within the National Union of Conservative Associations.

For this body, which had its origin in the Conservative organisational drive of the 1860s, was never the coherently organised federation of local associations it appeared on paper; nor was the membership of the local associations that were affiliated to it representative of any kind of 'popular' toryism.[54] Its objects were defined as disseminating information and popularising the party at a local and provincial level. But though its early publications show some preoccupation with the working-class tory voter, this soon faded into the realm of things hoped for. What the National Union never did, despite some initial ambitions, was to raise funds or choose candidates: the only two activities whereby it could have gained any real influence. ('Both [party organisations] are shams', wrote Lowell in 1900, 'but with this difference, that the Conservative organisation is a transparent, and the Liberal an opaque, sham'; and Mackenzie has more recently emphasised how the organisation of the Conservative party *outside* parliament was concieved of as a servant of the party *inside* parliament.[55]) Socially, moreover, Joyce's analysis of the Ashton Conservative Association is symptomatic: the committee broke down (in 1885) into one-third large manufacturers, one-third lesser manufacturers and shopkeepers, and one-third clerical and artisans; workingmen's involvement in a 'polling district committee' was simply a 'plaything'.[56] The National Union in Lancashire as a whole, heartland of provincial toryism, still emerges as dominated by traditional interests and local notables; its subjects of debate were religion, fair trade and foreign policy—never social reform. When Lancashire defied London, it was in order to assert diehard values.[57]

Nonetheless, it was on the National Union, that muddled and spancelled organisation, that Churchill and Gorst had fallen in the summer of 1883, when their election to the Council provoked considerable acrimony. Gorst was determined to revive the ideas of popular organisation and control with which the National Union had originated. Churchill echoed this, telling the conference that the interests of the Conservative party were 'perfectly safe in the hands [of the working classes], if we will trust them... you must invite them to a share and a real share in the party government' and in parliament. But, more importantly, he was determined to define himself aggressively against his leaders—at a time when he was seriously considering the possibility of changing parties.[58] As the campaign developed, he worked hard trying to establish some degree of financial independence for the National Union, while Gorst privately emphasised the need to flatter the desire of local notables for recognition by the central politicians.[59] But throughout the following months, his tactics can be seen as defined by how he wanted to relate to Salisbury and cut out Northcote; and it is notable both how he left the National Union offensive on ice when distracted by political events, and how when he came to negotiate with Salisbury in February 1884 those who supported him tended to be opponents of Northcote rather than exponents of tory democracy. By February, political journalists were drawing the conclusion of a Salisbury–Churchill combination.

Why, then, did Churchill at this very point move implacably against Salisbury by taking up an intransigent line on the question of extending the powers of the National Union in the name of tory democracy? The answer is that he didn't; or at least, didn't want to. His tactics, when examined day by day, show a pattern of public irreconcilability masking private negotiations, which never really paused: all directed at Salisbury, not Northcote. Winston Churchill's selective quotations from his father's supposedly 'defiant' letters conceal how much Lord Randolph was trying to keep matters open, and often actually backing down. And, most importantly, he was warned that provincial toryism would not support a complete breakdown between the National Union and the leaders. Again and again, private moderation and compromise accompanied grand public repudiations; and what set Churchill's pace, in Westminster and out of it, can most clearly be seen as Northcote's failure in the commons over the crisis in Egypt and the Sudan (on which Churchill wanted a grand confidence debate). There was also the reason he produced to Lord Dartmouth, president of the National Union, which was that he could not stand successfully for Birmingham unless the National Union's powers were reformed. And he went on to mount his campaign of speeches in Birmingham in April 1884—in which, as has been said, Gorst's advice to go for social reform was ignored, Churchill's own personal position was emphasised, and his rhetoric (often diehard) was cast at what he himself called 'the influential residents of the town'. Indeed, as his running-mate Burnaby pointed out to him with military forthrightness, the only point of coming to the provinces to 'address the plebs' was to alarm his rivals.[61]

And this was not missed by contemporaries. Gorst was privately researching the extent of support, and the organisational state, of local associations; and he found, to his chagrin, a very uneven pattern of affiliation to the National Union—and to tory democracy as conceived by the front line. The leaders of provincial conservatism had, indeed, been warned by circular letters that the National Union's original and legitimate ambition to broaden the basis of Conservatism had been perverted into Churchill's drive for personal power.[62] And in fact, even during his Birmingham campaign, Churchill was negotiating with his leaders indirectly, having let Abergavenny know that he did not intend to claim control of seat nominations, and would accept the presence of the party whips on the National Union council if the central committee were dissolved. At the end of April the leaders decided to vote the National Union £3000 a year and to meet Churchill on 1 May.

Again, however, Churchill's bargaining hardened: not, as his biographers state, because he was forced into it by an unexpected rebellion on the council, but because he deliberately set up a carefully orchestrated disagreement.[63] As usual, however, Churchill had a strong lobby working behind the scenes for rapprochement; and significantly, he used his Birmingham and Liverpool tory democrat contacts, Satchell Hopkins and Forwood (by now an ally), to approach Salisbury a few days later—by which time he had been allowed to appear the champion of provincial toryism against the Conservatism based on land, church and metropolitan grandees. The *éclat* with which he had publicised his disagreement with Salisbury concealed the fact that his emissaries were allowed concede to the leaders full control over 'general party finances, questions of public policy, and matters appertaining to the selection of candidates'—in other words, all that mattered. This was just what Salisbury had wanted, and Churchill had refused, a month before.

Why this sudden rapprochement, after the display of independence? Again the reasons are to be found in high politics, far removed from the world of tory democracy. Churchill's support in the commons was vital for Beach's motion censuring the government for their Sudan policy. He was also needed to arrange an accomodation with Parnell and Healy over this manoeuvre.[65] In this light should be seen Churchill's threats at this very time to desert the party and contest Birmingham as an independent.[66] As usual, he had publicly demonstrated his strength at a time when his party could not do without him, and then allowed himself be privately reconciled (the very strategy which would be his downfall at Christmas 1886). The

Sudan debate, his public reconciliation with his leaders, and his re-election as National Union chairman, concealed the fact that he had now climbed down over any real demand for independence on the part of the National Union. Churchill's argument, when he had to produce one, was that any real trial of strength with the leaders must be postponed until the National Union Conference at Sheffield in July, though Gorst wanted to drive ahead, worried that the moderates were gaining the upper hand. But in fact, Churchill was already losing interest, and returning to the central arena where his parliamentary weight could be thrown in the balance—not only over the Sudan debate but also, and far more potently, in the fast-approaching crisis over parliamentary reform. This supplied the catalyst that decided the fate of the National Union's attempt at independence and 'tory democracy's' bid for influence in parliament.

V

This was because the summer of 1884 was dominated by the deadlock over the Liberals' decision to extend household franchise to the counties and the tory split about the advisability of holding the measure up in the lords or compromising on a simultaneous redistribution scheme which would safeguard their own strongholds. And in the brinkmanship and negotiations which occupied politicians that summer, Churchill's part was vital. In this light should be seen his activities throughout these months. Both sides knew that if Churchill split openly with Salisbury, Gladstone would survive; hence the avalanche of letters from correspondents, tory democratic as well as old guard, begging Churchill not to split the party. The lords rejected the Reform Bill in July, but Churchill maintained an enigmatic low profile. And when the National Union conference opened in Sheffield on 23 July, though it was officially a struggle between tory democrats and aristocratic elitists, those in the know saw it as breaking along the lines of those who supported the lords' intransigence and those who did not. Churchill was known to be among the latter. And the former needed to win him back, if they were to bring off the compromise which was now their only option; and even more so, if Gladstone called a dissolution on reform in August.

This was the scenario articulated by Churchill's enemies on the council, to which they added expressions of mortal terror lest Salisbury, Northcote and Beach abandon them in order to conciliate Churchill.[67] Though his candidates won a majority of seats on the council at Sheffield, what followed was an anti-climax: a speedy agreement between Churchill and Salisbury, which while abolishing the central committee in name, and giving the party whips seats on the National Union council, ignored all ideas of democratising the party in parliament by giving financial or candidate-choosing powers to the local associations. In other words, Churchill's direct challenge to Salisbury had been bought off at an un-named price. Both Churchill's biographers produced rather lame explanations endeavouring to show that he won the day for a democratised parliamentary party. Gorst's son presented it as a betrayal by Churchill of tory democracy, which it was, and of his father—which it was not. The elder Gorst's wish to democratise the party organisation was obviously sold out; but no-one has been able to explain why he acquiesced, in a muted letter to Churchill declaring his readiness to 'rest on our laurels' (what laurels?)[68] He had, indeed, been fortuitously absent on the Isle of Wight when Churchill capitulated to Salisbury at a London garden party. But why did he not repudiate the arrangement on his return? The answer is, because he too had been bought off; and we happen to know *his* price, recorded by the indefatigable Loulou Harcourt in his diary. Sir Algernon Borthwick, who had been involved in the negotiations throughout, confided to Loulou that Gorst had been promised the solicitor-generalship in the next tory government 'if he makes his submission to Randolph and the tory party'.[69] He did; and he received his reward in June 1885, though it turned to ashes in his mouth.

Churchill, on the other hand, appeared to have reached his apotheosis. Reconciled to his leaders for the express purpose of the delicate negotiations over reform, he played his part by overt acts of party loyalty. He even attacked Gorst in public. There was to be one last twist: when all preliminaries were over, Salisbury neatly excluded him from the final negotiations with the Liberals—to his fury. Churchill retaliated with an extraordinary newspaper interview, not much noticed before, on 27 November. Here he suddenly reverted to the tory democratic line: and it is extremely ironic that at *this* stage he suddenly pressed the only logical end to the tory democratic faith, a fully-fledged policy of Bismarckian social reform. He called for local government reform based on fully elective democracy, full licensing control for these new bodies, working-class housing provided by 'a large investment of public money and a large amount of state intervention for the benefit of the masses of the people', protectionism and tariff reform, a government expenditure target of £100,000,000, and a complete overhaul of Dublin Castle ('a nest of political corruption'); he ended with a broad hint about universal suffrage.[70]

Flashy as this was, it came too late; it was little noticed in the metropolitan press, and within a week Churchill was en route to India, for which continent he would provide an impeccably tory secretary of state in Salisbury's caretaker government the following June. Tory democracy was something he continued to discover when beleagured, or merely piqued; his most consistent exposition of Conservative social reform would come when he was long out of office, speaking to declining audiences, and increasingly erratic. His correspondence shows that the tragic attempt at the end of his life to contest Bradford was at first welcomed by archetypal local tory democrats (middling manufacturers begging him to visit them at houses with names like 'The Acacias'). But even by November 1884, it was too late to recapture their confidence.

For the local notables who had provided the real backbone of 'tory democracy' felt aggrieved and deserted after Sheffield. More than one local association chairman told Churchill they would never have worked so hard if they had known this was to be the outcome.[71] Financial independence was as far away as ever; by the end of the year the Birmingham association in fact had to send obsequious requests for money to the central agent, ironically asking Churchill to intercede. Tory democrats like Maclean, reviewing things long afterwards, consoled themselves with the thought that Churchill's flawed career had irretrievably broken down, not with his resignation in 1886, but in 1884, when he agreed to the 'euthanasia' of the provincial conservative associations.[72] And when Salisbury entered his temporary kingdom in June 1885, and Gorst became, as promised, solicitor general and Churchill Indian secretary, they were members of a government whose personnel was noticeably lacking in representatives of aspiring middle-class toryism. Metropolitan grandees had won out once more. An embittered old supporter from the National Union struggle put it to Churchill with brutal accuracy:

> I cannot tell you, my dear Randolph Churchill, how deeply I regret that your undoubted ability to lead an advanced tory party, which I was one of the first to recognise, should be thus shelved if not closed... We find you helping to place in power all those, and those only, whom we turned over at Sheffield as not truly representing the views of the majority of the party. It will be difficult to justify this to your friends in the country.[73]

Politics being what they were, and are, Churchill—having succeeded—was not in a position where he needed to justify anything to his friends: at least, not yet. And the question which arises is whether a letter like this, and tory democracy at large, represented anything except the self-delusion of the self-important. By the end of 1886 (and the end of Churchill's official career), the National Union had been reorganised to embrace all local associations and connect them up to the council; but financial independence and the power to choose candidates were still a chimera, and Salisbury frequently told them their functions were, and must remain, local and limited.[74] Not only did the occupational and social structure of British government elites remain the same;[75] but also, given that what defined Conservatism from the 1870s (not only from 1886) were resistance values and the defence of property, its 'revival'—for all the hopes of people like Forwood who wrote in the reviews—would depend upon this, not a departure into progressivism. Conservatism, as defined by Salisbury and the fifteenth earl of Derby, 'placed no confidence in theories for the regeneration of mankind':[76] which was, then as now, its attraction for pessimistic intellectuals. Nor had 'democracy' ever been in question; Disraeli's dictum that 'the distribution of political power in the community is an affair of convention, and not an affair of moral and abstract right',[77] held good within the party as well as in the political world at large. The attitude of the centre to the periphery remained that indicated by Salisbury's brutal remark that his epitaph should be 'Died of writing inane letters to empty-headed Conservative associations'.[78] In 1884 Churchill, and even Gorst, showed that they subscribed to the conventional attitude when they sold the National Union and tory democracy down the river.[79]

Indeed, Churchill's mission to the provinces had mostly been for the purposes of entertainment (besides self-advancement), and the chief function of local toryism had been to provide an audience. Music-halls had become a vital forum for the propagation of John Bull opinions, chauvinism, xenophobia and all; and a superbly deadpan *Spectator* obituary of Churchill in 1895 would apostrophise him as 'the best music-hall orator of recent times'.[80] That was the level upon which he appealed to his audiences, which cloaked the fact that much of what he was saying in the early 1880s (as over Egypt and Ireland) was highly unwelcome to provincial Conservative opinion. But political imaginativeness was, in fact, as suspect to tory democrats as to Carlton Club mandarins, both of whom made common cause from the mid-eighties in a hegemony where any genuinely popular element there might be in toryism did not have to be represented in parliament. As for those working-class elements who voted Conservative, where they continued to do so they did it for the same sectional and peculiar reasons they had always done. Salisbury's party was in 1886 already prepared to capitalise on a national constituency which hardly needed the Irish issue that came as a fortuitous fillip. The threat was already perceived to come not from Parnell, but from Hyndman and Henry George. In this connection, the key text of 1886 was not Gladstone's *The Irish question* or Dicey's *England's case against home rule*, but something more like W. H. Mallock's bizarre novel *The old order changes*, inspired by the West End riots of that year. In it he attempted to hypothesize a stabilized social order where a new Tory party runs the factories like monasteries. Or, for the purposes of this paper, one might consider the equally strange production from Standish O'Grady in 1886, entitled *Toryism and the tory democracy*. In the accents of a latter-day Carlyle, O'Grady preached his version of the peculiar faith that went by this name. But his implicit conclusion was that propertied interests must, no matter how abused by platform performers, remain Conservative for self-preservation; and the democratic excesses of orators like Churchill, aimed at a mass audience, were only intended as tongue in cheek. 'Such is the law of the game as laid down by the democratic development of modern England'.[81]

Thus far, we may agree. The odd thing is how far the rhetoric reached, not only at the time, but also in the reminiscences of politicians who were involved and—until very recently—in the work of historians who were not. But the real importance of the stalking-horse of an appeal to tory democracy was not so much in an effort to cajole a new electorate, as in the attempts of ambitious and impatient men to take over the direction of affairs in the corridors of Conservative power; when they had used their equivocal appeal to its full potential, they deserted back to the parliamentary fold and received their own short-term rewards. However, even in this more visceral arena, the old elite were eventually too strong for them; which was probably some small comfort to the disgruntled provincial leaders who were left playing second fiddle in the inevitably hierarchical orchestra of national Conservatism.

Notes

1. See H. J. Hanham, *Elections and party management: politics in the time of Disraeli and Gladstone* (London, 1959), pp 105 ff. The Lancashire case is argued over in J. R. Vincent, 'The effect of the Second Reform Act in Lancashire', *Hist. Jn.*, xi (1968), pp 84–94, and J. C. Lowe, 'The Tory triumph of 1868 in

Tory democracy and political elitism

Blackburn and in Lancashire', ibid., xvi (1973), pp 733–748. Also see R. L. Greenall, 'Popular Conservatism in Salford 1868–1886', in *Northern History* ix (1974), pp 123–38.

2. A recent discussion of the historiography of class in Victorian politics is provided by Tom Nossiter, 'The middle class and nineteenth-century politics: notes on the literature' in J. Garrard *et al.*, (ed.), *The middle class in plitics* (Farnborough, Hants., 1979), pp 67–91.

3. Not that his ideas always measured up to the grand theory. 'Let us show the people, i.e. the lower orders, by adding to their comforts in the only legitimate way a legislature can do, *viz.*, by voting money to building public baths . . . that we are their real friends.' Charles Whibley, *Lord John Manners and his friends* (2 vols., London, 1925), i, 137.

4. See J. Cornford, 'The transformation of Conservatism in the late nineteenth century', in *Victorian Studies*, vii (1963), pp 35–66.

5. Paul Smith, *Disraelian Conservatism and social reform* (London, 1967), p. 157.

6. Ibid., p. 16, n. 2; also Cornford, op. cit., p. 62. On Manchester and its significance for the nineteenth-century imagination see Steven Marcus, *Engels, Manchester and the working class* (New York, 1974).

7. P. Smith, op. cit., pp 217–8.

8. See W. S. Blunt, 'Randolph Churchill: a personal recollection' in *Nineteenth Century* (Mar. 1906), pp 408–9.

9. See for instance Fabian Ware, 'Conservative opportunism and imperial democracy', in *Nineteenth Century* (Mar. 1907), pp 405–18.

10. See for instance Lord Henry Bentinck, *Tory Democracy* (1918).

11. P. Smith, op. cit. (1967); E. J. Feuchtwanger, *Disraeli, democracy and the tory party* (Oxford, 1968); M. Cowling, *1867, Disraeli, Gladstone and revolution* (Cambridge, 1967); F. B. Smith, *The making of the second Reform Bill* (Cambridge, 1966); Cornford, op. cit. (1964).

12. Quoted in Cornford, op. cit., p. 41.

13. E.g., E. A. Nordlinger, *The working-class tories* (London, 1967); R. T. Mackenzie and Allan Silver, *Angels in marble: working-class Conservatives in urban England* (London, 1968); D. Kavanagh, 'The deferential English: a comparative critique' in *Government and Opposition*, vi, no. 3 (1971), pp 333–60; W. Guttsman, *The British political elite* (London, 1968); F. Parkin, 'Working-class Conservatives: a theory of political deviance' in *Br. Jn. Sociology*, xviii (1967), pp 278–90. 'Deviance' as a concept was used by hostile contemporaries regarding working-class toryism. 'Mythic as a mermaid', remarked John Morley; 'a monstrosity', said a Blackburn reformer (quoted in Lowe, op. cit., p. 741). *Truth* referred to them as 'loafing traitors to their order' (28 Aug. 1884), adding that they were the same small band paid to move from meeting to meeting all over the country. Thorold Rogers said that if the genuine Conservative working-man could be found he ought to be preserved in a glass case (Greenall, op. cit., p. 124). But Frederic Harrison took the phenomenon more seriously than his allies; see 'The Conservative reaction', in *Fortnightly Review*, no. 88 (Mar. 1874), pp 297–309.

14. See e.g. J. Garrard (ed.), op. cit.; also G. Crossick (ed.), *The lower middle class in Britain 1870–1914* (London, 1977).

15. See A. Frisby, 'Has Conservatism increased in England since the last Reform Bill?', *Fortnightly Review*, no. xxx (1881), pp 727–9. Also Feuchtwanger, op. cit., pp 82–3.

16. P. Smith, op. cit., p. 317; also E. J. Feuchtwanger, 'The Conservative party under the impact of the Second Reform Act', *Victorian Studies*, ii (1958–9). p. 304.

17. See e.g. Salisbury's speech at Littlehampton and Northcote's at Hereford, reported in *Pall Mall Gazette*, 19 July 1882, 19 Sept. 1882; also Lytton to Stanhope, 8 June 1883, Stanhope MSS 0295; and many scattered references in 'old guard' Conservative correspondence at this time.

18. Feuchtwanger, *Disraeli, democracy . . .* , p. 62.

19. See R. C. K. Ensor, 'Some political and economic interactions in later Victorian England', *R. Hist. Soc. Trans.* (4th ser.), xxxi (1949); contradicted by Cornford, op. cit., pp 57–8.

20. See *Truth*, 4 May 1882, for a typical article stating that 'hard-headed Conservatives' were forecasting a scenario whereby the Irish would hold the balance at the next election and, with the Conservatives, put the Liberals out; the Conservatives declining to take office under these conditions, Conservatives and moderate Liberals would form a coalition under Derby or Argyll. This was exactly the kind of outcome Northcote wanted (see A. Lang, *Letters and diaries of Sir Stafford Northcote, first Earl of Iddesleigh* (London, 2 vols., 1890), ii, 150.

21. See Foster, *Lord Randolph Churchill: a political life* (Oxford, 1981), pp 101–2.

22. T. E. Kebbel, 'The spirit of party', *Nineteenth Century* (Jan–June 1882), pp 385–6.

23. See Feuchtwanger, *Disraeli, Democracy...* , pp 98, 170, for references to Forwood causing this reaction among older tories.

24. H. D. Wolff, *Rambling recollections* (London, 1908), ii, 128–9.

25. Stanley to Disraeli, 28 Nov. 1853, quoted in P. Smith, op. cit., p. 22.

26. 'Their foremost wish is to be isolated from the class out of which they came . . . [and to be placed] *en rapport* with the territorial gentry'. W. A. Abram, 'Social condition and political prospects of the Lancashire workingmen', *Fortnightly Review*, iv (1868), pp 439–40. Also see J. Morley, 'The Chamber of Mediocrity', ibid. (Dec. 1868), p. 690: 'For the new feudalism is only just beginning to organise itself... the Lancashire towns are turning to what they consider the politer faith... the man who began life as a beggar and a Chartist softens down into a Radical when he has got enough for a weaving shed; a factory of his own mollifies him into what is called a sound Liberal; and by the time he owns a mansion and a piece of land he has a feeling of blue blood tingling in his veins, and thinks of a pedigree and a motto in old French'.

27. T. W. Freston to A. J. Balfour, 3 Jan. 1883 (Balfour MSS at Whittinghame, 28). The class nature of the 'masses', however, was more accurately analysed by A. Egerton, writing to W. H. Smith on 9 April 1880 and castigating his canvassers for ignoring the 'miles of new streets just outside of Manchester and other boroughs... when the county and borough franchise is assimilated, which it will I suppose be this session, these suburban voters may very possibly strengthen instead of weaken the conservative party, as they are a very different class from the workingmen householders in the county'. (Hambleden MSS, PS/6/580).

28. *Quarterly Review*, ccix (1866), p. 55.

29. 'The state of the Opposition', xxii, p. 668. Balfour thought Wolff and Gorst were responsible, and most authorities (including the Wellesley Index) have followed this; but Escott, who edited the magazine, records that Churchill was

one of the co-authors (*Randolph Spencer-Churchill as a product of his age, being a personal and political monograph* (London, 1895), p. 158; and the style of the second section bears him out. For the background see Foster, op. cit., pp 103–6.

30. Gorst to Churchill, 10 Sept. 1882 (Lord Randolph Churchill MSS, hereafter RCHL, i/76).

31. See, e.g., H. Raikes, 'The functions of an Opposition', *Nineteenth Century* (Jan. 1883), pp 140–54, and St John Brodrick, 'The functions of Conservative Opposition', ibid., pp 155–65.

32. He suggested publishing his speech against Bradlaugh because 'it might be widely circulated in the large towns'; Churchill to Escott, 6 May 1883 (Escott MSS, BL Add. MSS 58793). Smith had been told in August 1881 that a Conservative victory at Preston was caused not by Fair Trade but by Roman Catholic feeling against Bradlaugh; R. Mowbray to Smith, 10 Aug. 1881 (Hambledon MSS PS/7/80).

33. See *Vanity Fair*, 1 May 1880, 16 Oct. 1880, 5 July 1881, for probable contributions; Chamberlain referred in parliament to Churchill's articles in the journal, and was not contradicted. For presentation of Churchill as a future leader see ibid., 10 July 1880; also reaction to Churchill's speech at Hull at Christmas 1881.

34. See *Truth*, 8 Dec. 1881, on Churchill at Manchester. Smith repeated exactly this point in a letter to Harrowby, 17 Jan. 1883: 'Liverpool and Preston prove that men care more than we had supposed possible for themselves rather than for principles and very much of the action of the 4th Party and the Review and Newspaper articles are prompted by a resolve to push personal interests at all hazards. Who is to lead if Northcote ultimately fails?' (Harrowby MSS, LIV/209).

35. Balfour is as responsible as Winston for concealing this strategy. His own *Chapters of autobiography* (London, 1930), puts Churchill's ambition for a total takeover at the improbably early date of 1881. Thus he glossed over both his own early desertion of his Fourth Party allies, and the extent to which that 'party' was a front group to advance Salisbury against Northcote.

36. See Alan J. Lee, 'Conservatism, traditionalism and the British working class, 1880–1918' in D. E. Martin and D. Rubinstein (ed.,), *Ideology and the labour movement* (London, 1979), pp 84–102.

37. See review article of E. P. Thompson, *The making of the English working class*, *Hist. Jn.* viii (1965), p. 278.

38. These have been brilliantly delineated in P. Joyce's D. Phil. thesis, 'Popular Toryism in Lancashire, 1860–1890' (Balliol College, Oxford, 1975), to which I am indebted for much of what follows; see also his *Work, society and politics: the culture of the factory in later Victorian England* (Brighton, 1980).

39. Joyce, op. cit., p. 214.

40. And Gladstone was presented as a secret convert to Papism, for Lancashire platform purposes; Hanham, op. cit., p. 215.

41. Feuchtwanger, *Disraeli, democracy...*, pp 209–11. Churchill, however, pressed Salisbury hard for honours for his Birmingham supporters.

42. Cornford, op. cit., p. 59.

43. *The political writings of Richard Cobden* (London, 1867), i, 131. Cf. Walter Bagehot, in *The English constitution* (1867; 1961 edition), pp 235, 263–4. 'It has been thought strange, but there *are* nations in which the numerous unwiser part wishes to be ruled by the less numerous wiser part. The numerical majority—whether by custom or by chance, is immaterial—is ready, is eager to delegate

its power of choosing its rulers to a certain select minority. It abdicates in favour of its elite, and consents to obey whoever that elite may confide in...if [their representative] was rich, they respected him much; and if he was a lord, they liked him the better'. Or again, Leslie Stephen, also in 1867: 'The country is aristocratic because the whole upper and middle, and a great part of the lower, classes have still an instinctive liking for the established order of things', quoted in Hanham, op. cit., p. xv.

44. J. Robb, *The Primrose League: 1883–1896* (New York, 1942), p. 89.
45. Ibid., *passim*. The Countess of Malmesbury, in the *National Review*, May 1885, emphasised that the success of her habitation was due to the fact she 'gave my whole time and energy to canvassing among the middle classes', and Loulou Harcourt noted that on 19 April 1883 'no cabmen were wearing primroses, and they are very good barometers of opinion' (Lewis Harcourt's Journal, Harcourt MSS B, vol. 350, p. 176).
46. See R. V. Price, 'Society, status and Jingoism: the social roots of lower middle-class patriotism 1870–1900' in G. Crossick, op. cit., pp 89–112.
47. *Fortnightly Review*, cxcvii (May 1883), pp 613–21.
48. *Truth*, 3 May 1883.
49. For a discussion of the provincial middle-class's reluctance to enter the metropolitan political world see J. Garrard, 'The middle classes and nineteenth-century national and local politics' in J. Garrard, op. cit., pp 35–66. And for a personal vignette which bears this out see Hanham's biography of J. W. Maclure of Manchester: Hanham, op. cit., pp 314–5.
50. See Foster, 'To the Northern Counties Station: Lord Randolph Churchill and the prelude to the Orange Card' in F. S. L. Lyons and R. A. J. Hawkins (eds), *Ireland under the Union: varieties of tension* (Oxford, 1980), pp 274–5.
51. See *Morning Post*, 17 April 1884, for a full report of this speech (there are many excisions in the collected edition, which was edited by Louis Jennings, an embittered tory democrat ideologue determined to reclaim Churchill for the faith).
52. Gorst to Churchill, 15 Apr. 1884 (RCHL iii/345).
53. For the roots of Birmingham Conservatism see Feuchtwanger, *Disraeli, democracy...*, pp 193–4, and C. Green, 'Birmingham's politics, 1873–1891: the local basis of change', *Midland History*, ii (1973–4), pp 84–98. This shows that, though some working-class municipal candidates were forced upon the local Conservative party, this was not an indication of a popular identification with Conservatism as such.
54. Cf. Feuchtwanger, pp 122 ff: 'It was desired to attract the support of the masses, yet preserve and accept the supremacy of the upper classes, a feat easier to accomplish in literature than amid harsh realities of political life'. The fullest account is in R. T. Mackenzie, *British political parties* (2nd, revised edition, London, 1964), pp 146–231. Also see Hanham, op. cit., pp 115–7, on how local associations relegated the influence of workingmen's 'clubs' associated with them.
55. Mackenzie, op. cit., p. 146.
56. Joyce, op. cit., p. 260.
57. As over the choice of Raikes, a go-ahead progressive Tory, to succeed a traditional grandee at Preston in 1882. That Gorst and Churchill realised this may be indicated by the fact that when Raikes abandoned Preston in November both Gorst and Churchill refused to succeed him; *Pall Mall Gazette*, 9 and 11 Nov. 1882.

58. Or so he told his family, who tried desperately to dissuade him; see Lady Rosamund Fellows to Churchill, 15 Aug. 1883, and Lord Wimborne to Churchill, 14 Aug. 1883, (Blenheim MSS K/IV).

59. See J. M. Maclean, *Recollections of Westminster and India* (Manchester, 1902); also Gorst to Churchill, 22 Sept. 1883 (RCHL i/170).

60. See Satchell Hopkins (Churchill's chief contact at Birmingham) to Churchill, 16 Mar. 1884 (RCHL ii/319); Maclean to Churchill, 18 and 20 Mar., ibid., 322–3. The National Union was not representative of all associations which were in turn not representative of all Conservatives in their localities. See Hanham, op. cit., p. 20.

61. Burnaby to Churchill, 8 May 1884 (RCHL iii/371).

62. See Gorst's report to Churchill (RCHL iii/345) and draft of Percy's circular letter in Balfour MSS at Whittingehame, 63.

63. See Foster, *Churchill*, pp 147–50.

64. Balfour roughed out a formula for future arrangements on 7 May, which is in the Whittingehame MSS, 63. An important clause read 'that in the event of the head whip making a written protest against any action taken by or on behalf of the National Union, as inconsistent with the welfare of the party, the matter be referred to the recognised leaders of the party, whose decision shall be final'.

65. See letters from Beach to Churchill, 2 May 1884, Long to Churchill, 8 May 1884, and Abergavenny to Churchill, 12 May 1884 (RCHL iii/355, 372, 389).

66. See Burnaby to Churchill, 8 May 1884 (RCHL iii/371); V. Hicks Beach, *The Life of Sir Michael Hicks Beach, Earl St Aldwyn* (2 vols., London, 1932), i, 213; A. Jones op. cit., p. 135; Lewis Harcourt's Journal MSS B, vol. 358, p. 58.

67. See RCHL iii/411, 414, 416 for reports of affairs in the provinces. He was also personally exhausted, and his ally Wolff incapacitated by a nervous breakdown. For his opponents' fears, see Percy's desperate letters to Balfour, n.d., and to Wortley (copy), 28 June 1884, in Whittingehame MSS.

68. Gorst to Churchill, 27 July 1884 (RCHL iii/455).

69. See Lewis Harcourt's journal, Harcourt MSS B, vol. 361, p. 22. Gorst assuaged his conscience by preaching 'the land for the people' to the Scottish crofters that autumn, to general amazement; see *Pall Mall Gazette*, 27 Aug. 1884.

70. *Pall Mall Gazette*, 27 Nov. 1884.

71. See letters from Forwood, 28 July 1884, Wainwright, 29 July 1884, Slade, 30 July 1884, in RCHL iii/457, 459, 460.

72. See Maclean's review of Winston Churchill's *Life in east and west* (Bombay), v (1906), 292 ff.

73. RCHL v/652; Staveley Hill to Churchill, 26 June 1885.

74. Mackenzie, op. cit., pp 175–6. On p 257 he quotes Winston Churchill in 1945, delivering exactly the same admonition.

75. See Guttsman, op. cit., pp 82–3, 100–101, for the remarkable preponderance of the landed aristocratic elite in Conservative cabinets well into the twentieth century.

76. See *Speeches of the 15th earl of Derby*, i, 267 (delivered on 18 Dec. 1875). Also P. Smith, *Lord Salisbury on politics: a selection from his articles in the Quarterly Review 1860–1883* (Cambridge, 1972), passim (especially 'Disintegration').

77. *Hansard 3*, ccix, 250.

78. Cecil, *Salisbury*, iii, 108.

79. For an interesting variation on this see E. T. Raymond, *Portraits of the nineties* (New York, 1921), p. 109. 'The career of Lord Randolph Churchill was founded on a hatred and an illusion. The illusion was that the conservative party was still

the party of the aristocracy, that the old quarrel between the landowners on the one side and the bankers, the manufacturers and the tradesmen on the other, yet persisted. He failed not because he was before, but because he was behind his time'. Churchill's governing hatred, in Raymond's view, was for the middle class.

80. For Toryism and music-halls see A. Lee, op. cit., pp 93–4, and L. Senelick, 'Politics as entertainment: Victorian music-hall songs' in *Victorian Studies*, xiv (1975), pp 149–80. The *Pall Mall Gazette*, prescient as ever, had remarked on 21 February 1884, *à propos* Churchill: 'The Toryism of the music-hall will supersede the Conservatism of the drawing-room'.

81. P. 126. For a modern academic argument that English Conservatism *does* (or can) represent a genuinely popular cause see Harvey Glickman, 'The toryness of English conservatism', *Jn. Brit. Studs.* (Nov. 1961), pp 111–43; but this unsurprisingly tries to cramp varieties of historical context and experience into theoretical frameworks (the Fourth Party, for instance, is grouped with the tory reform committee—and much else—as an instance of 'tory evangelism'). And even Mr Glickman remarks that 'as *social theory*, tory democracy is about as illuminating as "Conservative Communism"' (p. 132). He concludes more relevantly that 'Flexibility reinforces the emphasis on the non-rational, which... is at the heart of tory beliefs; Conservatives agree that policy arises from circumstances, that it may be altered by the acquisition of new recruits, and that it is less important to a party than tradition and organization' (p. 141).

The role of the peace movement in German parliamentary politics 1890–1933

Karl Holl

Historians prefer to state the existence of a phenomenon rather than to state its nonexistence. In the case of the German peace movement and its role in parliamentary politics one is in such a position, namely, one is forced to say that the peace movement was of minor importance in German parliamentary politics, at least for long phases of the period under consideration. This point is emphasised if a comparison is made with other western European countries, like Great Britain and France, where the movement of organised pacifism, having regard to the number of members and the parliamentary role it played, has always enjoyed a quite different and a larger dimension.[1]

That the role of the German peace movement, compared with other countries, was weak is a relevant historical statement, which gives significant information about the internal situation in Germany in this period. The reasons for this situation are apparent. If one regards pacifism as an ideology stemming philosophically from rationalism and the enlightenment, and politically as an emancipatory movement, then it is quite clear why its growth was limited in Germany. In Germany rationalism did not reach its total application; a revolutionary process struck three times without achieving its aims, namely in the modest results of the great French revolution, in the revolution of 1848–49, and in the revolution of November 1918. These circumstances gave too weak a stimulus for the stabilization of the peace movement in Germany. In addition to these obstacles there was no stimulus of the kind given by religious dissent, e.g. by the Quakers and Mennonites in the U.S.A. and in

England. In Germany it was of secondary or of no importance at all.

On the whole the preconditions in Germany for organised pacifism were much more disadvantageous than in other European countries and in the U.S.A. Whereas in the U.S.A. and in England peace societies existed since the beginning of the 19th century, the initiative of Arnold Ruge for a united Europe and for universal peace at the Frankfort National Assembly of 1848, as well as at the second universal peace congress in Frankfort in 1850, produced no significant reactions in Germany, with the exception of certain local peace activities which were stimulated in Koenigsberg and other centres by the English pacifist Hodgson Pratt, who travelled in Germany making speeches on peace themes.

It was only after the publication of Baroness Bertha von Suttner's novel *Down arms!*, in 1890, that the founding of the German Peace Society covering the whole territory of the Reich took place. Its establishment was mainly the work of a friend of Baroness Suttner, the Viennese journalist Alfred Hermann Fried. Berlin was both its birthplace and its centre. A broad, but transitory feeling in favour of peace arose among the educated classes as a reaction against the military bill brought before the Reichstag in 1892, and was apparent at the time of the dissolution of the Reichstag and the subsequent electoral campaign. All this had created for a short time a comparatively favourable climate for peace activities in Germany; but it was not to last.

It became evident, also, that the location of the headquarters for the German Peace Society in Berlin—the residence of the Reichstag, the capital of the empire as well as of Prussia—was no guarantee of the success of the peace agitation and of its organisational stability. On the contrary, it was in Prussia, where the conditions for peace work were extremely bad, that the pacifist agitation met with militaristic counter-propaganda which defined pacifism as weak, unmanly and unpatriotic, and where pacifism was confronted by conservative and feudal social structures that resisted the peace movement. This hostility is so much more surprising in that the social structures of the peace movement were such that it recruited its members mainly from the middle and lower middle classes and from the educated middle class of the so called 'Bildungsburgertum', not from the proletariat. Its social philosophy was by no means a revolutionary one. On the contrary it contained obvious socially conservative elements. It took its aims from the arsenal of arguments going back to Immanuel Kant's writing 'On perpetual peace' of 1795—arbitration within the framework of international courts, arms reduction and limitation, international treaties for every kind of state relations etc. Social changes were not regarded as necessary preconditions for a peaceful foreign policy. There was no notion of interrelations between internal and external factors in foreign policy. The German peace movement was in fact not un-patriotic in the sense of betraying the interests of the fatherland. For example, German pacifists were strictly in favour of the preservation of the actual status of Alsace–Lorraine and rejected re-annexation by France even on the basis of a plebiscite. This demonstrates their inclination towards the *status quo* in politics.

Nevertheless the peace movement in Germany, though weak, was regarded by the leading circles in society, under the auspices of German imperialism, as a threat to an expansive foreign policy, and therefore it was attacked by the 'patriotic' agitation societies and ignored by public opinion. It was left alone, without support, by the state.

Politically the German peace movement stood, as can be seen from such a profile, close to the left-wing of liberalism.[2] The few members of the Reichstag who belonged to the German Peace Society, and who occupied leading positions within it, stemmed from the *Deutschfreisinnige Partei* and its two successor parties, the Liberal People's Party and the Liberal Association. In southern Germany organised pacifists were members of the German People's Party, a left-wing democratic party of the petty and middle bourgeoisie. But their pacifist activities in support of the Anglo-American trend in favour of the establishment of international arbitration remained weak and half-hearted. As one would expect, the peace movement did not find any support among the other par-liamentary groups in the Reichstag. The national liberals were much in favour of the imperialistic colonial policy and the massive armaments policy, in which they were deeply involved economically. The two conservative parties were closely identified with German military policy and its social implications, while the Catholic Centre Party did not support the peace movement because it identified that movement, not without reason, with hated left-wing liberalism, and because, since Bismarck had left the political scene, it followed a policy of tactical adaptation in order to escape from the political ghetto.

The peace movement was not supported by German social democrats and their attitude deserves to be examined a little more closely.[3] German social democracy refused for a long time—until the eve of World War I, in contrast to socialism in Great Britain and

France—to cooperate with the peace movement, because it felt the pacifist programme was meant to stabilize the existing social structure and to disguise the social conditions of peace and war. Given its dogmatic basis, it expected the achievement of the welfare of mankind as well as of universal peace from a social revolution. It could not cooperate with an organisation, no matter how sympathetic it might be, that ultimately did not see any necessity to change the political and social framework as a precondition for peace and a peaceful foreign policy. The German pacifists themselves very much regretted the attitude of rejection shown by the social democrats, the more so because it confirmed their social exclusiveness and the narrow basis of their support. They could only have become a mass movement with the aid of the social democrats.

Under these circumstances, the German Peace Society had to be satisfied with the support of a small parliamentary nucleus of pacifists and with commenting on all events that seemed to be relevant to peace. They sent petitions to the Reichstag, which ignored them, they sent addresses to the chancellor and the Kaiser, who gave no response at all, they commented on the Boer War and other events of public interest and were glad whenever they could observe some manifestations of the Kaiser's willingness to act as a 'peace-Kaiser'.

The German friends of peace had to be content with modest successes. They remained a movement of outsiders with a very small number of adherents, not more than ten thousand, of whom probably only a small number was really active. In a great many cases they encountered obstacles and threats, particlarly if they were state officials.

All this was, of course, in contrast to the influence of the mighty associations and pressure groups of economic interests, such as the Farmers' League and the Central Association of Industrialists as well as the so-called 'patriotic' agitation societies such as the Pangerman League, the Colonial Association of the Eastern Marches, the Navy League etc., all of which flourished more or less under protection by the state.

In the circumstances, one should not be very surprised to find that the German Peace Society had to be content when a small, weak group of Reichstag-members participated in the work of the Inter-parliamentary Union. When in 1911, under the very active chairmanship of Otfried Nippold, the 'Association for International Understanding' was founded,[4] it met with the approval of the German Peace Society. Its aim was to overcome anti-pacifist resentments in the leading social circles, and by so doing, to recruit partisans for peace among university professors, and to promote actions in favour of international understanding, mainly with Great Britain.

In Prussia, in spite of the best efforts of certain pacifists who tried to stimulate agitation throughout the country, the organisational strength remained modest. Local branches existed only in Berlin and in Frankfurt on Main, a city that maintained an anti-Prussian tradition, having been annexed as one of the last free cities in 1866.

On the other hand, organised pacifism grew stronger in southern Germany, in Baden, Wuerttemberg and Bavaria, in a context that was close to left-wing liberal bourgeois democracy. It was here that the number of local branches of the German Peace Society was much bigger and the membership in the smaller towns was very often identical with that of the German People's Party, that is with the democratic party of the petty and middle bourgeoisie. In the second chamber of the Badian Diet, a parliamentary initiative inspired by the German Peace Society against excessively nationalist school-teaching and school-books was adopted by a small majority, whereas a similar initiative in the second chamber of the Prussian Diet was rejected by a great majority. As a consequence of these developments, the German Peace Society moved its headquarters from Berlin to Stuttgart in 1900.

These discouraging circumstances improved slightly when the revisionist and reformist wing of the Social Democrats, in the course of the general ideological development of the party, became increasingly aware of the growing danger of war. After the party won electoral successes at the Reichstag election in 1912, the Social Democrats began to approach the bourgeois peace movement. It seemed encouraging that the leading figure of revisionism, Eduard Bernstein, published articles in the central pacifist review *Friedens-Warte*. This was seen as evidence of a change of mind. It was significant, indeed, that the German–French meetings of M.P.s in Basle in 1912 and 1913, which were intended to encourage an understanding between Germany and France, were attended more frequently by socialist parliamentarians than by members of the left-wing liberal parliamentary group of the Reichstag, not to speak of other parliamentary groups who were not represented at all.[5]

The outbreak of the first world war found the German peace movement, like those in other countries, rather unprepared. Until the last moment, the German Peace Society had nourished the illusion that the growing interdependence of world society, in the sense of Norman Angell's hypothesis explaining the economic folly of a worldwide war, would banish the war danger. But it was not only psychologically that the outbreak of the world war proved a shock for the German Peace Society. In terms of organisation as well the German Peace Society was not in the least prepared to meet the new challenge. Under the restrictive conditions of martial law, the so-called 'minor state of siege', the Society was subjected to strict controls. Meetings were prohibited, its publications and letters subjected to censorship and its speakers spied upon. It was only after a certain time that it found new methods and new organisational forms which enabled it to escape from the stranglehold of the military authorities and the provisions of the martial law against pacifists.[6]

It also took a long time for the German peace movement to win support within the Reichstag itself for its campaign against the official policy of territorial annexation (the 'peace by victory' programme) and for its advocacy of mutual international understanding and a new international order for the postwar period. This was mainly accomplished by a whole series of leaflets for mass agitation and by petitions addressed to the Reichstag dealing with all essential aspects of German foreign policy.

Interactions of the kind to be mentioned here prepared the way for structural changes, which later influenced the image of the German Peace Society. Significantly there sprang up new peace organisations such as the 'League of the New Fatherland'[7] or the 'Women's Association for Peace and Freedom', similar to bodies in Great Britain, U.S.A. and the Netherlands. Just after the end of the first world war, the centre of gravity moved within the German Peace Society. Now the majority of the membership was no longer committed more or less to left-wing liberalism, but to social democracy and to independent social democracy. In addition to this, the peace efforts of Pope Benedict XV had legitimised Catholic advocates of peace and encouraged them to come forward. Members of the Centre Party also participated in the peace movement. From this time one can speak of a specific Catholic peace movement in Germany as a sector of the whole of organised pacifism.

The changes in the structure of membership caused, on the other hand, ideological changes. In the executive bodies of the peace organisations there were still exponents of left-wing liberal political convictions like the historian and later Nobel prizewinner, Professor Ludwig Quidde, who had been President of the German Peace

Society since 1913. But in contrast to the pre-war situation these positions were now contested by more radical pacifists. The sharp contrast between the internal and the external fields of politics was now disputed more openly, and the abolition of the existing structures of social and political power was claimed as a pre-condition for a new peaceful Germany.[8]

With such a new image the German peace movement entered into the Weimar republic. It was quite natural that the peace movement should no longer take a neutral position towards the concrete form of the state. Organised pacifism openly expressed support for the republic. It regarded itself as a movement supporting the new state. The three parties of the Reichstag which formed the first coalition government, the government of the so-called 'Weimar coalition', the Social Democratic Party, the German Democratic Party, a newly founded left-wing liberal party, and the old Centre Party, all had members within the ranks of the German Peace Society. In a short transitory period after the revolution of November 1918, the German peace movement was relatively influential, the more so as the majority of its members stressed their national solidarity by attacking the Versailles peace treaty, which in their minds was quite in contrast to all pacifist principles. This reflected the fact that only a small minority of German pacifists believed that Germany was to blame for the outbreak of the world war, one example being the pedagogue and philosopher Friedrich Wilhelm Foerster.

The greater organisational flexibility and the great possibilities for recruiting members in a more extended field led to the emergence of individual peace organisations, existing side by side with the traditional Peace Society. There was now a broad spectrum from the left to the moderate right wing, which was represented by the newly founded League of Nations Union. In order to coordinate the activities of all these separate peace organisations an umbrella organisation was founded, the German Peace Cartel.[9] Pacifist mass-agitation in the form of mass meetings under the slogan 'no more war!' (as in other countries) was the peace movement's gesture to the new democracy. But the favourable conditions for the peace movement and for pacifism did not last for long.

In practice, the old social structures, spared by the revolution, had maintained their vigour. How strong they were was proved by the Reichstag elections of 1920, when, after the Kapp coup, the Weimar coalition lost its majority. This meant, at the same time, that all hopes the German peace movement had entertained for a peaceful transformation of German policy were gone. The old clichés, directed against the pacifists, were soon renewed: pacifists were unmanly, they were incapable of defending themselves by arms, and they did harm to their country by using the arguments of the victors. Pacifism was accused of preventing the revision of the Versailles peace treaty. This was untrue, for many in the peace movement were in favour of a peaceful revision of Versailles. They were even in favour of the union of Austria with Germany. They endorsed defensive wars, which signified that they did not agree with the military articles of the Versailles treaty, and they agreed with wars by way of sanctions within the framework of the League of Nations. But, on the other hand, they protested untiringly against the numerous signs of an illegal remilitarization in Germany, against the uncertain allegiance of the German army to the republic, and they tried to remind the parties of the Weimar coalition of their duties towards a peaceful foreign policy and a home policy free of militarism.

The existence of illegal military formations, e.g. the so-called 'Schwarze Reichswehr', and of illegal armaments, both incompatible with the provisions of the Versailles treaty, remained for a long time the main target of pacifist criticism. The pacifists were more successful than before the war in finding parliamentary spokesmen in the pacifist M.P.s But, of course, they were not in the majority within their respective parties. In the German Democratic Party for example, the prominent pacifist Ludwig Quidde had no chance of winning a seat in parliament since he had been a member of the Constitutional National Assembly of 1919.[10] The excellent liberal pacifist Walther Schucking, a professor of international law, was a member of the Reichstag until 1928, when he became a judge in the International Court in The Hague. He was without a strong following in his party. As the German Democratic Party was among the parties of the Weimar coalition and the most committed advocate of a peaceful revision of Versailles, and as the minister of defence, Otto Gessler, came from the party, it was obviously in a difficult position. Every change in the direction of pacifism would, as the party feared, cause a significant loss of voters, as in the catastrophic elections of 1920. However, every change of course in favour of a decided policy of rearmament would have irritated leftist liberal voters. So the party was forced to adopt a policy of permanent manoeuvring, and, as a result, it declined to almost total unimportance. In doing so, the party had an effect on prominent liberal members of the German Peace Society, mainly Quidde, whose position was so much undermined that finally he had to give up the leadership of the Society and to leave it to more radical elements.

In the Catholic Centre Party pacifism did not play a major role. In this party it was mainly members of the left wing, like the physicist and radiologist Friedrich Dessauer, who represented pacifism, whilst the more radical and leftist exponents of political Catholicism, so far as they were pacifists, agitated within splinter groups outside the Centre Party. The growing coolness of the Centre Party towards the peace movement was only the reflex of the gradual development of the party towards the right. This was characterised by the fact that in the late twenties the prelate Ludwig Kaas took the chairmanship of the parliamentary group of the party.[11]

The Social Democratic Party, as far as its self-image was concerned, was a genuinely pacifist party. It took a very cool position towards the army from the beginning, so that the party was the main vehicle of pacifist protests and claims. The pacifist activities, on the other hand, caused certain difficulties for the SPD because of the attitude of the two other republican parties. This was the case with the agitation in favour of the expropriation of the German princes in 1926[12] and mainly in the campaign against the building of armoured cruisers in 1929.[13] In such cases the SPD, when using clearly pacifist and socialist arguments, ran the risk of going too far to the left and thus being compelled to make an arrangement with the Communist Party.

The attempt by the Social Democratic Party to draw a strict line of division between itself and the Communist Party while not alienating its own left wing, created by the return of the Independent Social Democrats to the fold, caused difficulties. These were compounded by the efforts of the party to maintain its links with the middle-class republican parties. The outcome was a situation characterised by very contradictory and inconsistent attitudes, as well illustrated by the discussions on the armoured cruiser issue.

As for the nationalist parties and the National Socialist Workers' Party there could, of course, be no doubting their strictly anti-pacifist attitude, and this is also true of the Communists, who were not against war, if war was revolutionary and anti-capitalist. The majority of the German Peace Society, therefore, rejected the offer of the Communist Party for partnership in certain political actions, the more so as the German Communist Party was undoubtedly very dependent on the Soviet Russian sister party in Moscow. In addition to this, the Communists were discredited once the close contact and effective cooperation between the German army and the Red Army became known.

The weakening of the base of the republican forces, as demonstrated by the fact that the parties of the Weimar coalition had lost their majority for the first time in the Reichstag since 1920, naturally influenced the attitude and the self-confidence of the German Peace Society. As a result of a deep frustration those elements in the Reichstag who mistrusted the traditional instruments of the bourgeois peace movement asserted themselves. They wanted to abolish the individualistic character in the organisation of the movement in order to stimulate mass-agitation instead. They wanted to have more proletarians as pacifist partisans. Such elements even rejected defensive wars, and advocated conscientious objection instead. Imitating the example of Arthur Ponsonby, the German Peace Cartel, inspired by left-wing pacifists, organised activities in several towns and communities in central Germany with the city of Zwickau as a centre. In the course of this agitation more than one thousand people signed pledges that they would refuse every kind of military service in the future in the event of war.[14]

These developments were, in fact, just the opposite to the tendencies of remilitarization and hidden rearmament going on at the time. At least in the two bourgeois parties of the Weimar coalition this question was discussed in a very controversial manner and the result was a growing suspicion of the German Peace Society. Even if one allows that conscientious objection under the premises of the Versailles treaty seemed to be a question of more academic than practical importance, there was nevertheless the pressure of the *principiis obsta*, which was organised by the army and those elements within the parties that were interested in rearmament. The radicalisation of the German peace movement is indicated by the fact that the German section of the League of Nations Union, the right wing of the German Peace Cartel, had been compelled to leave the Cartel in the mid-twenties. It was also a similar indication when Quidde gave up his leading position in the pacifist organisation in 1929. It was thus much easier for the parties of the Weimar coalition to shake off the German Peace Society. Even the moderage Ludwig Quidde left the German Democratic Party, because he did not accept the amalgamation of his party with the so-called 'Young German Order', a moderate rightist and for a time openly anti-semitic and anti-pacifist organisation, into a new party called the 'German State Party'. Things went from bad to worse for pacifists of left-wing liberal views. The new party, which evidently had an orientation more to the right, was not at all attractive for pacifists. Most of them followed Quidde's example and founded a new splinter party, the

'Radical Democratic Party'. For those who remained, the German State Party declared membership in the German Peace Society to be incompatible with party membership.

The Social Democratic Party, which had seen the exodus of radical pacifists and socialists in the early thirties to found the 'Socialist Workers' Party', introduced the same procedure regarding incompatibility. For the Centre Party this was not necessary at all, since pacifism no longer played any role in the party.

At the end of the Weimar Republic, organised pacifism seemed to become a *quantité negligeable*. Whereas the German Peace Society vehemently directed its agitation against rising fascism, thus becoming the special target for the hatred of the National Socialists, it no longer found an outlet in the Reichstag.

The role of outsiders, which the pacifists had to play before the world war and which was their situation once more, became visible on the parliamentary level too, after the German judiciary, one of the pillars of the ancien regime that had survived the revolution without any damage, produced legal decisions obviously hostile to pacifism. This was made manifest in that all reporting and commenting on the occurrence of illegal rearmament as a violation of the Versailles treaty was prosecuted as high treason. The most sensational case of this kind had been an article with the title 'Windy things from aeronautics' in Carl von Ossietzky's famous weekly *Die Weltbühne*,[15] where the illegal connections between the German army and the Red Army in the field of aircraft production and testing were exposed. Ossietzky, as the editor responsible, was accused of high treason and sent to prison.

It is quite clear that German pacifists, moderates as well as radicals, did not feel that the transition from the authoritarian practices of the last phase of the Weimar Republic to the National Socialist regime was a decisive break. They were accustomed to having difficulties with state authority. Very soon, however, they were compelled to realise that there were indeed real differences between the Weimar Republic and the new state with respect to the treatment of pacifists. Pacifism of whatever kind was now outlawed and persecuted. A great many German pacifists, some of them with an international reputation, were forced into exile or thrown into prison and concentration camps, where they were cruelly tortured.[16] The case of Berthold Jacob, for example, whom the Nazis lured back from Switzerland in order to murder him,[17] or the case of Theodor Lessing, whom the Nazis discovered in Czechoslovakia and shot, showed how seriously the threat had to be taken that the new regime would persecute pacifists and other opponents and eliminate them, even in exile. A great number of German pacifists in exile never came back to their home-country, having died before the end of the Nazi regime or being too disenchanted to return.

If we summarise the results of fifty years of organised pacifism in Germany, we can discover no great success for it between 1890 and 1945. A heavy political and ideological burden, a kind of mortgage, was the main obstacle for pacifist achievements in Germany. It was responsible for the fact that there was never effective public support for pacifism. Pacifist success in parliamentary politics in Germany was, of course, never comparable with the success of economic pressure groups. Pacifism lacked the power of a religious faith and instead could prove its truth for every new generation only by the negative effect of war. It lacked the irresistibility of its own message.

Notes

1. For a general survey see: Roger Chickering, *Imperial Germany and a world without war. The peace movement and German society 1892-1914* (Princeton and London, 1975); Friedrick-Karl Scheer, 'Die Deutsche Friedensgesellschaft (1892-1933). Organisation-Ideologie-Politische Ziele. Ein Beitrag zur Entwicklung des Pazifismus in Deutschland' (Dissertation Bochum 1974, unpublished); Dorothee Stiewe, 'Die bürgerliche deutsche Friedensbewegung als soziale Bewegung bis zum Ende des Ersten Weltkrieges' (phil. Diss. Freiburg i. Br. 1972); Karl Holl, 'Die deutsche Friedensbewegung im Wilhelminischen Reich. Wirkung und Wirkungslosigkeit' in Wolfgang Huber, Johannes Schwerdtfeger (editors), *Kirche zwischen Krieg und Frieden. Studien zur Geschichte des deutschen Protestantismus* (Stuttgart, 1976), pp 321–372.
2. See Holl, op. cit., pp 336–341 and Karl Holl, 'Krieg und Frieden und die liberalen Parteien' in Karl Holl, Günther List (editors), *Liberalismus und imperialistischer Staat. Der Imperialismus als Problem liberaler Parteien in Deutschland 1890-1914* (Göttingen, 1975), pp 72–88; Lothar Albertin, 'Das Friedensthema bei den Linksliberalen vor 1914: Die Schwäche ihrer Argumente und Aktivitäten', ibid., pp 89–108.
3. See Hans-Josef Steinberg, *Die Stellung der II. Internationale zu Krieg und Frieden* (Schriften aus dem Karl-Marx-Haus, Trier, Heft 8), (Trier, 1972).
4. Roger Chickering, 'A Voice of moderation in Imperial Germany: the "Verband für internationale Verständigung" 1911-1914', in *Journal of Contemporary History*, 8 (1973), pp 147–164.
5. Adolf Wild, Baron d'Estournelles de Constant (1852-1924), *Das Wirken eines Friedensnobelpreisträgers für die deutsch-französische Verständigung und europäische Einigung (Hamburg, 1973), pp 399–421;* Alwin Hanschmidt, 'Die französisch-deutschen Parlamentarierkonferenzen von Bern (1913) und Basel (1914)', in *Geschichte in Wissenschaft und Unterricht* (1975), pp 335–359.
6. Wilfried Eisenbeiß, *Die bürgerliche Friedensbewegung in Deutschland während des Ersten Weltkrieges. Organisation, Selbstverständnis und politische Praxis 1913/14-1919* (Frankfurt a.M., 1980), pp 138–148; see also the assessment of

Karl Holl

an insider: Ludwig Quidde, *Der deutsche Pazifismus während des Weltkrieges 1914–1918. Aus dem Nachlaß Ludwig Quiddes herausgegeben von Karl Holl unter Mitwirkung von Helmut Donat* (Boppard a. Rh. 1979), esp. pp 95–112, 144–148, 207–216.

7. See Otto Lehmann-Rußbüldt, *Der Kampf der Deutschen Liga für Menschenrechte vormals Bund Neues Vaterland für den Weltfrieden 1914–1927* (Berlin, 1927); Erwin Gülzow, '*Der Bund "Neues* Vaterland". Probleme der bürgerlich-pazifistischen Demokratie im ersten Weltkrieg (1914–1918)' (Diss. Berlin, GDR, 1969).

8. This is the general impression if one reads, e.g., the record of 'Achter deutscher Pazifistenkongreß einberufen von der Deutschen Friedengesellschaft und der Zentralstelle Völkerrecht. Berlin 13. bis 15. Juni 1919' in *Preußischen Herrenhaus. Verhandlungsbericht* (Charlottenburg, 1919).

9. See Reinhold Lütgemeier-Davin, 'Pazifismus zwischen Kooperation und Konfrontation. Das Deutsche Friedenskartell in der Weimarer Republik' (Diss. Kassel, 1979/80); for the problems of pacifism in the Weimar Republic see also Karl Holl, Wolfram Wette (editors), *Pazifismus in der Weimarer Republik. Beiträge zur historischen Friedensforschung* (Paderborn, 1981), with articles of different authors on specific aspects.

10. See Karl Holl, 'Pazifismus oder liberaler Neu-Imperialismus? Zur Rolle der Pazifisten in der Deutschen Demokratischen Partei 1918–1930' in Joachim Radkau, Imanuel Geiss (editors), *Imperialismus im 20. Jahrhundert. Gedenkschrift für George W. F. Hallgarten* (München, 1976), pp 171–195; id., 'Die Deutsche Demokratische Partei im Spannungsverhältnis zwischen Wehrpolitik und Pazifismus' in Holl and Wette, op. cit., pp 135–148; Werner Schneider, *Die Deutsche Demokratische Partei in der Weimarer Republik 1924–1930* (München, 1978), pp 113–123.

11. For the problems of Catholic pacifism in the Weimar republic see Dieter Reisenberger, *Die katholische Friedensbewegung in der Weimarer Republik* (Düsseldorf, 1977); id., 'Der "Friedensbund Deutscher Katholiken" und der politische Katholizismus in der Weimarer Republik' in Holland Wette, op. cit., pp 91–111.

12. See Ilse Kelbert-Girard, 'Die große Volksbewegung für die entschädigungslose Fürstenenteignung—Volksbegehren und Volksentscheid 1926' (Diss. Berlin, GDR, 1960).

13. See Jost Dülffer, *Weimar, Hitler und die Marine, Reichspolitik und Flottenbau 1920 bis 1939* (Düsseldorf, 1973), pp 109–130; Wolfgang Wacker, *Der Bau des Panzerschiffes "A" und der Reichstag* (Tübingen, 1959); Ernst Laboor, 'Der Kampf der KPD gegen den Panzerkreuzerbau' in *Zeitschrift für Geschichtswissenschaft 1958* (Sonderheft), pp 170–189.

14. See Franz Kobler (ed.), *Gewalt und Gewaltlosigkeit. Handbuch des aktiven Pazifismus* (Zürich, Leipzig, 1928), p. 36.

15. Heinz Jäger (Walther Kreiser), 'Windiges aus der deutschen Luftfahrt', in *Die Weltbühne* (1929), pp 402–407.

16. A contemporary documentation is given in *Das Deutsche Volk klagt an. Hitlers Krieg gegen die Friedenskämpfer in Deutschland. Ein Tatsachenbericht* (Paris, 1936), spec. pp 15, 282.

17. See Jost Nikolaus Willi, *Der Fall Jacob-Wesemann (1935/1936). Ein Beitrag zur Geschichte der Schweiz in der Zwischenkriegszeit* (Bern, Frankfurt, 1972).

'Rats' versus 'Ditchers': The die-hard revolt and the Parliament Bill of 1911

Ronan Fanning

'I am afraid I shall have to show myself very vicious, Mr Asquith, this session. I hope you will understand'. So remarked Andrew Bonar Law as the two party leaders left the house of lords after listening to the king's speech at the opening of the 1912 parliamentary session. And by April 1912 Asquith was already angrily denouncing the 'new style' of opposition.[1] What the 'new style' meant, the resort to direct, extra-parliamentary methods of political action involving courses of ever-increasing violence in the conservative and unionist party's opposition to the third home rule bill, is too well-known to bear repetition. The purpose of this paper is rather to seek the origins of the 'new style'—how it grew out of the mounting frustration and bitterness among Unionists during Arthur Balfour's last months as opposition leader; how Balfour differed from a majority of his followers in his conception of the right role for an opposition and the manner in which that role should be enacted; how the die-hard revolt and the events leading to Balfour's resignation from, and Bonar Law's succession to, the leadership marked a shift in the balance of power within the party and presaged that partiality for extremism which so characterised Unionist opposition to the third home rule bill. It seeks, in short, to show that the dimensions of the 'new style' were already apparent in 1911 and that home rule was as much the occasion as the cause of the strategy of opposition so relentlessly implemented in 1912–14.

The outline of events providing the backdrop against which the die-hard revolt was acted out may be briefly outlined. After the second general election of 1910—a uniquely galling experience for the modern Conservative party in that never before or since have they lost three elections in a row—the new parliament assembled on 6 February 1911, and on 21 February the Parliament Bill was again introduced. The bill did not pass the commons until 15 May and there followed a truce in party politics on account of the celebrations for the coronation of George V on 2 June. Not until July, therefore, were the lords' amendments removing all organic or constitutional legislative changes from the bill's terms of reference rejected by the government. On 14 July the government informed the king that, if the lords were to prove intractable in their opposition to the bill, they would advise him to create whatever number of peers might be necessary to secure its enactment. On 19 July, Lord Knollys, acting on behalf of the king, informed the tory leaders 'that the king had consented to make the peers that might be necessary to secure the enactment of the parliament bill'.[2]

The knowledge that the government had already obtained guarantees from the king posed an inescapable dilemma for Balfour and Lansdowne, the unionist leader in the lords: they could advise their followers in the lords to abstain on the crucial vote in order to avoid the creation of peers and so retain their majority in an enfeebled, but not yet impotent, upper house; or they could advise them to carry their opposition to the point of voting against the bill and forcing a creation of peers. Balfour and Lansdowne recommended retreat. But the shadow cabinet split at a stormy meeting on 21 July and a section of the unionist peers, who became known as the die-hards or 'ditchers' (who would die in the last ditch), decided to reject their leaders' advice and vote against the bill. Another group of unionist peers—the 'rats' in die-hard parlance— determined to go beyond what their leaders asked in their anxiety to avoid the creation of peers and voted with the government in the fateful division on 10 August. The support of the 37 'rats' and the 2 archbishops and 11 bishops was decisive and enabled the government to carry the bill by the slender majority of 17 votes (131 to 114).[3] The composition of the majority caused one die-hard[4] to remark that they had been 'beaten by a combination of the twelve apostles (the bishops) and Judas Iscariot (the recreant peers)'.

The most telling argument against the Unionists forcing a creation of peers was that the loss of their majority in the lords would 'hasten home rule, Welsh disestablishment, one man one vote and all the rest'. The preservation of the lords' capacity at least to delay the enactment of home rule had been a fundamental consideration with Balfour since the end of 1910.[5] But Balfour and Lansdowne failed to prepare their supporters for such a sudden switch of strategy. Indeed before June 1911, when the die-hard movement began,[6] there had been no relaxation in the party's official policy of unswerving opposition to, and denunciation of, the bill. To urge his followers to give way was both difficult and disagreeable to Balfour and the passive, waiting policy of postponing the evil hour of action was typical of his leadership. Many of his front-benchers were pledged to a policy of 'no surrender'. Austen Chamberlain, for example, addressing a meeting of leading Unionists in Lansdowne House as early as January 1911, 'made a great plea that the 500 peers should be made if necessary'.[7] Lord Salisbury and his brothers, Balfour's kinsmen in the so-called 'Hotel Cecil', felt similarly.[8]

Lansdowne, as the whig leader of tory peers, was even more vulnerable than Balfour. 'The peers', noted the editor of *The Spectator*, 'will not follow Lansdowne on a constructive course, though they will on a destructive one'[9] and he predicted that Lansdowne would

> allow things to go so far that he will not in the end be able to control them... If for weeks and weeks he in effect declares that unless concessions are made the peers will have to be created, and that when no concessions are made... he tells the peers that they have got to yield, hands down, and without any of the concessions which were previously declared absolutely essential, he will find he has greatly over-estimated his powers.[10]

And Lansdowne himself, once he learnt of the guarantees, immediately feared a revolt of his followers.[11]

In these circumstances it was hardly surprising that he and Balfour took refuge in the passive policy of waiting on events in the vain hope that the government might, in the end, refrain from seeking guarantees. But what they did not know, and what stultified their strategy during the first half of 1911, was that the government had sought and obtained the guarantees before the second election of 1910 under a pledge of secrecy which was so strictly interpreted that the Unionists did not learn of the guarantees until the following July.[12]

The government's *fait accompli* left Balfour and Lansdowne no room for manoeuvre and—as the editor of *The Spectator* had predicted—demanded so sudden a reversal of policy as seriously to erode their influence. Suspicion of collusion between opposing party leaders was widespread if unwarranted and contributed materially to the vehemence of the die-hard revolt: 'Balfour, if not actually in league with Asquith', wrote one die-hard, 'consistently behaved this year as though he were in league'.[13] Resentment at alleged ill-treatment of the crown and infringement of the constitution accelerated the breakdown of the normal courtesies of party politics, and weakened tory inhibitions against embracing unprecedented courses in opposition.

The die-hard revolt showed just how weak those inhibitions had become by 1911; it marked the beginning of a trend that was to culminate in such happenings as the Ulster gunrunning and the Curragh incident. 'We should always remember that we are now for the first time given a chance of resisting the Parliament Act in operation', declared F. E. Smith in 1913. 'That act was revolutionary, perhaps we have our one and only chance of destroying it by counter revolutionary means'.[14] In 1911 such opinions found their strongest public expression in the pages of the *National Review* which argued against the opposition persisting

> in the farce of treating the coalition factions as honourable men honestly contending for high, though possibly mistaken principles. If you go out to shoot game it is right enough not to shoot at a pheasant which is sitting or running, but it is ridiculous to hamper yourself with artificial rules when you are merely engaged in the destruction of vermin.[15]

In private, some die-hards were still more violent. 'Nothing will save us', wrote F. S. Oliver to Lord Milner, 'except the sight of red blood flowing pretty freely; but whether British *and* German blood, or only British, I don't know—nor do I think it much matters. "Blood" is the necessity'.[16] And George Wyndham thought war with Germany both possible and desirable.[17]

A readiness to regard violence, even civil war, as a legitimate political weapon, which was to be so characteristic of Unionist opposition to the third home rule bill, was common among die-hards; 'they are ready for actual armed resistance, or rather they would like that', noted Wilfrid Blunt in his diary.[18] And, as Lord Willoughby de Broke declared at the height of the die-hard campaign, 'we have used every weapon save personal violence. I should not be averse to using even that'.[19] The tradition of normal social intercourse between parliamentary opponents began to crumble and some tories criticised Balfour's close personal friendship with the Asquiths; Sir Almeric Fitzroy, who noted this development, also recorded that two of the most prominent die-hard families, 'the Salisburys and the Selbornes... had refused to dine in Downing Street'.[20]

One notable manifestation of the breakdown of customary political usage occurred on 24 July 1911—three days after the shadow cabinet split—when a small group of unionist backbenchers headed by Lord Hugh Cecil, F. E. Smith and Edward

Goulding shouted down Asquith in the commons. This unprecedented demonstration was widely recogised as being 'undoubtedly meant quite as much to keep Balfour up to the mark as to defy Asquith',[21] and to warn the Unionist leader of the likely reaction if he attempted to reach a compromise with the government.

Rejection of compromise in any shape or form was central to the die-hards' political philosophy. Witness, for instance, Willoughby de Broke's reaction to the unsuccessful constitutional conference of 1910:

> Most people take much comfort in the idea of a conference. It seems to them to be something safe and reasonable which will save them the trouble of taking sides, and spare them the disagreeable experience of having to think for themselves. Not so the die-hards... A real quintessential die-hard, although he may not say so, never entirely trusts his leaders not to sell the pass behind his back... The thing would end in a compromise; a great principle was at stake; and there is nothing so wicked as a compromise about a principle. Indeed, to a certain frame of mind, a compromise about anything is an unspeakable piece of poltroonery.[22]

Such sentiments inspired the die-hards to denounce the Parliament Bill as the latest and most striking instance of their party leaders' 'foolish temporising' with the radical-socialist party. 'Our leaders', declared one die-hard, 'have already sacrificed everything to what they supposed was expediency but which in fact was folly'.[23]

The difference between Balfour's political ethos and the die-hards' was too wide to admit of reconciliation; and, in a memorandum which (although it was suppressed on the advice of colleagues who feared it would make a bad situation worse) serves to underline the extent of this difference, Balfour declared that

> the policy which its advocates call 'fighting to the last'... [is] essentially theatrical, though not on that account necessarily wrong. It does nothing: it can do nothing: it is not even intended to do anything except advertise the situation... Their policy may be a wise one, but there is nothing heroic about it; and all military metaphors which liken the action of the 'fighting' peers to Leonidas at Thermopylae seem to me purely for music hall consumption.
>
> I grant that the music hall attitude of mind is too widespread to be negligible. By all means play up to it if the performance is not too expensive. If the creation of X peers pleases the multitude and conveys the impression that the lords are game to the end, I raise no objection to it, *provided it does not swamp the house of lords.* [24]

But the theatricality, which Balfour perceived as weakness, was seen as strength by his critics within the party who admired the die-hard style of opposition. Balfour's memorandum was similar in tone to his projected open letter to the Irish unionists (also suppressed) during the Wyndham–MacDonnell imbroglio;[25] in each case Balfour was so scathingly intolerant of the stupidity of his critics as to provoke the charge of failing to understand, let alone to sympathise with, a section of the party.

Die-hard peers were still less amenable to Balfour's authority than Irish Unionists. Lansdowne, not Balfour, was their official leader, and he—as we have seen—had but small claim on their allegiance or their affections. And their membership of the house of lords made them immune to threats of disciplinary action; to be denied the party whip could not result in their losing their seats as might happen to schismatic Unionists in the commons. A further consideration was the die-hard conviction that it was only by forcing a massive creation of peers and thereby destroying the character of the upper house that a thorough-going reform of the lords could be secured. George Wyndham, emerging from comparative obscurity for the first time since his resignation as chief secretary for Ireland in 1905[26] as a die-hard leader, stressed this point: 'after insisting on the vital necessity of preserving the principle of two effective chambers', he wrote, 'the house of lords cannot acquiesce in the virtual destruction of that principle without losing the respect of all thoughtful men... If the house of lords give way they will not only connive at the destruction of our existing constitution, they will also make it impossible to erect any stable substitute'.[27]

The die-hard revolt did not merely divide the party along the factional lines of the previous five years in opposition, but revealed increasing antagonism to Balfour's leadership within all factions. Many Irish Unionists, for example, did not accept that the preservation of the lords' power at least to delay the passage of home rule was all-important: although some of the most prominent (Lansdowne, Midleton, Londonderry and Long) backed Balfour, others (Carson and Craig) were die-hards. The Irish peers were similarly divided, and only 7 of the 28 representative peers of Ireland took the die-hard line in the crucial division on the Parliament Bill: Ashtown, Farnham, Kilmaine, Massy, Muskerry, Templetown and Wicklow. A comparable proportion of peers who held nearly all their land in Ireland, 16 out of 60, were die-hards: Clanricarde, Clonbrock, Erne, DeFreyne, Farnham, Gormanston, Holmpatrick, Kilmaine, Leitrim, Limerick, Massy, Muskerry, Ranfurly, Templetown, Vaux of Harrowden and Wicklow.[28]

Nor did the split follow the lines of division on fiscal policy which had wracked the party since 1903. Free fooders, notably Salisbury and his brothers, joined with such staunch tariff reformers as Austen Chamberlain and Lord Selborne in the die-hard campaign. Other prominent tariff reformers, such as Bonar Law and Henry Chaplin, supported Balfour. 'The "excursions and alarms"', noted Balfour's secretary, Jack Sandars, 'have their amusing side when they exhibit Chamberlains and Cecils as bedfellows'.[29]

Yet analysis of the split at the crucial shadow cabinet meeting on 21 July suggests that the old groupings were not without significance. The die-hard faction (Carson, Austen Chamberlain, Selborne, Balcarres, Salisbury, Wyndham, Halsbury and F. E. Smith) was markedly tariff reform in its sympathies; with the notable exception of Salisbury, it included none of the leading opponents of tariff reform. Balfour's supporters (Lansdowne, Curzon, Londonderry, Midleton, Akers-Douglas, Lyttelton, Chaplin, Long, Derby, Ashbourne and Steel-Maitland), on the other hand, included nearly all those who had been most opposed to the tariff reformers' capturing the party's policy and organisation— men such as Londonderry, Midleton and Derby. And while others of Balfour's supporters were tariff reformers in theory, they had tended to put loyalty to Balfour before loyalty to tariff reform.[30] With the exception of Carson, moreover, all those most closely associated with the cause of Irish unionism—Londonderry, Midleton, Long and Ashbourne—supported Balfour. Broadly speaking, therefore, the split in the shadow cabinet reflected something of the struggle for power since the party went into opposition between those who consistently placed the cause of the union before tariff reform and those who favoured the contrary ordering of priorities.

Even more revealing, perhaps, was the way in which (despite Salisbury's defection) the 'Hotel Cecil' or the 'old gang', held together. Of the nine members of the shadow cabinet present at the meeting on 21 July who had at some time served in the ministry of the third marquess of Salisbury, all but one—Halsbury—backed Balfour. Three of the eight die-hards, by contrast, had never held cabinet office, namely Carson, Smith and Balcarres.[31]

The die-hard revolt, then, can be seen as a direct attack on both the personnel and style of the Balfourian system of party leadership. It marked the beginning of the ultimately successful attempt at a takeover by the new men who were to favour Bonar Law's new style of opposition—he too, it should be noted, had no cabinet experience. The struggle, observed Strachey, the editor of *The Spectator*, is whether the will of Lansdowne and Balfour is to prevail or the will of Austen Chamberlain and F. E. Smith... The Chamberlainite tradition, and it is one that F. E. Smith is sure to support, is that you must give no quarter in politics, and that the spoils are to the victors, and these tactics will soon be put into operation.[32]

Winston Churchill saw it rather differently and commented that the Hotel Cecil 'would rather inflict any amount of injury upon the tory party than share power with any able man of provincial origin'.[33] And Balfour's secretary commented that 'the unorthodox group has the best of our fighting men; while AJB has to count on Londonderry, Ashbourne, Long and H. Chaplin as his officers, loyal men though they be'.[34]

This demand for a 'fighting' opposition, denounced by Balfour as 'essentially theatrical', set the pattern for unionist opposition in 1912–14. It was crucial to Carson's attitude: 'I think the action of the leaders in the present crisis is lamentable', he wrote to James Craig; 'it will damp down enthusiasm for a long time—and the open way in which the official party is joining hands with the government is a calamity';[35] and he argued that Lansdowne's policy 'will create a permanent breach in the party... it will be looked upon as a tacit arrangement with the government'.[36] Carson and his Irish unionist allies were fearful, above all, of the implications for Irish policy of the growth of those conciliatory, inter-party conference techniques which Professor John Fair has recently analysed[37]—the 1910 constitutional conference was a case in point; their worst fear was that if the party leaders were ready to compromise on the Parliament Bill they might be equally ready to compromise on home rule. 'Men who surrender over the Parliament Bill, which as Asquith himself told us involves home rule', wrote Leo Maxse, the editor of the *National Review*,

> are equally capable of surrendering home rule. I loathe home rule as much as anybody but I entirely agree with Carson. Unless we can get this wretched flag pulled down from the two front benches, they had better definitely undertake to help the government in carrying all their legislation, and we can have a definite and decent split.[38]

But Carson, the southern unionist leader of Ulster unionists, as we have seen, was the solitary die-hard among the Irish unionists in the shadow cabinet; this facet of the split foreshadowed the growing divergence between Ulster unionists and southern unionists which was to characterise Irish unionist politics in the next decade. Thus Midleton, the official leader of the southern unionists and a leading advocate of compromise at the time of the Irish Convention of 1917, played a prominent part in rallying opposition to the die-hards.[39] The southern unionists were understandably more anxious than their Ulster colleagues not to lose the advantage of being able to delay home rule under the terms of the Parliament Bill. Lord Arran, for instance, conditionally pledged himself to vote with the die-hards 'unless I in the meantime see reason to think that the creation of peers will accelerate or increase the likelihood of home rule'.[40] But even the Ulster unionists were not united behind Carson on this issue. The duke of Abercorn, an immensely influential figure in Ulster unionist politics, withheld his support from the die-hards.[41] Lord Milner, on the other hand, although later one of the staunchest opponents of home rule, supported the die-hards partly because he did not accept that the Irish issue was paramount in 1911, and did not 'at all agree with the idea that home rule should be made the crucial point about which we should fight to the death, abandoning all else. It is abandoning far too much'.[42]

Nevertheless the die-hard revolt is the first manifestation of Carson's powerful influence as a force for extremism within the upper echelons of the unionist hierarchy. His first concern was the *quality* of Unionist opposition; to what lengths would the party go in its opposition to home rule—would they stand out against all compromise? He clearly saw the die-hards as a ready-made power base on which he could mount his campaign to capture the party's support. 'We must not disband', he urged Lord Willoughby de Broke, after the battle against the Parliament Bill had been lost;

> I know you will help us in the pitched battle over home rule and we must find out where the party stands and to what extent they will go. I fear more private council tactics over this and we cannot afford it. There is a splendid fighting spirit in the north of Ireland only waiting for a lead.[43]

Carson's efforts quickly won success: by the end of October Austen Chamberlain and his supporters 'had decided to back Carson for all they are worth in his resistance to home rule'.[44] Although not all die-hards shared Carson's exclusive concern with the Irish issue, they were, in George Wyndham's words, 'closely bound by kindred passions for *definite* fighting'.[45] Given that the next great struggle between the parties would clearly centre upon home rule, that the die-hards should endorse the most uncompromising of Irish policies was but an example of their determination to influence the strategy of opposition in general.

Lord Selbourne enunciated these wider ambitions when he declared that the die-hards should try 'to capture the party and unionist machine lock, stock and barrel';[46] or, as another die-hard, the duke of Northumberland, observed, they had 'by the force of circumstances discovered who are the die-hards... and who are not, and if it were possible to keep them in some way together, and in touch with one another... [it] might be of great use in the future in putting backbone into our front bench'.[47]

The outcome of these die-hard deliberations was the formation at the beginning of October 1911 of a group known as the Halsbury Club, named after their most venerable member, the former lord chancellor, Lord Halsbury. The Halsbury Club, although its existence was short-lived, perpetuated the spirit of the die-hard revolt and institutionalised the disaffection with the party leadership for long enough to serve as the catalyst which triggered Balfour's resignation. Although he did not publicly announce his decision to step down until 7 November, Balfour had explained how his mind was moving in an uncharacteristically intense outburst to Jack Sandars even before the lords's vote on the Parliament Bill. Sandars's summary of their conversation on that occasion is worth recounting as it amounts to an apologia for Balfour's leadership in opposition:

After Mr Chamberlain's famous pronouncement for tariff reform in 1903, the party was practically rent in twain. It would have been easier to take side with the extremists of either school of opinion, but the consequences would have been fatal to the party, as fatal as the rupture in 1846... he had strained every nerve to prevent party disunion. In accents which showed how deeply he felt it, he referred to the abuse which had been poured upon him and the imputations which had been made upon him between 1906 and January, 1910. But he had seen the success of his Fabian methods, and it would be admitted that he had saved the party from breaking up, and that we went into the general election of 1910 a united party. 'Now observe', he said, 'our men were entitled by tradition to call themselves protectionists, they were equally entitled to hold fast to the creed of free trade ... It was worth everything to try and reconcile these conflicting opinions. And whatever it cost me, I was rewarded by practical success. But now, on a question which is not one of principle, but of mere party tactics, I am confronted with a deep schism among my leading colleagues. In a cabinet, if there is a division of opinion, the rule is that the majority must prevail; and if the view of the majority is not accepted, those who will not accept the decision of the majority have no alternative but to leave the government. But here, after full discussion, a minority decline to accept my advice which commanded the majority of votes at the shadow cabinet, and the dissentient members have gone out into the world proclaiming their differences and embarked upon a policy of active resistance. I confess to feeling I have been badly treated. I have no wish to lead a party under these humiliating conditions. It is no gratification to me to be their leader. If they think that someone else is better able to discharge the duties of leadership, I am quite willing to adopt that view. It is useless for me to attempt the duties of leadership if my leadership is not accepted.[48]

The die-hard revolt was in three particulars quite different from the earlier revolts against Balfour's leadership in opposition: first, it caused the gravest *public* split in the party since Chamberlain had launched his tariff reform campaign; second, it disclosed a fundamental difference between Balfour's political ethos and that of many of his followers, and it alienated Balfour from those followers as nothing had done before; and, third, because what was at issue was not policy so much as the strategy of opposition, it drew support from all sections of the party and left Balfour in a peculiarly isolated and vulnerable position. Given Balfour's obsession with party unity—the main theme of his leadership in opposition—the significance of the first particular is immediately apparent; but the other two require more detailed analysis.

Balfour's embittered outburst to Sandars and the tone of his suppressed memorandum reveal a sense of isolation which was reinforced by a certain aloofness which had always divided Balfour from his rank-and-file with whose main sections he had no close ties of either interest or affection. His enemies, observed one of his backbenchers, protested that,

> though possessing a country estate, he was in no real sense a country gentleman, had few interests in country life, and chose his friends from among a small, exclusive, and by no means typical section of London society. In private conversation his detractors would say, 'our party is mainly composed of country gentlemen and the British *bourgeoisie*. A successful man of the middle classes, like Joe Chamberlain, or a *grand seigneur*, as old Salisbury was, understands thoroughly at least one of those sections; a philosopher and a dilettante like Balfour has no point of contact with either; they don't understand him, and he doesn't understand them'.[49]

When criticism of Balfour's leadership reached its peak in 1911, there was no substantial body of party opinion ready to declare that his departure was unthinkable; and it was the absence of a demand that he should stay as much as the demand that he should go which led him to resign.

Balfour, who always took great pains to prevent political differences intruding on his personal relationships, was especially irked by the antics of his cousins, the Cecils, and he told Lady Elcho that 'fragments of the unionist party seem to have gone temporarily crazy to the great detriment of the party as a whole. As usual the leading lunatics are my own kith and kin.'[50] Indeed, such was Balfour's distaste for the passions dividing his party on the Parliament Bill that he did not even wait in London for the result of the lords' division but instead left for a continental holiday. 'Politics have been to me quite unusually odious', he wrote from Paris; 'I have, as a matter of fact, felt the situation more acutely than any in my public life—I mean from the personal point of view.'[51] Balfour's premature departure further enraged the die-hards.[52]

The most committed tariff reformers, whose aspirations Balfour had long thwarted and whom he had infuriated by his pledge that he would submit tariff reform to a referendum if he were returned to government during the second election campaign of 1910, were particularly hostile. As far back as January 1911, a cabal of prominent tariff reformers had dined together at the Café Royal to discuss 'the political situation—mainly... the "Referendum" and its bearing on tariff reform'; those present were Lords Milner, Selborne and Ridley, Austen Chamberlain, F. E. Smith, Sir Joseph Lawrence, Edward Goulding, J. L. Garvin (the editor of *The Observer*), Henry Chaplin and W. A. S. Hewins.[53] Many of this group later occupied key positions in the die-hard movement. Selborne, for example, was the most prominent unionist peer to attach himself to the die-hards from the outset, and he played a leading part both in setting up their organisation and in dictating their tactics; he was also appointed chairman of the Halsbury Club.[54] F. E. Smith became a secretary to the die-hard committee; and of the remainder, Chamberlain, Milner, Garvin, Goulding and Lawrence were all influential die-hards.

Men like Lawrence interpreted Balfour's referendum-pledge as the ultimate betrayal of tariff reform.[55] They were consequently much less ready to acquiesce in his leadership and to accept the argument—as propounded, for example, by Austen Chamberlain—that, whatever Balfour's deficiencies, he was the only leader available to the party. Only Chamberlain's determination not to participate in any open repudiation of Balfour's leadership deprived the group of a leader and prevented the Halsbury Club from assuming a much stronger anti-Balfourian character.[56] But the difficulty of finding a suitable substitute now came to mean much less. A hard core of embittered and frustrated tariff reformers began to insist simply that 'Balfour must go', a slogan coined by Leo Maxse, the editor of the *National Review*, in September;[57] they cared less who might succeed him, as we can see from the extraordinary emergence of Bonar Law, a man innocent of any cabinet experience. The deterioration in Balfour's relationship with Austen Chamberlain, notwithstanding the latter's selflessness in refusing to challenge for the leadership, further undermined his position. Chamberlain's enduring sense of dissatisfaction with the referendum policy caused him to take a stronger and more independent line than previously and he was no longer disposed to play his accustomed role of mediator between the party leadership and the tariff reform wing of the party.

It was their common hostility to Balfour's leadership rather than any agreement on a successor, however, that united the members of the Halsbury Club. Milner, Wyndham and Amery, for example, took this opportunity of proposing a detailed constructive programme for the party[58] which reflected the gulf that had always divided their notion of opposition strategy from Balfour's. But there was little support for such schemes among their fellow Halsburyites. 'Members of this club', Balfour himself observed, 'differ on all constructive questions, but they are united in dis-approval of their leader's advice'.[59] One prominent die-hard, Lord Lovat, doubted the wisdom of their continuing to act together in the autumn of 1911, and he supported this view of Balfour's: 'a body of men who are divided on essentials and who are only united in their determination to sit tight against court and cabal, church and Curzon,[60] cannot hold together once the fight which froze them together is over'.[61] Certainly, hostility to Balfour seems to have been crucial, for when he resigned as leader the club immediately dissolved.

But the overt hostility of the Halsburyites, many of whom were long-standing critics of Balfour, was less important than the erosion of support he had formerly enjoyed among the more moderate sections of the party such as the Free Fooders. As long as the crisis over fiscal policy was acute they had judged Balfour's leadership to be their best guarantee of survival, but the fiscal issue no longer dominated their political thinking. His differences with the Cecils in particular—given Balfour's marked aversion to political tensions obtruding on his social or familial relations—was another factor calculated to dispose him to resignation. Lord Salisbury had voted with the die-hards and flirted, albeit briefly, with the Halsbury Club; Lord Robert Cecil had actively urged Balfour's resignation;[62] and Lord Hugh, another convinced die-hard, had also been one of the main instigators of the notorious commons' row on 24 July—so much so that the participants were generically labelled the 'Hughligans'.[63]

The Cecil connection had been a mainstay of Balfour's leadership; he was heavily dependent, too, on loyal party managers; on his relationship with Lansdowne; on the support of Walter Long and the party moderates. All now failed him simultaneously.

A change of party managers had inevitably followed in the wake of the second election defeat of 1910 and Alec Hood had resigned as chief whip in June 1911. He was replaced by Lord Balcarres and a new appointment as chairman of the party organisation was also announced—Arthur Steel-Maitland. The changes effectively ended the system whereby the Conservative Central Office and the party machine had been effectively, if informally, managed by the triumvirate of Sandars, Hood and Akers-Douglas, a former chief whip. Now, Balfour could count on whole-hearted support from neither his new nor his old advisers. Both Hood and Akers-Douglas, although siding with Balfour out of loyalty, sympathised with the die-hards.[64] Balcarres and Steel-Maitland were even less helpful, and a memorandum of Steel-Maitland's, which 'dwelt upon the disaffection in the ranks of the party and upon the necessity of drastic efforts being made by Mr Balfour to bring his colleagues and the party into line... had the effect of confirming Mr Balfour's dissatisfaction with his position as leader'.[65]

Nor was Lansdowne much of an ally. Shattered by the revelation that the government had obtained guarantees, he refused to believe it until he had received official confirmation from the king.[66] Moreover, his health throughout this period was poor,[67] and this may have worsened what even an understanding biographer saw as his chronic disability: 'that he was of too fine a grain to make the requisite impression upon the public and upon the party as a fighting man. There was not enough of the hearty contempt for opponents and of the blunt self-confidence and pugnacity which is expected from a party leader'.[68] The enactment of the Parliament Bill confirmed tory fears of Lansdowne's whiggery and destroyed what prestige and authority he had previously possessed. Balfour suffered by association, and his inability to act independently of Lansdowne on an issue that involved the constitution and composition of the upper house lessened his already poor chances of repressing die-hard disaffection.[69] Balfour, complained Austen Chamberlain, 'in his anxiety to be loyal to Lansdowne, ... has been much less than loyal to us and I cannot say how bitterly I feel such treatment from a leader for whom I have made great sacrifices of opinion and some of reputation'.[70]

But Walter Long's was perhaps the most critical of all the defections among Balfour's supporters. He interpreted a memorandum from Long at the end of September as 'a bold and brutal invitation to retire' and observed that it came from 'my oldest colleague, my *professed* friend and upholder. Nothing of the die-hards could be compared with this for what is called disloyalty'.[71]

The die-hard revolt, then, even if it failed in its immediate objective, precipitated the disintegration of the Balfourian system of party leadership. So long as there was a real danger of the party splitting on the fiscal issue Balfour's compromising, uncommitted leadership was almost invulnerable. Ironically, it was largely due to Balfour's own efforts that the danger had passed. In the early years of opposition, criticism of Balfour's leadership was nearly always related to differences on policy; tariff reformers, free fooders and Irish unionists alike pointed to the deficiencies which seemed to preclude Balfour from vigorously propounding their respective policies. Now these sectional divisions were no longer crucial but the odium that Balfour had incurred for his past failures to satisfy sectional ambitions remained. In particular, the tariff reformers were not disposed to forgive or forget.

And there were others. Resentful of, and embittered by, repeated party disappointments and electoral defeats more and more unionists came to concur in the long-standing verdict of Balfour's tariff reform critics: that Balfour's genius for compromise, which he would yet again put to great effect when he served in the coalition governments of 1915–22, was rather a vice than a virtue. The die-hards demonstrated the strength and prevalence of the counter-vailing conviction among unionists that total commitment was necessary. Such a commitment was as alien to Balfour's political philosophy as it was to his temperament, and it was not surprising that Selborne should write of receiving 'a series of letters from different people, all written uncontroversially but with the obviously genuine belief that Arthur is not really in earnest about this question at all'.[72] Balfour recognised his handicap in this respect but he could not remedy it. 'I know I cannot be evicted from the leadership', he confided in his secretary, 'and if I resigned I could make trouble, which of course is absurd; but Long asks me to change and I cannot change'.[73]

In three successive general elections the unionists had failed; and they had failed not only to withstand what they denounced as the government's revolutionary legislation but they failed also (at least the tariff reformers did) to secure their own party's unqualified acceptance of their fiscal policy, let alone the enactment of that policy. In their frustration it seemed there was only one course left open to them: to change their leader and to change the conventions that determined that leader's approach to politics. 'No one', a tariff reformer once wrote in criticism of Balfour, 'has done more to reduce politics to the level of a party game'.[74] But, as Belloc and Chesterton noted in their book on *The party system* published, incidentally, in 1911, tariff reformers missed the point when they condemned Balfour as weak: 'the real difficulty is not that he is weak, but that he is strong—strong in the traditions of party, the complex system of relationships and alliances that cover English politics like a net, much too strong to allow his hands to be forced by the tory democracy'.[75]

The passage of the Parliament Bill without the creation of peers marked the last triumph for this Balfourian system of alliances and for the counsels of moderation in the unionist party before the coming of the Great War. But the portents of change were unmistakable: the house of commons had already witnessed the first of those violent and unruly scenes which were to become increasingly common in the years ahead; and in August 1911 the revolutionary proposal that the lords should hold up the Army Annual Act in an attempt to subvert the very basis of government was first mooted.[76]

Austen Chamberlain highlighted the inadequacies of Balfour's leadership at such a time when he attacked it as too frequently depending upon 'a mere splitting of hairs, a quibble unworthy of the ingenuity with which he sustained it and of the serious issues at stake. He was not content to make a broad statement of his views without at the same time giving expression to all the qualifications which to his mind it required'.[77] And Chamberlain was far from alone in this opinion of his leader. More and more unionists (Carson, Milner and Willoughby de Broke were but some of the most prominent) despised the rules and conventions upon which Balfour's approach to politics reposed. But under Andrew Bonar Law rules would be broken, conventions abandoned, inhibitions scorned; the die-hard style, if not the die-hard policy, would triumph. In Bonar Law the party had now a man ready to supply the demand for forceful leadership that had created him: his speeches would not be qualified; moderation would hold no appeal for him; and under him the conservative and unionist party would adopt a course that for violence and extremism had no parallel in modern British history.

Notes

1. Robert Blake, *The unknown prime minister—the life and times of Andrew Bonar Law 1858–1923* (London, 1955), pp 95–6.
2. See J. S. Sandars's memorandum in the Balfour papers, 12 Aug. 1911, entitled 'A diary of the events and transactions in connection with the passage of the Parliament Bill of 1911 through the house of lords' (hereafter cited as *Sandars diary*).
3. See Gregory D. Phillips, *The die-hards—aristocratic society and politics in Edwardian England* (Cambridge, Massachusetts and London, 1979), pp 139–40.
4. Lord Hugh Cecil; see Sandars to Balfour, 11 Aug. 1911 (Balfour papers).
5. See A. M. Gollin, *The Observer and J. L. Garvin 1908–14: a study in a great editorship* (London, 1960), p. 319.
6. See A. Wilson-Fox, *The earl of Halsbury* (London, 1929), pp 231 ff.
7. Midleton to Salisbury, 18 Jan. 1911 (Salisbury papers).
8. See W. Ormsby-Gore to Willoughby de Broke, 29 Dec. 1913 (Willoughby de Broke papers) for an account of a conversation during a house party in Hatfield on 19–21 Dec. 1910 when Salisbury, Hugh Cecil, Curzon and Derby all took the die-hard line. Selborne did likewise in a letter to Balfour of 23 Feb. 1911 (Balfour papers).
9. Strachey to Cromer, 31 Mar. 1911 (Cromer papers, P.R.O., FO 633/34/9–10). See also Fitzroy papers, (B.L. Add. Mss. 48374, f. 60), where (early in 1906) Fitzroy wrote of Lansdowne as the man whose recent action 'is the most conspicuous claim of the unionist party to national confidence. I hope it may have the effect of consolidating behind Lord Lansdowne the unionist forces in the house of lords, as the experiment of whig leadership for tory peers is one that has many risks and will be watched with great interest'.
10. Strachey to Cromer, 6 Apr. 1911 (loc. cit., 633/34/13–19).
11. Lord Newton, *Lord Lansdowne* (London, 1929), p. 419.
12. The government seem to have broken their pledge of secrecy to the king in at least one respect: they informed the Irish parliamentary party of the agreement in December 1910. See T. P. O'Connor to Redmond, 22 Dec. 1910 (Redmond papers): 'I had a long talk with the master of Elibank yesterday. He gave me an account of the interview between Asquith and the king. It is quite satisfactory. Bigge, the king's secretary, has been complaining that the liberals had played unfairly with the king in demanding and getting guarantees—I believe in writing—before the election instead of trusting to the word of the king. All good news for us ... The master insisted strongly on an attitude of reticence and reserve with regard to the king; and was a little frightened, he said, at one passage in one of your speeches which seems to lift the veil a little. I tell you this for your guidance.' The government presumably told the Irish of the guarantees because they feared they might otherwise jeopardise their plans by pressing publicly for a more vigorous policy. Certainly, between then and the enactment of the Parliament Bill—in distinct contrast with the early months of 1910—the Irish proved the most amenable of allies. See Ronan Fanning, 'The Irish policy of Asquith's government and the cabinet crisis of 1910' in Art Cosgrove and Donal McCartney (eds), *Studies in Irish history presented to R. Dudley Edwards* (Dublin, 1979), pp 279–303.
13. Leo Maxse to Arthur Steel-Maitland, 15 June 1911 (Steel-Maitland papers); see also W. S. Blunt, *My diaries 1888–1914* (London, 1932), p. 770.

14. John D. Fair, *British interparty conferences—a study of the procedure of conciliation in British politics 1867–1921* (Oxford, 1980), pp 103–4.
15. *National Review*, March 1911, p. 53.
16. Oliver to Milner, 31 March. 1911 (Milner Papers, 194).
17. Blunt, *Diaries*, p. 771.
18. Ibid.
19. Wilson-Fox, *Halsbury*, p. 250.
20. B.L. Add. MSS. 48376, f. 116.
21. L. S. Amery, *My political life* (London, 1953), i, 380. See also Elibank papers, diary of Arthur Murray, M.P., f. 29: 'it is difficult to write calmly of the unprecedently insolent behaviour of Lord Hugh Cecil, F. E. Smith and the small band of tories responsible for this outrage upon parliamentary decencies and traditions. It was a deplorable degradation of the British parliament, an insult to the leader of the house—and at the same time, an outburst against the leadership of Arthur Balfour, who showed himself utterly incapable of controlling the Hughligans.' Cf. Lady Victoria Hicks Beach, *Life of Sir Michael Hicks Beach* (London, 1932) ii, 268–9; and R. S. Churchill, *Winston S. Churchill: young statesman, 1901–14* (London, 1967), ii, 431–3.
22. Lord Willoughby de Broke, *The passing years* (London, 1924), pp 270–1.
23. Galloway to Willoughby de Broke, 12 July 1911, Willoughby de Broke papers.
24. 22 July 1911; printed in Blanche Dugdale, *Arthur James Balfour, first earl of Balfour* (London, 1939), ii, 50–1.
25. See J. R. Fanning, 'The unionist party and Ireland, 1906–10' in *I.H.S.*, xv, no. 58 (Sept. 1966), pp 147–71.
26. Sandars suggested that Wyndham's sensibilities were so bruised by the events of 1904–5 that he never recovered—'it has been pathetic to watch his attempts at recovery... his copious rhetoric has become an unmeaning verbosity... He seems to have acquired—perhaps unconsciously—a certain artificiality of style and manner which suggests a note of insincerity... cultivated opinion has always found in him more to admire as a man of letters than as a man of affairs'—A privy councillor [J. S. Sandars], *Studies of yesterday* (London, 1928), pp 56–7. See also Blunt, *Diaries*, p. 780 (entry for 15 Oct. 1911), which suggests that Wyndham's 'political prospects... might yet be retrieved in his party if he could only be less self-indulgent. He is the imaginative brain of them all, having engineered the whole revolt against Balfour, and might have the leadership if he would amuse himself less'.
27. Wyndham's memorandum, 'A note on the political situation', 4 Jan. 1911 (Balfour papers).
28. See Phillips, *The die-hards*, pp 9 & 176 (notes 19–20). See also James Craig to his wife, 25 July 1911 (P.R.O.N.I., D. 1415/13/38): 'Walter Long is cross, and Lord Londonderry is going one way, and Carson and ourselves another. Charlie [Craig] takes a different view to me, while Edward Goulding is hand in glove with the free traders like the Cecils'. See also below, n. 41.
29. Sandars to E [?sher], 26 July 1911 (Balfour papers).
30. *Sandars diary*; both Bonar Law and Finlay, who were thought to be neutral during the meeting, later supported Balfour.
31. The legal connection was also marked among the die-hards: Halsbury, Carson and Smith were all lawyers and Selborne, too, came of a distinguished legal family—his father, the 1st earl, was lord chancellor in 1872–4 and 1880–5.
32. Strachey to Curzon, 1 Aug. 1911. Cf. Strachey to Rosebery, 26 Aug. 1910: 'the truth is that so English an Englishman from many points of view, he [Joseph

Chamberlain] is in other ways utterly un-English. Almost every Englishman has a touch of the essential whig in him and liking for moderation and the *via media*. Joe has none. Once a Jacobin, always a Jacobin' (Strachey papers).

33. 5 June 1911, cited in R. S. Churchill, *Winston Churchill*, ii, 354.
34. As note 29 above.
35. Montgomery Hyde, *Carson* (London, 1953), pp 286–7.
36. Carson to Sandars, 2 Aug. 1911 (Balfour papers).
37. See Fair, *British interparty conferences*, pp 3 & 90–1.
38. Maxse to Sandars, 24 July 1911 (Balfour papers).
39. See Ampthill to Willoughby de Broke, 26 June 1911 (Willoughby de Broke papers).
40. Arran to Willoughby de Broke, 28 July 1911, Willoughby de Broke papers. In the event Arran did not vote with the die-hards.
41. See Abercorn to Halsbury, 27 July 1911, (Halsbury papers, box file 7–19, env. 8). Only 15 of 'between 25 and 30' who attended a meeting of Irish peers were listed as sympathetic to the die-hards and 4 of the 15 (including Abercorn and Arran) defected before the decisive vote on 10 August—see letters from Scarbrough (27 July 1911) and Mayo (28 July 1911) in the Willoughby de Broke papers.
42. Milner to Willoughby de Broke, 21 June 1911 (Willoughby de Broke papers).
43. Ibid., Carson to Willoughby de Broke, 21 Aug. [1911].
44. Austen Chamberlain, *Politics from inside—an epistolary chronicle 1906–1914* (London, 1936), p. 358.
45. J. W. Mackail & Guy Wyndham, *Life and letters of George Wyndham* (London, 1925), ii, 730.
46. Selborne to Willoughby de Broke, 18 Aug. 1911 (Willoughby de Broke papers). See also Selborne to Halsbury, 31 Aug. 1911, (Halsbury papers, box-file 7–19, env. 13); and Selborne to Austen Chamberlain, 4 Sept. 1911 (Austen Chamberlain papers, AC 9/3/56), for evidence of Selborne's key role in the formation of the Halsbury Club. See also above, n. 8.
47. Northumberland to Willoughby de Broke, 11 Aug. 1911 (Willoughby de Broke papers).
48. See Sandars's memorandum, 8 Nov. 1911, 'Note on the events leading up to Mr Balfour's resignation'—hereafter cited as *Sandars note* (Balfour papers).
49. Lord Winterton, *Pre-war* (London, 1932), pp 17–18.
50. Balfour to Lady Elcho [Blanche Dugdale's transcript?], 30 July 1911 (Balfour papers).
51. Dugdale, *Balfour*, ii, 61.
52. See, e.g., Amery's comment to Sandars that 'he was very sorry that Mr Balfour had gone to Gastein before the issue was cleared up. He thought the effect on the party would be bad' (*Sandars diary*).
53. Lord Milner's diary for 10 Jan. 1911 (Milner papers, 274).
54. See Wilson-Fox, *Halsbury*, pp 234–5; also above, n. 46.
55. Lawrence to Willoughby de Broke, 15 Aug. 1911 (Willoughby de Broke papers); see also George Peel, *The tariff reformers* (London, 1913), p. 79.
56. On 7 October, Neville Chamberlain wrote to Austen who was then holidaying on the continent, telling him that Amery had telephoned him 'to say that Milner, Carson, Selborne, Wyndham, F. E. Smith, Willoughby de Broke and other die-hards had met and had determined to act together and go for a forward policy. They did not want to form a separate party or organisation, but by working together to ensure that their views would have a fair chance. They were all (I still quote A.) ready and anxious to follow you if you would

lead them, and were extremely anxious to get in touch with you... I hear from so many quarters expressions of dissatisfaction with A.B. and L... that I was very glad to hear of this move. It seems to me serious, and that now is the time for you to come forward and give them a lead... This is the critical point of your career as well as that of the party. Of course, I am not suggesting any open revolt at present, but no doubt a difference of opinion will arise some time (if A.B. does not resign first) and you will get your way if you have the die-hards behind you.' (Austen Chamberlain papers, AC 9/3/14).

57. *National Review*, Sept. 1911, p. 16; see also Oct. 1911, pp 214–19.
58. Amery's summary of Milner's views (after they had both met with Wyndham on 18 Sept. 1911) is printed in Chamberlain, *Politics from inside*, pp 369–70.
59. *Sandars note.*
60. Curzon was 'generally believed' responsible for party tactics on the night of the crucial division and was bitterly attacked by die-hard speakers during the debate; see Willoughby de Broke, *The passing years*, p. 302. The die-hards particularly despised him, because he had at first supported them and then switched sides—see above, n. 8.
61. Lovat to Willoughby de Broke, 17 Aug. 1911, Willoughby de Broke papers.
62. Viscount Cecil of Chelwood, *All the way* (London, 1949), pp 118–19.
63. See above, n. 21.
64. *Sandars diary.*
65. *Sandars note.*
66. Lucy Masterman, *C. F. G. Masterman* (London, 1939), p. 201.
67. See Newton, *Lansdowne*, p. 415 and Randolph Churchill, *Winston Churchill*, ii, 351.
68. Newton, op. cit., pp 492–3.
69. There is some evidence that Balfour was disappointed by Lansdowne's attitude during this period—see Masterman, loc. cit., where it is recorded that when Balfour went to see Lloyd George (on the morning after the unionists had received confirmation that the government had the guarantees and told him that he and his colleagues had decided to give way) he 'made a rather curious comment. "You see what Lansdowne is like"'. Lansdowne was also largely responsible for the suppression of Balfour's memorandum attacking the die-hards (*Sandars diary*).
70. Chamberlain to his wife, 26 July 1911 (Austen Chamberlain papers, AC 6/1/88).
71. *Sandars note.*
72. Selborne to Salisbury, 18 Aug. 1911 (Salisbury papers).
73. *Sandars note.*
74. H. Morgan-Brown, *Balfourism–a study in contemporary politics* (London, 1907), p. 2.
75. H. Belloc and C. Chesterton, *The party system* (London, 1911), p. 24.
76. Wolmer (Selborne's son) to Willoughby de Broke, 15 Aug. 1911 (Willoughby de Broke papers).
77. Austen Chamberlain, *Down the years* (London, 1935), pp 214–15.

A parliamentary state at war: France 1914-1918

John Horne

Introduction

Shortly after the first world war, the historian Pierre Renouvin began a book on the forms of French wartime government by making two key points. First he observed that the democratic system of the Third Republic had reached a point of 'equilibrium and stability' by the eve of the war. It was the parliamentary system established in the 1870s and early 1880s, with its own distinctive balance of powers, consolidated by forty years of parliamentary practice, and reinforced by the trauma of the Dreyfus affair, which confronted the experience of the first world war.

He pointed out secondly that the principal characteristic of wartime government was the extension of executive power (of 'governmental functions'), accompanied by the erosion of customary procedures of accountability and of individual liberties.[1] But pre-war norms and arrangements were not totally suspended. There were degrees to which the authority of different states, and their authoritarianism, were developed during the first world war. France did not experience a virtual military dictatorship, as did Germany from 1916 to 1918. By comparison with Russia there remained considerable freedom of expression and organisation. It is perhaps worthwhile, therefore, picking up the threads of Renouvin's enquiry to explore further the ways in which the war did extend and alter the powers of the pre-war state. For despite the torrent of writing on the war up to 1939, the research since on the wartime state has been spread very unevenly across the different problems, and there has been virtually no attempt at a 'vue d'ensemble'.[2] There is only room here to suggest three among many possible lines of investigation, but each raises a fundamental aspect of the state.

First is the impact of the war on the democratic system of political representation. For if the war shifted the balance of power in favour of the executive, this inevitably ran up against the considerable authority of the elected representative in the system as it normally functioned—a system known to some political scientists as the 'deputy-centred republic'.

Second is the ideological dimension of the state's activity. The French state, like others by 1914, had developed a powerful educative and persuasive capacity (especially in the primary school system); but even more significant was the activity—often in connection with the state—of those organisations in civil society (including the press and political parties) which helped develop the cultural assumptions and political values which legitimised the state and underpinned its authority. The war at this level was a critical test for the state since (as the Russian example showed) survival against external threat depended on the initial breadth and depth of the state's legitimacy, and on its subsequent maintenance, as much as on military or economic capacity. The persuasive attempt by the state to bolster 'morale' and renew public support for the long war effort arguably constituted a 'political mobilisation', no less important in its way than the military or economic mobilisation. It both extended the state's power and involved it in new relations with private institutions and organisations.

Finally, the wartime state obviously intervened on an unprecedented scale in the economy. In doing so it developed new relationships with organised economic forces—notably labour and business (especially manufacturing)—which in turn raise the important questions of the degree of autonomy which the state possessed in relation to them, and of whether there was a shift (real or perceived) in the relationship of economic power to the state between 1914 and 1918.

The military effort: the impact of war on the representative political system

The military effort raised in acute form the question of the balance of power between the principal institutions of state, and presented the wartime expansion of executive power in its most obvious form. Generals, government ministers and parliamentary deputies all had varying views on who should control the military effort.[3]

Initially the army was placed in an immensely strong position. The war was expected to be short, and nothing seemed more urgent than to give the high command full power over military affairs to repulse the impending invasion. The government retained ultimate control, but with Paris menaced, it withdrew temporarily to Bordeaux and parliament suspended its sitting.

The form of the military mobilisation added greatly to the high command's powers. It was not just a question of the massive call-up of men. The 'state of siege' legislation, which defined the state's powers in an emergency, had originally been envisaged as limited in both time and geographical application. But in early August 1914 it was implemented by government and parliament for all of France for the duration of the war. The 'state of siege' did not supersede the basic constitutional laws and the supremacy of parliament, but it juxtaposed the military with civil administration and in certain domains, such as police powers, censorship and law courts, made it predominant.[4]

In 1914, therefore, the power of the French high command was considerable: first, because with the initial invasion and near conquest of France, it was almost totally in charge of the war effort; secondly, because the army acquired a vital role in the domestic administration of France.

The extent of the army's domestic involvement raises the first question in civil–military relations, and the balance of power within the state. Was there any real danger of a full-scale military dictatorship? Or was it at least possible that the high command might use the 'state of siege' if not to overthrow the republic, to remodel it in a conservative mould?

The fear was not necessarily far-fetched. Within living memory two generals had threatened the infant republic, MacMahon in 1877 and Boulanger in 1887–9. But the evidence is against it in 1914–18. The government of Viviani had no difficulty in restricting the military's administrative powers in September 1915, allowing them to operate to their full legal limit only in much reduced 'army zones'.[5] As civilian control was re-established over the military effort proper, there was never any suggestion of real insubordination by leading generals.[6]

This is not to deny that there was much latent hostility among the often Catholic and monarchist senior officers to the republic and to the politicians, frequently anti-clerical, with whom they had to deal.[7] But as the Dreyfus Affair had shown, their predominant characteristic was their isolation from the real centres of French political power rather than an active commitment to overthrow the republic. By insisting as much as possible on professional autonomy, they hoped to maintain their sense of authority and hierarchy at least in the military sphere.

This meant that the real conflict occurred over the degree of independence of the high command from government and parliament in managing the military effort. For many leading soldiers, and most obviously Joffre, the French commander-in-chief until December 1916, it seemed essential to reduce the meddling of an inefficient parliamentary system. For the parliamentary deputies, especially those of the centre-left, it gradually came to seem equally indispensable that control by the elected representatives should be imposed on a virtually unfettered high command. The governments of Viviani and Briand (down to March 1917) were caught in the middle.

The conflict would not have arisen had the war been short. But as it ceased to be a hiatus, a national emergency, and turned into a long and complex process, it became increasingly difficult to rule off military affairs into a separate compartment. The high command opposed any outside interference in the 'army zone', either in the organisation of the military effort or in strategy. On questions of military organisation, however, the deputies and senators had the right to investigate the army (as they did various other aspects of executive power) through the system of parliamentary commissions. In a long and difficult battle in 1915 and 1916, the potent army and budget commissions, especially in the chamber of deputies, gradually imposed on the government and on a furiously reluctant high command their prerogative to investigate all aspects of army administration, from the hospital system to conditions in the trenches.[8]

Rather more slowly, the deputies forced the government to take the initiative from the high command on questions of strategy. This was the heart of the matter. In principle, the division of responsibilities was clear. Stemming from the constitutional laws, the government had 'political direction' of operations while the high command was responsible for their execution.[9] In practice, the dividing line was extremely unclear, partly because the high command interpreted the 'execution' of operations to include almost all matters of broad strategy, partly because the changing nature of the war genuinely eroded the distinction between 'direction' and 'execution'. Specific questions of tactics became more and more entangled with factors of the highest political importance—manpower reserves, the quality and quantity of armaments, the morale of the troops, and relations with France's allies.[10] Governments until 1916 were reluctant to redefine the relationship between the direction and execution of operations in their own favour, preferring to endorse the autonomy claimed by the high command. Many deputies, however, as the war dragged on, wanted the government to decide on broad matters of strategy—if necessary with parliamentary debate.

Until 1916, Joffre was able to conserve much of the autonomy which his victory on the Marne in 1914, and the reluctance of governments to meddle in unfamiliar matters, had bestowed on him.[11] But his failure, despite warnings, either to strengthen or abandon the salient of Verdun (in his belief that it would not be attacked), made him directly responsible for the costliest French campaign of the war. Verdun, militarily useless, was defended at the cost of 315,000 French casualties simply because it was politically and psychologically impossible to abandon it under German attack. This gave a minority of deputies the issue they needed. A number of the warnings about Verdun's inadequate defences had come from soldier-deputies to the chamber's army commission, thus vindicating the parliamentary right of enquiry into military organisation. Furthermore, the tactics of attrition employed at Verdun crystallised two fundamental problems—the protection of French soldiers from unnecessary wastage, and shrinking national manpower reserves—both of which suggested that the government needed to take a more active role in military planning. Individual deputies like Abel Ferry had raised these criticisms since 1915, but Verdun generalised them amongst deputies to the point where, in June 1916, the government was forced to concede the first secret session of the chamber during the war.[12]

In the event formal censure of the government and high command was avoided. But Briand was obliged to promise tighter control of the military and the chamber of deputies formally resolved to strengthen its investigative powers into all aspects of army organisation. By the end of the year, Joffre had been dismissed from active command and governmental control of strategy (as well as parliamentary surveillance of the army) had been fairly clearly implemented—although no completely harmonious definition of the respective spheres of government, parliament and the army was ever established during the war.[13]

The restoration of the primacy of the elected civil authority over the army was thus won by the deputies, not the government, and in this it reflected the political system of pre-war France. Characteristically, this system lacked strong parties (apart from the Socialists) linking government to electorate. The deputy, once elected, enjoyed considerable autonomy in his parliamentary decisions. In particular, it was the deputies who made and unmade governments, without recourse to a general election. The parliamentary function of the deputy was to reduce the frequently strong electoral divisions by acting as a political broker, seeking out the consensus which would permit a government to emerge. The principal cleavage in parliament, therefore, was less between government and opposition on the basis of electoral programmes, than between government and the deputies as such, with the latter exercising a close and critical surveillance over the executive.[14]

The wartime reaction of the deputies was in many respects a defence of this system, a reassertion of the 'deputy-centred republic.' Their authority was demonstrated by their ability to challenge the autonomy of the high command and to force the government into more active control of military affairs; and their principal instrument, besides the innovation of the secret sessions of the chamber and senate, was the system of parliamentary commissions developed between 1876 and 1914 as the means of continuous surveillance of government by parliament.[15] Significantly, when parliamentary inspection of the army was reinforced after the June 1916 secret session of the chamber, various proposals for a new mechanism of control (loosely inspired by the revolutionary 'représentants en mission') were rejected lest they weaken the existing commissions.[16]

Of course, parliamentary opinion was far from unanimous in criticising the high command and reasserting the authority of the deputies. The source of these moves tended to be deputies of the centre-left—that is, precisely those who most identified with the political culture of republicanism and its revolutionary traditions.[17] They were highly sensitive to undue concentrations of power, especially if these hinted at escaping accountability to parliament, and stressed that between elections popular sovereignty resided in the deputies. From these ideas, key figures in the battle for parliamentary control, such as Abel Ferry, developed the underlying notion of a people's war—constantly referring to the republican military effort during the French revolution as a symbol for the liberation of popular energies, and urging the deputies to participate both in unleashing these energies and protecting the interests of the soldier–citizen. As Ferry typically commented in his notebook:

The spirit of 1793 is underneath, bureaucracy is on top. That is the trouble.[18]

Conversely, even when the chamber and senate in their majorities had endorsed the implicit criticisms of the high command in June–July 1916, there remained deputies, especially on the right, who continued to uphold the autonomy of the high command and the need for 'authority' in war.

If the relative weakness of parties in France helped strengthen the parliamentary representatives against the executive, this could also be a source of vulnerability. In normal circumstances, government leaders in the 'deputy-centred republic' tended to be skilled in negotiation and compromise. This was essential in a system where the nexus of power between government and electorate was fragmented at the level of the deputies—and where in consequence corridor alliances and parliamentary manoeuvres were essential in the formation of new governing coalitions. Until October 1917 changes in wartime government followed just such a pattern, including the traditional counter-weight to governmental instability of certain ministers who occupied posts (sometimes the same) in successive governments (notably Louis-Jean Malvy, a Radical who held his party's traditional fief of the ministry of the interior from 1914 to September 1917). In moments of crisis, however, an alternative type of leader emerged—the 'consul'— whose authority derived not merely from the deputies but from a broader sense of public unease, which in turn allowed him unusually bold and autonomous executive action.[19] In the shape of Clemenceau just such a figure emerged from November 1917 to the end of the war, over whom the deputies had far less influence.

In 1917, several distinct problems shook French society. The new commander-in-chief, Nivelle, who was firmly under civilian control, launched an ill-conceived and quite unwinnable offensive in the Champagne region which only served to produce serious mutinies. Simultaneously there was an outburst of strikes soon surpassing even high pre-war levels. An important current of 'pacifism' developed, drawn from the intellectual middle class, some industrial workers (including women), and certain rural areas. At its simplest, it expressed war-weariness, while at its more articulate it usually demanded an immediate negotiated peace as an alternative to the seemingly impossible pursuit of military victory. Finally a rash of scandals erupted, in some of which certain 'pacifists', among them deputies and leading journalists, were found to be receiving (knowingly or not) German funds.

These currents were fairly distinct. But in much of the press, in a good deal of public opinion, and also within parliament (especially on the centre-right), they provoked a strong reaction which tended to see only a widespread 'pacifist' plot, or cancer, manipulated by the Germans, whose elimination required strong government action. The full extent and nature both of German involvement in France and of the currents of industrial protest, war-weariness, pacifism etc. have yet to be established.[20] It seemed clear to many at the time that the mutinies had primarily (though not solely) military causes, that Malvy's negotiations with strike leaders did not amount to complicity with the enemy, or that Caillaux, *bête noire* of the right, was not necessarily a traitor because he actively symbolised certain hopes for a negotiated peace. Nonetheless, Malvy was forced from office by attacks in parliament and Caillaux was arrested on Clemenceau's instruction.[21] The extreme right, notably Léon Daudet and the Action Française, deepened into an almost manichaean division the distinction between a 'jusqu 'auboutiste' commitment to military victory and 'pacifism', with the latter interpreted as anything which weakened or questioned the former. But a broader mood beyond parliament shared the basic assumption, stimulated by the graphic press presentation of the 'treason' (Bolo Pacha, Pierre Lenoir *et al*) which had undoubtedly occurred.[22]

It was Clemenceau who encapsulated (and perhaps manipulated[23]) this mood. His 'ministerial declaration' to the chamber of deputies, for example, strongly hinted that anti-patriotism did not only consist of formal treason:

> We take an oath... that justice will be done according to the rigour of the law... Feebleness would be (treated as) complicity. No more pacifist campaigns, no more German intrigues. Neither treason, nor half-treason: war. Only war.[24]

Clemenceau also incarnated the response in the only politically feasible form, that of the Jacobin tradition of firm (though parliamentary) government in times of national crisis, which could simultaneously appeal to the more authoritarian heritage of the right. It was at this critical juncture that the absence of firm party structures made it difficult for deputies with different views on the aims or running of the war to resist Clemenceau.

The Socialists, who did have a relatively firm structure and doctrinal identity, argued that the strikes had as much to do with living standards as with pacifism (a point Clemenceau privately accepted).[25] An increasingly large segment of the party (and a clear majority from October 1918) demanded the active search for a negotiated peace, while still proclaiming their support for the national defence and rejecting the label of 'traitor'. The national executive pressed the parliamentary group to withdraw completely from governmental participation towards the end of 1917, in order to mark the growing qualifications to Socialist support for the war effort.[26]

Other parties on the centre-left, however, and notably the Radicals, found it hard either to make these distinctions, or even to decide on them, precisely because their party identities and national structures were so weak. The Radicals were the largest single group in the chamber and they held at least 50 per cent of ministerial positions in all wartime governments, including Clemenceau's. They were normally strong champions of the deputy's authority; and pre-war they had increasingly avoided an aggressive brand of republican patriotism, which was certainly in their heritage, beginning instead to emphasise the liberal internationalism which was to characterise their foreign policy between the wars. But the war itself fragmented the Radicals' international aims. Their difficulty in acting nationally (even the executive committee did not meet before 1917) prevented them from imposing their own interpretation on the events of that year. Having thoroughly submerged themselves in the 'Union sacrée', they found it impossible as a party to repudiate or qualify Clemenceau's version of it in 1917–18.[27]

Where deputies, besides the Socialists, did express critical views on war aims and conduct in 1917–18, they not infrequently sought organisational support in extra-parliamentary bodies which they joined as individuals rather than party representatives. Among the most notable of these were the League of the Rights of Man, which campaigned against censorship and repressive domestic measures (while dividing over a negotiated peace), and the Republican Coalition, a loose left-wing pressure group which emerged in opposition to Clemenceau early in 1918 specifically to express an alternative, left republican approach to the war effort.[28] But these alternative voices remained feeble. Clemenceau, supported by the centre-right in parliament plus many of the left (though not the Socialists), and above all confident of broad popular support, established an extremely powerful, 'consul' type of government in the last year of the war, which firmly controlled both the high command *and* the deputies.[29]

The state and the political mobilisation of the war effort

The shifting balance of power between high command, parliament and the government raised issues familiar in pre-war politics, even if their wartime form was novel. The political mobilisation of the war effort (that is, the mobilisation of opinions and ideologies) involved substantially new questions—at least in the experience of the Third Republic—about the relationship between state and society.

After the war, academic studies of propaganda tended to assume that European societies could not have sustained such an unprecedented effort for so long without the manipulation of popular consciousness.[30] Recent French work on public opinion, however, has tended to emphasise the relatively autonomous sources of its support for the war, as well as the highly differentiated qualification of that support (by region and social class) in 1917–18.[31] H. D. Lasswell pointed out in his pioneering study of war propaganda techniques that public opinion was not just passively structured by official propaganda, nor was the state the only source of propaganda.[32] There were many unofficial propagandas, from churches, business and political organisations, specially created patriotic leagues and committees, and so on. The 'political mobilisation' of the war effort might thus be seen as involving the self-mobilisation of a series of national identities (more or less identified with the preservation of the republic) among major social groups and classes, including (most problematically) the working class.[33] The state, in its ability to express and coordinate these, arguably responded to broader social and political support for the war as much as itself creating that support.

Only fuller study of how the principal social groups and organisations responded to the war will clarify the composition of the broader political mobilisation of the war effort, and permit a more precise evaluation of the state's contribution.[34] There is, however, no doubt that the state itself mounted a substantial effort to stimulate and sustain support for the war, and its basic mechanisms can at least be indicated. Civilian 'morale' was quickly identified as a legitimate government concern. This did not simply entail maintaining a broad commitment to the national effort. As consensus on the aims and significance of the war weakened, maintaining 'morale' meant maintaining support for rather more specific ideas—as we have seen in the case of Clemenceau in 1917–18 (military victory rather than negotiated peace; the refusal to specify war aims; condemnation of the October revolution for breaking the eastern front, etc.).

The most obvious source of the state's contribution to the political mobilisation is official propaganda. French governments directly produced a certain amount of this—poster campaigns warning against spies, or urging the purchase of war bonds, flag days, and so on.[35] There was a certain rhetorical militarisation of the civilian population. Millerand as minister of war in 1914–15 and Albert Thomas, at least initially, as under-secretary of war for armaments production, both urged workers (many of whom were mobilised) to consider themselves soldiers of production.[36] In July 1917 the government created a 'medal of French recognition' for civilian fortitude during the war. Undoubtedly more important was the republicanisation of the war—that is the extension to it of the symbols and rituals of the political culture of republicanism. The 14 July celebrations of 1919 and 1920, as the double celebration of military victory and the reversal of the defeat of 1870 by a republican regime, were the most sumptuous of the Third Republic.[37] But, by comparison with governments during the second world war, the amount of domestic propaganda directly produced and disseminated by the state remained limited. The information section of the second bureau of the high command produced photographs and some films for domestic purposes. But the larger proportion of direct state propaganda was aimed at enemy and neutral countries. One of the principal official propaganda agencies, the Maison de la Presse, founded by Briand in January 1916, was concerned exclusively with foreign propaganda.[38]

The state, however, possessed in the press a private collaborator which greatly reduced the need for direct propaganda. The French press had reached its apogee on the eve of the war in readership and diversity. In addition to a variety of small circulation papers, often supporting particular political organisations and causes, there were four mass circulation dailies with a combined readership of 3,787,000 in 1912, 71 per cent of the Parisian total; *le Journal, le Petit Journal, le Petit Parisien*, and *le Matin*.[39] It is true that during the war the press was by no means wholly compliant. Some of the smaller papers represented pacifist or even revolutionary positions, or within their support for the war effort were fiercely critical of particular governments. But most of them, and the mass circulation dailies almost without exception, not only supported the war effort but preached the 'Union sacrée' and patriotic resistance until military victory. This did not amount to specific endorsement of every government by each main paper; *le Matin*, for instance, was hostile to Clemenceau and not a little critical of parliamentary pretensions to 'control' the high command. But the mass dailies reinforced the broad parameters of government views on the significance and aims of the war.[40] They did so positively by articulating the principal themes of the political mobilisation (the democratic defensive war effort of the allies, the identification of German aggression with atrocities and 'barbarism' etc.), and negatively by operating a kind of self-censorship in accordance with official advice.[41] This dual approach reached a culmination in April 1917, when Nivelle's disastrous offensive and the mutinies were first hidden by optimistic press reports and then all but ignored, opening up a distinct gap between the reactions of the mass media and a good deal of the public.[42]

Le Journal was the only one of the four mass circulation dailies which remotely favoured a negotiated peace and showed itself pessimistic on the outcome of the war, and it is at least possible that this was due to the German money which had secretly bought it.[43] (The revelation of the scandal in 1917 resulted in a drop in circulation of 50 per cent, to well under half a million). Otherwise, the broad cooperation between the main dailies and the state remained close, as, frequently, did the personal links with politicians (though in their substance these appear to remain unexplored[44]). *Le Petit Journal* was owned by Stephen Pichon, Clemenceau's foreign minister from 1917 to 1920.[45] Jean Dupuy, as the owner of the highly influential *Le Petit Parisien*, was the virtual spokesman of the two Briand governments from 1915 to 1917, and he also fully backed Clemenceau during the final period of the war (his political editor paid daily visits to Georges Mandel, Clemenceau's cabinet chief for domestic affairs.[46]). At least one contemporary close observer of the wartime press underlined its importance in 1917 in creating Clemenceau's authority in the country before it was established in parliament.[47]

In many respects, then, the line dividing the major papers from the state became blurred during the war. Apart from *Le Journal* in 1916–17, they collaborated with the state—although the state, through censorship, was itself an active partner. Indeed in many ways the mass press and censorship were complementary aspects of a single system of political mobilisation.

Censorship operated at several levels, both offering guidance and acting as a powerful repressive weapon against the recalcitrant sections of the press which fundamentally threatened the mobilisation of opinion. The state exercised a basic control of information through the cable system (where it censored incoming international news) and through the army, which controlled military news through official communiqués and the strict regulation of war correspondents. Beyond that, the official press bureau issued daily lists of sensitive news inviting cooperative self-censorship by the press (there was no formal censorship in advance of publication). But if papers disobeyed, the issue could be impounded and the paper suspended. In principle, censorship at whatever level applied to military and diplomatic information, not political comment. But ambiguity was present from the outset. The law of 5 August ratifying the 'state of siege' allowed censorship

....of information or articles... exercising a harmful influence over the spirit of the army and the population.[48]

As the consensus on the war and the way it was being fought was eroded from 1915, censorship became obviously political—both in its definition of militarily sensitive information and in its explicit control of editorial opinion. According to the memoirs of two of the press bureau censors:

(In the crisis of mid-1917) we no longer talked in any detail of strikes, sabotage, explosions, brawls, bombardments, visits by Gothas and Zeppelins... We cut everything... But can one really believe that the inhabitants of the suburbs and provinces did not notice the strikes?[49]

Clemenceau's new censorship directives when he assumed power included the instructions:

Be very severe on pacifist articles...
Be generous for political articles and news items,

but the press and the censor were unwilling to use all the latitude he appeared to have given them.[50]

The partnership of the press and censorship clearly amounted to an important, perhaps key, element of the political mobilisation, although until the censorship has been analysed in detail (both the *consignes*—or notices to the press of information to be suppressed—and the measurement of how censorship of opinion, and suspensions, fell across the spectrum of papers) it will be impossible fully to assess the weight of state control. But it all obviously amounted to an unprecedented state interference in what had counted as one of the principal freedoms of the pre-war political system, and there was an instructive reaction within parliament. By late 1915 when Briand took office, a debate on censorship had become unavoidable in the wake of numerous protests. It was launched by Paul Meunier, a Radical–Socialist deputy who was highly critical of political censorship while accepting the need for control of sensitive information. His proposal (reformulated by the commission on legislation) envisaged an explicit censorship in advance but restricted exclusively to military and diplomatic news. It was defeated for two reasons. Many deputies feared to legalise censorship as such (the 1914 law technically only established an *emergency* 'press regime' which would automatically disappear with the 'state of siege')—and the struggles of the mid-19th century republican press against the political censorship of the Second Empire were evoked. Even Briand blandly denied that any political censorship was in fact in operation. Just as importantly, however (if somewhat in contradiction), Briand argued persuasively that the protection of 'morale' from alarm and division distinguished war from peace, was indispensable to the war effort, and justified a certain control of press opinion. His statement was echoed by almost every French government during the war.

> In war, there are not only rifles, cannons, munitions and the soldiers' heroism—there is also the 'morale' of the country. When the war has lasted a long time... the principal ammunition is calm, the 'sang-froid' of the country... It must be understood that certain discussions may constitute a danger... the right to public meetings cannot be exercised without constraint, as in peacetime, ...the same rule must exist for newspapers; disseminated in thousands and thousands of copies, they can present an even greater danger than that resulting from public meetings... That is the essence of the problem.[51]

Meunier's bill was defeated by 349 to 158 and the *status quo* of a *de facto* political censorship was maintained. The troubling paradox that governments had to restrict formal democracy in order to fight the war 'for democracy' was only exacerbated, as consensus on the war diminished; but the majority of deputies accepted it either as justified in an emergency or as preferable to establishing the precedent of formal, if more limited, censorship.

The state and the war economy

Parliament was a forum, and a principal participant, in the struggle to establish effective direction of the war, and was preoccupied with the relationship between the state and the press to the extent that censorship infringed liberties of which deputies and senators normally considered themselves custodians. The economic activities of the wartime state occurred essentially outside parliament and they centred on the relationship of government ministries with individual businesses and with the representative organisation of the principal economic forces.

In the initial invasion crisis, normal business activity was suspended and the replenishment of munitions was left to the state arsenals and the military authorities. By late 1914 it was becoming obvious that the war would be won by continuous industrial as much as military strength, and it was equally clear that private enterprise would have to shoulder the burden. Parliament intervened in the automatic flow of men to the army, and began to distribute increasingly scarce manpower between military and industrial needs.[52] In May 1915, the reformist socialist Albert Thomas was appointed under secretary of state for munitions at the ministry of war, with the responsibility for organising the entire field of armaments production. By the end of the war, well over 50 per cent of all French workers were engaged directly in work for the national defence.[53]

State intervention in the economy went further. It extended to the control of foreign trade, the importing and allocation of scarce raw materials, price controls on some domestically-produced necessities, and eventually by 1918 (after much hesitation) to limited rationing. In many respects France by 1917–18 had a state-directed economy.

All of this involved unprecedented state contact with business and labour, those 'occult forces' whose organised and political strength grew considerably during the war.[54] The benefits and disadvantages of the new relationship with the state were not necessarily distributed evenly between them. Ministers and civil servants naturally stressed the impartiality of the state between major economic interests; especially in wartime, the supreme emergency, governments tended to talk in terms of the 'national' interest. It is important, therefore, to look more closely at how state regulation of the economy affected labour and business, in economic terms and in their respective organisational strengths.

By comparison with the pre-war economy, both labour and business could argue that they made sacrifices during the war. Although all workers retained the right to belong to trade unions, those mobilised for the army and seconded to factories came under restrictive military discipline (though they received normal wages), while the government possessed an arsenal of repressive measures against labour dissidence or pacifism, from censorship to courts martial.[55] Nor were grievances just political. The hesitancy and tardiness of the government in controlling soaring prices meant that living standards for most of the working class almost certainly declined.[56] At the same time, women entered the industrial workforce on an entirely new scale, and almost always at lower wages than men (causing tension among both men and women workers). All this, combined with an acute labour shortage, contributed to the mass strikes of 1917–18.[57]

Labour leaders could thus argue that labour bore an unfair burden in the war effort.[58] The idea of sacrifice was not itself shunned—at least not among the majority of the national leadership of the General Confederation of Labour (CGT). Rather it seemed that the state spread the sacrifice unevenly, producing an uncomfortable tension with its constant appeals to a 'national' interest overriding sectional concerns. Declining real wages contrasted sharply with high war profits which governments were reluctant to tax. They also refused to nationalise industries such as coal and the railways which were obviously essential to the war effort and, in the eyes of Socialist and trade union leaders, more clearly public utilities than ever before.[59] In the labour movement, the 'war profiteer' became a stock figure of odium.

There was, however, another side to the war experience of national labour leaders. After the government, on the outbreak of war, abandoned its emergency plan to imprison key labour leaders (frequently associated with pre-war anti-militarism), the latter received an unprecedented degree of recognition and consultation.[60] True, French trade union leaders were not party to substantial negotiations on dilution and industrial relations such as those which occurred in Britain in 1915. French trade unions were less powerful; customary work practices defended by the skilled engineering unions in Britain were less well-established in France; and with the immediate, massive mobilisation of August 1914, the French trade unions were decimated, for more than a year. Nonetheless trade union leaders were consulted on a range of issues (by Malvy, for instance, as minister of the interior on the 1917 strikes; or by Thomas on matters such as the welfare of women munitions workers). Moreover, the membership of the CGT in 1917–18 far outstripped pre-war levels.[61] The alteration of the CGT's relationship with the state was even more marked than was the TUC's in Britain in view of the hostility to the state which characterised the CGT's official doctrine before the war.

This combination among many national trade union leaders of a sense of unequal sacrifice in the impact of the war effort with optimistic expectations as to what organised labour might, with consultation and pressure, expect from the expanded activities of the wartime state, produced a particular 'war reformism' (in sharp contrast to the more radical labour protest movements against the war). As early as 1916 it had led the CGT to draft a comprehensive programme of post-war reforms, in which the trade union movement accorded itself a privileged role in helping the state introduce substantial economic and social changes, and eventually in running the economy.[62]

Business, on the other hand, could point to the gradual suspension of economic freedom. French industrialists, and the middle classes generally, were thoroughly imbued with the values of the *laissez faire* economy. Freedom of enterprise was an essential component of their definition of liberty. Most French businessmen saw the intervention of the state in the basic mechanisms of the market economy as at best a necessary sacrifice, and at worst a danger, to be ended as soon as possible after the war.[63] But a distinction has to be drawn between the real sacrifices made by business and the apparent sacrifices resulting from the infringement of basic economic and cultural values associated with the private enterprise economy.

Some sectors of the economy, notably those most marginal to the war effort, were obviously affected adversely. Too little is known about French business history during the war, but it is clear that building, some elements of the textile and clothing industry, the mass of luxury, frequently artisan, trades (for which Paris in particular was noted), and perhaps much of the retail trade, all suffered reduced activity. Many sectors, however, were just as obviously essential to the economic mobilisation or adapted themselves to it. Some industries, such as automobiles, aircraft, metallurgy and chemicals received a massive and permanent boost in importance from the war.[64]

Here, state intervention, for all its restriction of market forces, actually favoured them. It was a question of regulation and co-ordination rather than temporary state ownership. Socialist demands for nationalisation and the requisitioning of factories were ignored. So was the policy of the British ministry of munitions, of expanding state-controlled armaments production through the national factories. Indeed, the bulk of war production, along with technical control and profits, was left in private hands.[65] Albert Thomas summed up the French approach.

> The method employed consisted of... calling on the good will of all, and letting them set to freely. We encouraged the industrialists. We

showed them that they would not be ruined by working for the war, and that their initiative would find its reward. We supplied them with raw material, granted loans to expand factories or to build new ones... and found them the necessary manpower.[66]

Producers were guaranteed an outlet through state contracts. This in effect meant no-risks production for a high return. The size of the return obviously depended on the price negotiated, over which something of a tussle developed between the ministry of war's munitions service and the producers, who by late 1914 had grouped themselves into regional associations. But in essence it was difficult for the munitions service to make its own estimates of production costs and to limit gains to a 'fair' profit. War profits are one of the most under-researched of all aspects of French war-time economic history. But it seems that in most firms engaged in arms production profits were well above pre-war norms. The giant engineering company Schneider (Creusot) saw them jump from a pre-war average of 6.9 per cent to 10.8 per cent in 1915–16, and to 11.2 per cent in 1916–1917.[67] The profits of Renault seem to have declined from the very high 30.9 per cent of 1914–15 (close to the immediate pre-war average) to the more modest 15.7 per cent of 1918. A closer look indicates, however, that profits remained much higher but were partly disguised in the company's massive wartime expansion.[68] In 1917, the socialist Vincent Auriol, reporting for a chamber commission on the very limited excess war profits tax introduced in July 1916, concluded that abnormally high profits were widespread, that they were frequently disguised, but that even so, only a little over 10 per cent of the revenue due under the tax for the first eighteen months of the war had been paid.[69]

State intervention in the economy, then, seems to have favoured many sectors of privately-owned industry, assuring them of high and secure profits. Nor were the gains just material. As in the case of labour, the war greatly strengthened business organisation and its power as an interest group. New organisations were founded; in 1915 the National Association for Economic Expansion (ANEE) was organised with state encouragement to turn Germany's exclusion from world markets to the benefit of French industry. In 1919, again with government encouragement, the General Confederation of French Production was established to counter the CGT. Business organisations and individual business leaders were far more important than trade unionists in the actual organisation of the war effort. A group of engineering, metallurgical and chemical industrialists was in constant touch with Thomas as minister of munitions and with his successor, Loucheur (himself a leading industrialist), while businessmen and business organisations (especially the chambers of commerce) seem to have been far more integrated locally into the war economy than were the trade unions.[70]

The war thus broke down many of the barriers which had separated the pre-war republican state from industry—whether labour or business—and it benefited much of business in particular, both economically and organisationally. This arguably amounted to an early, but as it turned out temporary, instance of 'societal corporatism', or 'concentration'—that is, the development in industrialised societies of a powerful political nexus between the state and organised economic forces.[71]

There were figures within the state who hoped to consolidate this by translating some of the experiences of admittedly exceptional wartime economic arrangements into a corporatist reform of the peacetime economy. Although they considered that basic market mechanisms had to be freed, they felt that the state should retain a coordinating role in trade and economic growth, in close association with business organisations in particular. The two principal such voices were Albert Thomas, who advocated something of a mixed economy, with the state pioneering new means of production (developing the mass production techniques publicised by the war), and Etienne Clémentel, minister for commerce and trade from 1915 to 1919, who envisaged an early version of state planning, with the state encouraging rationalisation, the development of strategically important industries, and a more coordinated export drive.[72]

The response from business was limited (though its real extent and significance have yet to be analysed). Business in general demanded a return to traditional, limited relations with the state and full economic freedom, spurred perhaps by the strong corporate identity between big business and the large small-business sector— the latter having especially distrusted the state's wartime role. The government, too, in 1919–20, favoured decontrol as rapidly and completely as possible; Loucheur, when the ministry of armaments was converted into the ministry of industrial reconstitution, declined to take up the views of his predecessor, Thomas, while Clémentel and his civil servants at commerce and trade remained a rather isolated group in the immediate post-war state. There was, in consequence, very little interest in either business or government circles for the CGT's rather more radical programme of post-war reforms.

The war had proved something of a laboratory of experimentation and ideas for the reform of relations between the state and the major organisations of the industrial economy—but it was at the level of ideas that its longer-term influence remained.[73]

Conclusion

It might appear that the wartime state was dominated by emergency and improvisation, and that its study is therefore of limited interest, important only for the history of the war itself. But in a number of respects there are fundamental connections with the more normal operation of the state throughout the Third Republic.

The war demonstrated the basic resilience of the republican state. Accusations of inefficiency compared with more authoritarian regimes had been part of conservative criticism since the humiliation of 1870 and they became central to the new, anti-parliamentary extreme right which emerged in the wake of the Dreyfus affair. But in the event the republican state showed remarkable flexibility and resourcefulness in mounting the war effort. The restoration of basic civilian control over military affairs failed to solve the intractable problem of how to devise a successful offensive when the state of military technology and the even balance of opposing forces favoured the defensive—as the disastrous attack of April 1917 showed. This was a difficulty common to all the belligerents, however, and France was not more unsuccessful than others in facing it. But the fact that the republican state preserved its essential institutional form while mounting the military effort was of integral importance to the political mobilisation, which ideologically tended to stress the defence not just of France but of the republic. At the same time, the organisation of the war economy revealed that despite its limited pre-war relations with business and bitter clashes with the trade unions, the state had the capacity to develop new relationships with both, in order to stimulate an industrial production which became a major factor in the victory of the *Entente*. Each of these aspects of the war effort—military, ideological, economic—was a facet of the other, and the resilience of the state came partly from its successful adaptation to all of them.

This resilience is ultimately incomprehensible without reference to forces and structures in the pre-war state and society. An understanding of the state's preoccupation with 'morale', requires broader reference to the breadth and depth of the legitimisation of the Third Republic as the symbolic and organisational form of the state in the forty years before 1914. Similarly, the responses of organised labour and business to the economic effort were shaped by the growth and transformation of those organisations under the accelerated tempo of industrialisation after the mid-1890s. But this relationship also works in reverse. The war reciprocally provided these longer-term forces and structures with an interesting experience, doubtless often a distorting one, but one which also cast an original light on them. The shifting balance of power between parliament, government and the high command tested to the full the possible arrangements for apportioning power within the republican political system as such. The censorship was clearly exceptional. But the relationship of governments to the mass-circulation press raises important questions about the process of political mobilisation in peacetime. Finally, the various economic arrangements introduced during the war appeared to have been one more transient feature of the emergency, once it was over. But many of the themes emerged subsequently, during the Depression, under Vichy, after 1945—so that now, in terms of the economic role of the state, the first world war seems something of a turning point.

Notes

All books in French are published in Paris, and in English are published in London, unless otherwise indicated.

Abbreviations

BUG	*Bulletin des Usines de Guerre*	*JO*	*Journal Officiel*
FHS	*French Historical Studies*	*MS*	*Le Mouvement social*
JCH	*Journal of Contemporary History*	*RHGM*	*Revue d'Histoire de la Guerre Mondiale*
JMH	*Journal of Modern History*	*RHMC*	*Revue d'Histoire moderne et contemporaine*

1. P. Renouvin, *Les Formes du gouvernement de guerre* (1925), pp 3, 25.
2. More recent interest has centred on state intervention in the economy, and especially on the material contained in the copious private papers of Albert Thomas, under-secretary and later minister in charge of the munitions effort (Archives Nationales, Paris; see note 72 below). Propaganda, censorship and the press have received relatively little attention since G. Weill's pioneering article of 1933 ('Les gouvernements et la presse pendant la guerre', *RHGM*, April 1933, pp 97–118) at least from the angle of the political mobilisation of the war effort. Censorship records have been used to study public opinion by the late P. Renouvin and his followers (see esp. *RHMC*, XV, Jan–March 1968, special issue on 1917). The standard work on relations between parliament, government and the high command, which encompasses many of the memoirs and self justifications published up to 1939, though not the collections of

private papers opened only more recently—is itself rather old now (J. C. King, *Generals and politicians: conflict between France's high command, parliament and government, 1915–1918* (Cambridge, Mass., 1951). The work of G. Pedroncini (see notes 3, 10 & 20 below) has begun to remove these questions from the battefield of personalities, while M. Baumont ('Abel Ferry et les étapes du contrôle aux armées, 1914–18', *RHMC*, XV, Jan.–March 1968, pp 162–208) has used private papers to supplement the invaluable material on the struggle for parliamentary control over the army contained in Ferry's two published volumes (*La Guerre vue d'en bas et d'en haut*, 1920, and *Les Carnets secrets d'Abel Ferry*, 1957). Despite D. R. Watson's recent biography (*Georges Clemenceau*, 1974), there has been no serious, *comprehensive* analysis of the nature and significance of Clemenceau's assumption of power in November 1917, and of 'treason' and 'defeatism' as highly charged terms in a polarising wartime political vocabulary. Overall, there has been little attempt either to relate the different aspects of the wartime state to each other, or to see how the war explored and tested the parameters of the republican state as it had developed since 1870.

3. J. C. King, op. cit.; A. Ferry, *Les Carnets secrets d'Abel Ferry*; M. Baumont, op. cit.; G. Pedroncini, 'Les rapports du gouvernement et du Haut Commandement en France en 1917; *RHMC*, XV, Jan–March 1968, pp 122–32.
4. P. Renouvin, *Les Formes du gouvernement de guerre*, pp 3–50. The 'state of siege' legislation dated from 1849, and had been modified in 1878, after the MacMahon scare, to ensure that its application should be limited and kept under parliamentary surveillance.
5. Ibid., pp 31–2.
6. J. C. King, op. cit. esp. pp 138–9 on Joffre's acceptance in December 1916 of his effective dismissal from active command. See also P. Varillon, *Joffre* (1956), pp 516–23.
7. On this, see J. C. King, op. cit., for the 'Affaire Sarrail' (pp 67–88, 131–9).
8. General Pédoya, *La Commission de l'Armée pendant la Grande Guerre (1921);* G. Terrail, *Au sein des commissions* (1924); M. Baumont, op cit., A. Ferry, op. cit., J. C. King, op. cit., P. Allard, *Les Dessous de la Guerre révélés par les Comités Secrets* (1932).
9. P. Renouvin, *Les Formes du gouvernement de guerre*, pp 16–17, 76–77.
10. G. Pedroncini, 'Remarques sur la décision militaire en France pendant la Grande Guerre', *RHMC*, XX, Jan.–March 1973, pp 139–52.
11. For an inside view of the Vivani government's defence of Joffre (especially through Millerand, the minister for war), see *Les Carnets secrets d'Abel Ferry*, pp 34–120. For copious examples of the long, obstructive action fought by the high command against parliamentary investigation, see General Pédoya, op. cit., pp 17–40.
12. *Les Carnets secrets d'Abel Ferry*, pp 141–51; P. Allard, *Les Dessous de la Guerre révélés par les Comités Secrets*, pp 1–51; G. Suarez, *Briand. Sa vie, son oeuvre, avec son journal*, vol. 3, *Le Pilote dans la Tourmente, 1914–1916* (1939), pp 294–393; G. Bonnefous, *Histoire Politique de la Troisième République*, vol. 2, *La Grande Guerre 1914–1918* (1967), pp 130–56.
13. G. Pedroncini, 'Remarques sur la décision militaire…', op. cit.
14. P. Avril, *Politics in France* (1969) pp 47–90; D. Thomson, *Democracy in France since 1870* (1958), pp 75–115; R. D. Anderson, *France, 1870–1914. Politics and society* (1977), pp 61–87; P. Warwick, 'Ideology, culture and gamesmanship in French politics', *JMH*, 50, no. 4, December 1978, pp 631–59.

15. P. Guiral and G. Thuillier, *La Vie quotidienne des députés en France de 1871 à 1914* (1980), pp 221–55.
16. J. C. King, op. cit., pp 123–4.
17. When Ferry, on 18 February 1916, made an early (and premature) attempt to get the Chamber to impose on the government the obligation to restore parliamentary control over the army, 76% of his support came from Socialists and Radicals (85 and 32 votes respectively: see M. Baumont, op. cit., p. 184). The Socialist parliamentary group consistently demanded the reimposition of government and parliamentary control (*Le Parti Socialiste, la Guerre et la Paix. Toutes les résolutions et tous les documents du Parti Socialiste de Juillet 1914 à fin 1917*, 1918, pp 75–8).
18. *Les Carnets secrets D'Abel Ferry*, p. 69.
19. P. Avril, op. cit., pp 38–9.
20. P. Renouvin, 'L'Opinion publique et la Guerre en 1917,' *RHMC*, XV, Jan–March 1968, pp 4–23; G. Pedroncini, *Les Mutineries de 1917* (1967); J-J. Becker, *Les Français dans la Grande Guerre* (1980), pp 182–232.
21. L.-J. Malvy, *Mon crime* (1921), pp 270–83; D. R. Watson, op. cit., pp 286–9; G. J. Adam, *Treason and tragedy: French war trials* (1929); J. Caillaux, *Mes prisons* (1920), p. 64.
22. J. Caillaux, op. cit., pp 29–63 for a partisan but important view of this; E. Weber, *Action française* (Stanford, California, 1962), pp 103–12.
23. D. R. Watson, op. cit., pp 271–2; E. Weber, op. cit., pp 108–10.
24. G. Clemenceau, *Discours de Guerre* (1968), p. 132.
25. R. Poincaré, *Au Service de la France*, vol. 10, *Victoire et Armistice* (1933), p. 171; A. Kriegel, *Aux Origines du Communisme français* (1964), pp 193–4; D. R. Watson, op. cit., pp 284–7.
26. D. Ligou, *Histoire du socialisme en France, 1871–1961* (1962), p. 296.
27. S. Berstein, 'Le Parti radical–socialiste durant la Première Guerre mondiale', in P. Fridenson, ed., *1914–1918: L'autre front* (1977), pp 65–79.
28. H. Sée, *Histoire de la Ligue des Droits de l'Homme, 1898–1926* (1927), pp 143–65; J. Horne, 'Labour leaders and the post-war world, 1914—1919. A comparative study of wartime attitudes in the Confédération Générale du Travail and the British labour movement.' (Ph.D., University of Sussex, 1980), pp 322–5 for the republican coalition.
29. J. C. King, *Foch versus Clemenceau. France and German dismemberment, 1918–1919* (Cambridge, Mass., 1960).
30. G. Demartial, *La mobilisation des consciences* (1922; rev. ed., 1927), pp 116–7, for an example of this tendency, and for a criticism, H. D. Lasswell, *Propaganda technique in the great war* (New York, 1927), pp 4–6.
31. P. Renouvin, 'L'Opinion publique et la guerre en 1917', op. cit.; J.-J. Becker, *1914: Comment les Français sont entrés dans la guerre* (1977) and *Les Français dans la Grande Guerre*; J.-L. Robert, 'Chronique et réflexions: les luttes ouvrières pendant la Première Guerre mondiale', in *Cahiers d'Histoire de l'Institut Maurice Thorez*, no. 23 (Oct.–Dec., 1977), pp 28–65.
32. H. D. Lasswell, op. cit., pp 6–10, 184–6.
33. For working class and labour responses to the war see J.-L. Robert's summary, op. cit.; A. Kriegel, op. cit.; J.-J. Becker, *Le Carnet B. les Pouvoirs publics et l'antimilitarisme avant la guerre de 1914* (1973); J.-J. Becker and A. Kriegel, *1914, La Guerre et le mouvement ouvrier français* (1964); J.-J. Becker, *Les Français dans la grande guerre*.
34. There is a dearth of studies of the most important organisations in civil society

and their wartime relationships with the state (churches, labour, business etc.) For a beginning, see M. Fine, *Towards corporatism: The movement for Capital-labour collaboration in France, 1914–1936* (Ph.D., University of Wisconsin-Madison, 1971), chs. 1 and 2; J. Horne, op. cit.; H. D. Peiter, *Men of goodwill: French businessmen and the first world war* (Ph.D., University of Michigan—Ann Arbor, 1973); J. Godfrey, *Bureaucracy, industry and politics in France during the first world war: A study of some interrelations* (Ph.D. Oxford, 1974).

35. M. Hardie and K. Sabin, *War posters issued by belligerent and neutral nations* (1920).

36. See A. Thomas's speech to the workers at Le Creusot, late April 1916, in *BUG*, no. 1, May 1916, p. 2; Millerand was notorious for having rhetorically declared the wartime suspension of social welfare laws; for the medal, see *BUG*, no. 14, 30 July 1917, p. 107.

37. P. Ory, *La République en fête. Les 14 Juillet* (Paris, 1980), pp 19–21.

38. G. Weill, op. cit.

39. Figures from C. Bellenger, J. Godechot *et al, Histoire Générale de la Presse Française*, vol. 3, *De 1871 à 1940* (1972), p. 296.

40. Ibid., pp 407–55.

41. Ibid., pp 412–20; M. Berger and P. Allard, *Les secrets de la censure pendant la guerre* (1932); G. Demartial, op. cit., pp 145–64.

42. F. Amaury, *Histoire du plus grand quotidien de la 111e République. Le Petit Parisien, 1876–1944*. Vol. 2., *Le Petit Parisien. Instrument de propagande au service du Régime* (1972), pp 1073–6; G. Demartial, op. cit., p. 140; A. Billy, *La guerre des journaux Chronique de la presse parisienne, 1917–1918* (1919), p. 148, for further examples.

43. C. Bellenger *et al*, op. cit., pp 431–3; M. Berger and P. Allard, *Les secrets de la censure...*, p. 172.

44. This is true even of the apparently exhaustive study by F. Amaury, op. cit.

45. C. Bellenger *et al.* op. cit., p. 430.

46. C. Bellenger *et al*, op. cit., p. 431; F. Amaury, op. cit., p. 1106.

47. A. Billy, op. cit., p. 72.

48. F. Hennequin, *Du Régime de la presse pendant la Guerre* (1916), p. 6. See also G. Weill, op. cit., and P. Renouvin, *Les Formes du gouvernement de guerre*, pp 38–49.

49. P. Berger and M. Allard, *Les secrets de la censure...*, p. 208.

50. Ibid., p. 238.

51. *JO, Chambre des Députés, Débats parlementaires*, Jan.–March 1916, p. 101: F. Hennequin, op. cit., pp 12–28.

52. A. Fontaine, *L'Industrie française pendant la guerre* (1923) pp 49–85; General Pédoya, op. cit., pp 259–325.

53. M. Ferro. *La Grande Guerre, 1914–1918* (1969), p. 213.

54. See D. Halévy, *Pour l'étude de la Troisieme République* (1937), pp 39–42.

55. P. Baudry, *Guide de l'ouvrier militaire affecté dans une usine privée travaillant pour la défense nationale* (n.d.); circular of 16 October 1915 clarifying the position of the mobilised worker, in *BUG*, no. 12, 17 July 1916, pp 93–4.

56. J.-L- Robert, op. cit., pp 41–2; L. March, *Le mouvement des prix et des salaires pendant la guerre* (1925), pp 244, 297.

57. J.-L. Robert, op. cit., pp 47–62, and E. Shorter and C. Tilly, *Strikes in France 1830–1968* (1974), pp 122–7, for strikes. On women in the wartime labour force, see M. Frois, *La Santé et le travail des femmes pendant la Guerre* (1926); L. March, op. cit., pp 287–95, on women's wages; M. Dubesset *et al*, 'Les

Mutionnettes de la Seine' in P. Fridenson (ed), *1914–1918: L'autre front*, op. cit., pp 189–219; J. McMillan, 'The effects of the first world war on the social condition of women in France' (Ph.D., Oxford, 1976).

58. In reality, other social groups bore even greater hardship—notably the peasants (P. Sorlin, *La Société française*, vol. 2, *1914–1968*, 1971, pp 23–4).

59. See L. Jouhaux and M. Bidegaray, *Contre les Compagnies—Pour la Nation* (1917) for the views of the majority leaders of the CGT and the railway workers' federation. For parliamentary socialists' views on requisitioning, see *JO, Chambre des Députés, Débats parlementaires*, April–July 1917, pp 1091–2.

60. J.-J. Becker, *Le Carnet B...*, op. cit.; R. Picard, *Le Mouvement syndical durant la guerre* (1927); B. Georges, D. Tintant and M.-A. Renauld, *Léon Jouhaux*, vol. 1, *Dès origines à 1921* (1962); M. Fine, op. cit., J. Horne, op. cit.

61. J.-L. Robert, *La scission syndicale, 1914–1921. Essai de reconnaissance de formes* (Thèse de 3e cycle, Paris I, 1975), pp 350–2.

62. J. Horne, op. cit., pp 104–35.

63. A. François-Poncet, *La Vie et l'oeuvre de Robert Pinot* (1927), pp 223, 227; H. D. Peiter, op. cit., pp 150–1. For a survey of the post-war polemical discussion on state economic intervention, see C. Bloch, 'The literature of economic reconstruction in France,' in *Manchester Guardian Commercial Special*, no. 4, Jan 1923, pp 744–8.

64. C. Gide and W. Oualid, *Le Bilan de la guerre pour la France* (1931), pp 327–44; A. Fontaine, op. cit., pp 231–63, 367–403; P. Fridenson, *Histoire des usines Renault*, vol. 1, *Naissance de la grande entreprise, 1898–1939* (1972), pp 89–119.

65. G. Hardach, 'La mobilisation industrielle en 1914–1918: production, planification et idéologie', in P. Fridenson, ed., *1914–1918 L'autre front* op. cit., pp 80–109; A. Hennebicque, 'Albert Thomas et le régime des usines de guerre, 1915–1917'; ibid, pp 112–44.

66. Archives Nationales, 94 AP 141.

67. G. Hardach. *The first world war, 1914–18* (1973; Eng. tr., 1977), p. 106.

68. P. Fridenson, op. cit., p. 113.

69. *JO. Documents Parlementaires, Chambre des Députés*, 1917, annexe 3052, pp 252–6, and annexe no. 4053, pp 1852–6.

70. M. Fine, op. cit.; H. D. Peiter, op. cit (esp for local business participation); A. François-Poncet, op. cit., pp 192–228; R. Pinot, *Le comité des Forges de France au service de la Nation. Août 1914–Novembre 1918* (1919).

71. R. J. Harrison, *Pluralism and corporatism. The political evolution of modern democracies* (1980) pp 64–94; P. C. Schmitter, 'Still the century of corporatism?', in *Review of Politics*, 36, no. 1 (Jan. 1974), pp 83–131 (see esp. pp 103–4); C. S. Maier, *Recasting bourgeois Europe* (Princeton, New Jersey, 1975), pp 3–15.

72. On Thomas see note 65 above; M. Rebérioux and P. Fridenson, 'Albert Thomas, pivot du réformisme français', *MS*, April–June 1974, pp 85–97; M. Fine, 'Albert Thomas: a reformer's vision of modernization, 1914–32,' *JCH*, 1977, vol. 12, pp 545–64, and M. Fine 'Guerre et réformisme en France, 1914–1918,' in *Recherches*, no. 32/33, September 1978, pp 302–24; for Clémentel, see M. Trachtenburg, '"A new economic order", Clémentel and French diplomacy during the first world war,' *FHS*, X, no. 2 (1977), pp 315–41; H. D. Peiter, op. cit; J. Godfrey, op. cit.

73. M. Fine, *Towards corporatism...*, op. cit.; J. Horne, op. cit., pp 391–417.

A Protestant parliament and a Protestant state: some reflections on government and minority in Ulster 1921-43.

Paul Bew

> I have always said that I am an Orangeman first and a politician and a member of this parliament afterwards... All I boast is that we have a Protestant parliament and a Protestant state.
>
> Sir James Craig

In the spring and summer of 1920 it seemed to the Unionist leadership in Belfast that British power in Ireland was collapsing rapidly under the impact of guerilla war in the south and west. The Belfast Unionist leadership, known colloquially as the 'Old Town Hall' circle, demanded more repression from the British state. At the same time, their working-class supporters in the Ulster Unionist Labour Association (UULA) held meetings pledging support for the security forces and demanding more vigorous counter-insurgency measures. After one such gathering in the shipyards in July, attacks began on catholics and workers identified as Labour party members and socialists. They spread throughout the engineering industry and some sections of the linen industry to result in over 8,000 expulsions within a week.

Partly because of the new national situation, the employers and leading unionists not only acquiesced in such events but justified them—in sharp contrast to their attitude to previous expulsions (e.g. in 1893 and 1912). A shift in political relations within the Protestant class bloc had taken place. In its anxiety to reestablish a militant basis for resistance to the republican threat which could operate independently of the British authorities, the Unionist leadership had been forced to make considerable concessions to the Orange section of the working class. Inevitably, they strove to confer institutional and official status on this arrangement. Popular protestant practices of workplace exclusivism became linked to the successful efforts of Sir Edward Carson and Sir James Craig to secure British government funds for the UULA based constabularies in Belfast—the embryonic form of the 'B' Special constabulary.[1]

These developments had crucial implications for the process of state formation in Northern Ireland. The new apparatuses of the state acquired a decidedly populist stamp. Belfast catholics, perhaps less intransigent than their rural counterparts, were given no incentive to come to terms with partition. Furthermore, the in-built populist bias made it exceptionally difficult for any conciliatory tendencies within the Unionist leadership to develop.

The fundamental importance of religious and national identity is undeniable in Ireland. But it is clear, however, that in this instance class relations within the protestant bloc[2] did a great deal to determine the limits of its relationship to the catholic bloc. This essay is an attempt to follow up some of the implications of this thesis. At the same time, of course, it is impossible to ignore the role of factors external to the Irish social formation, in particular the British state. For the question immediately arises—what was the attitude of leading British politicians in government to these developments in Belfast in 1920? As Patricia Jalland has recently reminded us, by the time of the 1912 home rule crisis Winston Churchill and David Lloyd George had reached the unavoidable conclusion that Ulster could not be coerced into a united Ireland.[3] Nevertheless it should be noted that by 1922 the *prime* objective of British policy was to prevent a militantly republican government under de Valera being formed in Dublin. There was, it should be noted, a difference between Lloyd George and his circle—including the treasury—and Churchill in the colonial office about how to handle the problem. Lloyd George held that open oppression of the catholics in the north seriously undermined the new government in Dublin. The treasury for its part bitterly resented the expense of the Ulster security forces.

Churchill was equally concerned to prevent a de Valera government. Interestingly, he was a supporter of the concept of long term Irish unity, but this would have to be based on the coalescence of the conservative forces, north and south. However, for this benign development to occur, he reasoned, it was essential for the recently established provisional government in Dublin to smash de Valera. There was therefore nothing to be gained by strong criticism of the Unionist security forces in Belfast.

Churchill held the line against both Lloyd George's inclinations and the treasury's more fervent objections until June 1922 and the outbreak of the civil war in the south. This soon reached the point of no return in its intensity. There was no further need for the British government to interfere in the affairs of the Belfast regime.

The whole nature of London–Dublin–Belfast relations was transformed. There was no longer a political constraint on British policy towards the north, the constraint of maintaining the Dublin provisional government's credibility. Subsequent British attempts to interfere with the development of the northern state were fitful and individualistic rather than the product of concerted government effort. Internal division had prevented such action precisely at the time it would have counted for most.[4]

'Fitful' and 'individualistic' but not without interest. Patrick Buckland in one of his recent studies argues that anti-catholic discrimination in matters of law and order 'developed almost accidentally out of the confused troubles of the years 1921/2'.[5] Yet this thesis is difficult to sustain, when we consider, for example, the case of the Ulster government's military adviser, Major-General A. Solly-Flood.

In the spring of 1922 Solly-Flood had been appointed to his post on the advice of the former chief of the imperial general staff and ardent unionist, Sir Henry Wilson. It is quite clear that Wilson intended Flood to act as a counterbalance to those sectarian tendencies which he felt were implicit in such security forces as the 'B' Specials. Solly-Flood did indeed act in this way. He was a sharp critic of the 'B' Specials and called for their complete reorganisation. By September 1922 the Northern Ireland government had removed the troublesome Solly-Flood, though he and some of his staff were to plague the regime with complaints and 'leaks' for some years. The removal of Flood was skilfully presented at the time as simply an economy move, which it most decidedly was not.

After 1925 the Irish republican threat to the northern Irish state's existence had receded somewhat. Changes in electoral law had also strengthened the position of the Unionists. As H. Dixon, the Unionist chief whip, wrote to a parliamentary colleague—somewhat ominously—in this context: 'There is no room in Ulster for differences of opinion and people have got to learn this sooner or later'.[6] Sir Wilfrid Spender, the English officer who played a big role in the Ulster Volunteer Force and later became head of the Northern Ireland civil service from 1925–44, recalls being present at an interview on the boundary commission between his own premier,

Sir James Craig, and the Irish Free State leader, W. T. Cosgrave. 'Mr Cosgrave burst into tears and said that Lord Craigavon had won all down the line and begged and entreated him not to make things more difficult for him'.[7] Questions then remain—why did the northern Irish state retain its protestant and sectarian character in this epoch? Why did it not go along the path of compromise—of that political style of 'decency and consensus'[8] which Robert Skidelsky tells us characterised inter-war British politics? It is true that the state faced a large (one third), recalcitrant, catholic and nationalist minority who denied, with varying degrees of intensity, its right to exist. But as this was a time when the catholic nationalist challenge in the state was notably divided and incoherent, surely it was the time also for a conciliatory policy on the part of the Unionist leadership? The gains, in terms of increased security of the state, were potentially enormous.

An examination of the archives has revealed the dynamic of the state. This has shown not unanimity but a substantial degree of internal Unionist division. The present writer, in collaboration with others, has characterised this as a divide between 'populist' and 'antipopulist'. The populist grouping was based most firmly on the prime minister, Sir James Craig, the minister of home affairs, Sir R. Dawson Bates and, slightly more ambiguously, John Andrews at the ministry of labour. The anti-populist grouping was based mainly on the ministry of finance—in particular, Hugh Pollock, the minister for most of this period, and his chief aide, Sir Wilfrid Spender. The populist group sought to maintain the unity of the protestant majority at all costs, even that of visible and ritual exclusion of catholic minority. The anti-populist grouping feared the effect of this strategy, first and foremost on the British government, but secondly on the protestant community—who were in this view being 'molly-coddled'—and lastly, on the catholic community who would be confirmed in their nationalism. Populist strategies dominated but their excesses were modified by anti-populist pressures, thus giving the state a certain rather special type of resilience.

One obvious area of conflict between the two groups was security policy. Sir Wilfrid Spender shared Solly-Flood's distaste for the 'B' Specials.[9] But he was also deeply concerned about the cost of the Northern Ireland security forces in general. Yet despite the efforts of the ministry of finance to establish control over other government departments (in the manner of the British treasury) the Royal Ulster Constabulary enjoyed superior wages to those of their British counterparts in the period 1922–31. For a brief period parity was then achieved only to be undermined again. In October 1932, the ministry of home affairs 'forgot' to apply the recent British cut on police pay in Northern Ireland.[10] There were, of course, good reasons. In October 1932 Belfast experienced the outdoor relief riots, that unique occasion when catholic and protestant worker rioted not against each other but against an oppressive and niggardly system of outdoor relief.[11] As the Cabinet paper recently reproduced by Dr A. C. Hepburn in his valuable collection of documents has shown, the police were on their last legs.[12] Nevertheless, Britain too faced problems of public disorder and, it is clear, anyway, that the capacity of the ministry of home affairs to flout the ministry of finance was a consistent feature of the period.[13]

Nor was home affairs the only offender. The ministry of agriculture was also a target for bitter criticism. It is worth making this point as, in recent writing, agriculture has been taken as the one department of the Northern Ireland government which offered a successful example of devolution working 'to advance regional interests'.[14] Whatever the department's technical achievements, it remains true, as Spender noted in his diary in mid-1933, that no less than four administrative officers had resigned from agriculture rather than accept the department's haphazard and unprofessional style of work.[15] Sadly, the rancours of sectarianism afflicted agriculture as much, if not more than, other departments. This may be demonstrated by reference to the incident in March 1943, when Craig's successor as prime minister, John Miller Andrews (recently somewhat generously described as 'conscientious, energetic and humane'[16]), took Spender aside to tell him

> ...we could only take into our service those who were loyal. He then went on to refer to the position of the ministry of agriculture, where he said there was a large number of Roman Catholic inspectors. This caused a great deal of difficulty. In fact, he knew a case in Comber where it was shown conclusively that unfair discrimination had been made by one of these inspectors. He knew a branch of the ministry of agriculture in which practically the whole staff were Roman Catholics. I said that I thought he must be referring to the slaughterhouse branch, in which Protestants refused to work because of the conditions of employment. This was the case.[17]

Spender added:

> Personally I am of opinion that the prime minister is making a mistake in going into this matter at all ... he would find it a source of embarrassment if he produced any statistics or defended himself in this

matter. Offence would be caused in Great Britain if he took a bigoted point of view, and he would also further exacerbate the difficulties between the British government and Eire: on the other hand it was a mistake to encourage representations which showed any intolerance amongst his followers.

The present writer has laid considerable stress on this populist/anti-populist division. This line of argument is certainly open to criticism. Was this division, as the economic historian David Johnson has argued in a recent review, not simply a reflection of the 'natural' division in government between spending and non-spending departments[18]—a division which is chronicled skilfully for the rest of Ireland by Dr Ronan Fanning in his recent study of the Irish department of finance.[19]

David Johnson's argument is perhaps not entirely satisfactory—if only because it omits any consideration of the different attitudes of the two groups towards the catholic community. It is also vital to note that there is a fundamental difference between the finances of a subordinate parliament within the United Kingdom in Belfast, and that of a more or less independent state in Dublin. The point is—Dublin talked about spending its own money, Belfast talked more and more about the implications, as the 1930s progressed, of becoming increasingly dependent on British largesse.

As the treasury by various 'fudges', 'wangles' and 'dodges'—the precise words used by Sir Richard Hopkins, the treasury controller[20]—increased its subventions to Northern Ireland in order to maintain the standard of living in the province, attitudes in Ulster's ruling circles to this practice differed. Thus the dominant populist group—Craig, Bates and Andrews—were happy enough to take the risk of increasing loss of financial independence in order to maintain the political support of the protestant community. The anti-populist grouping in the ministry of finance was less than happy about this calculation. This attitude permeated the senior officials at finance, as may be seen from the memoirs of those involved.

Patrick Shea, in his moving and justly celebrated autobiography, has recalled his own unease:

> My concern was with the business of government. We were becoming agents where we had been principals. I felt that a community having been given authority in the management of its affairs, however limited that authority might be, should maintain and use it to the limit.[21]

When he became aware of the implications of Lord Beveridge's report for Northern Ireland, Shea was moved to observe:

The government should consider taking steps to hold our living standards somewhat below those in Great Britain. We might begin by looking at the possibility of applying a 'minus factor' to the very generous Beveridge proposals.[22]

G. C. Duggan, another prominent official, shortly after his retirement expressed himself in the same vein in 1950: 'Stormont sold itself by adopting socialist legislation... the dividing line between Ulster unionism and British socialism has become very tenuous; the paths of the fellow traveller and the socialist state... have become merged'.[23] It is possible to smile at the political naïvete of all this. Shea's 'minus factor' was hardly likely to be introduced by a Unionist government worried by war time electoral losses to Labour. Duggan's description of Ulster in 1950 as 'merged' in a 'socialist state' is at least controversial. Shea recalls one of his political masters commenting on the minus factor proposal: 'You know you are asking me to commit political suicide'. With his customary good humour Shea acknowledged: 'He was probably right'.[24]

Nevertheless it is quite clear that, politically, the anti-populist group had a more exalted view of the autonomy of the Belfast parliament and with that conception went a more fervent commitment to avoidance of overdependence on British money. Hugh Pollock, the minister of finance, had made it clear that he regarded Northern Ireland as 'an autonomous state with a federal relationship to the United Kingdom'[25] and with a responsibility for its own financial affairs. For the populists Stormont was merely a 'subordinate authority' which Westminster had set up for its convenience and which it had therefore an obligation to support.

It is also certain that even within the spectrum of inter-war non-socialist opinion, the anti-populist group's views on economic and social policy were well to the right of that of the populist groupings. A typical passage in Sir Wilfrid Spender's diary in late 1938 runs:

I was talking to the head of one of the big London banks last week who said that in his opinion 90% of the people were living above their proper incomes—a most alarming statement.[26]

On the other hand, the populist group tended to favour not the restrictionist views of the banks but the more pragmatic, 'productionist' outlook of the business community. They were capable at times of a certain vulgar practical Keynesianism. As Craig in 1931 had explained:

He had been spending the great bulk of his time recently in consultation with the heads of the great business concerns in Ulster, whose advice he always liked to take in preference to that of banks and stockholders, and although it might seem to be impertinent of him to say so, if Britain had obtained advice from the manufacturers, a great deal of misfortune might have been avoided.[27]

The populist/anti-populist division cannot be reduced simply to the division between spending and non-spending departments. It was too closely associated with the issues of anti-catholicism, the status of the local parliament—'federal parliament' or 'subordinate regional authority'—and more general views on social policy.

Nevertheless, David Johnson, makes a good point when he argues that 'the populist/anti-populist division within the government was by no means as rigid'[28] as the present writer and others have suggested. While it is clear that the populist/anti-populist division did fundamentally determine the working of the state, it is wiser to stress rather more a degree of unity of purpose within the government. Both populists and anti-populists had a shared nightmare called 'Connolly socialism'—the much rumoured thirty two county socialist republic. (It is not necessary to argue that these fears had any substantial basis in fact.) Let us consider the case of Sir Wilfrid Spender. Spender was increasingly plagued by the ambiguities of his own position. He had entered Irish politics partly in opposition to the 'Tammany Hall style' of Irish nationalist politics, yet he now found himself administering what he saw as a unionist variety of the same style of politics. Spender's other main motivation for his Irish involvement was his obsession with imperial security. He had always felt that Ireland was strategically vital for England. However, even his assumptions on this score were soon called into question. In 1937 Major-General H. Montgomery, whose pro-imperial credentials Spender fully accepted, publicly argued that some form of Irish unity on a dominion basis was essential to British security in the event of a second world war. Only then would the island of Ireland present no threat to Britain.

Spender was caught in a quandary. He admired Montgomery's resolute acceptance of unpalatable conclusions on the grounds of imperial necessity. Nevertheless he felt it necessary to write to Montgomery to dispute his arguments. Spender stressed both the alleged leftward trend in the Irish Free State (of which he knew little) and, more interestingly, assessed the implications for Ulster:

> If the news which reaches me from the Free State is true that communism is gaining ground every day and that both the church and the more conservative leaders are losing ground, I do not think that even the sacrificing of Northern Ireland and the creation of an Irish

Dominion would ultimately result in the strengthening of the Empire...

I am strongly concerned that the Ulster working classes appreciate the benefits of the British connection, but if this were severed a large proportion of those resident in Northern Ireland would change to socialistic tendencies.[29]

Spender thus revealed that one political calculation remained decisive—the anti-socialist one. In arguing this it is not intended to suggest—as Dr. Tom Garvin has suggested in an otherwise perceptive and acute discussion—that the northern Irish working class was 'hopelessly split by the manipulations of the bourgeois state'.[30] Nevertheless, this political calculation or fear was there, and if it was there in so principled (in a certain sense) and upright a man as Spender, it was certainly present in the rather less restrained anti-populist group. And if it was there it must have had effects on society in general.

An acknowledgement of the justice of David Johnson's point here may allow us to come to terms with another friendly critic. Patrick Hillyard, himself the co-author of an important book on the northern Irish state, has argued in a discriminating review article,[31] that the 'major problem' with the 'populist/anti-populist' analysis 'is how to reconcile the populists' dominance and their apparent extravagance with public funds with the very low levels of public expenditure which occurred in the inter-war years'.[32] For example, Hillyard is able to point to the fact that in social security and housing the Northern Ireland levels of public expenditure were lower than in the rest of the United Kingdom. The unemployment insurance scheme was far narrower in application than in Great Britain; it excluded a larger proportion of workers and their contribution conditions were more severe. As a result, a far larger proportion of people were forced to seek help from the Poor Law. Expenditure under the Poor Law, however, was considerably lower than in other parts of the United Kingdom. A similar pattern may be seen in housing. Local authorities provided only 15 per cent of all new housing built between the wars compared with 25 per cent in England and Wales.

Hillyard's point is well taken. However, it is vital to note that all the areas of low spending he mentions affected most directly the life chances of working class catholics and only a minority of working class protestants at the lower end of the scale. Populists and anti-populists were able to accept these policies because they conflicted with the political aims of neither.

It would always have been difficult for any Unionist leadership to pursue a softer policy towards catholics. The denial by the Irish nationalist body politic of the right to self-determination for the protestant community (a right so vigorously claimed for Irish nationalists) was a profound obstacle to any improvement in community relations. Nevertheless it is difficult not to feel that in so far as there was any opportunity for generosity in the epoch—though it would obviously have involved massive political risks—a chance was perhaps missed.

Notes

1. These passages are based on the work of Henry Patterson. See, in particular, his *Class conflict and sectarianism: the protestant working class and the Belfast labour movement* (Belfast, 1980). It is regrettable that the otherwise interesting work of Brian Barton dismisses these events in the shipyard in a couple of lines, see his *The government of Northern Ireland 1920–3: the development of Northern Irish government policy in relation to law and order* (Belfast, 1980), p. 5.
2. These have recently been reappraised in Peter Gibbon's discussion of Patterson's book in *Sociological Review*, 29, no. 3 (Aug. 1981).
3. Patricia Jalland, *The Liberals and Ireland: The Ulster question in British politics to 1914* (Brighton, 1980), pp 58–65.
4. See Paul Bew, Peter Gibbon, Henry Patterson, *The state in Northern Ireland: political forces and social class* (2nd ed., Manchester, 1980), pp 50–6. For a complementary analysis, see J. McColgan, 'Partition and the Irish administration 1920–22' in *Administration*, 28, no. 4 (1980), pp 147–182.
   More controversial and polemical is the work of M. Farrell; see his 'The Pro-treatyites and partition', *Papers presented to the seventh annual Sociological Association of Ireland* (April, 1980). That distinguished scholar John Grigg in his recent essay 'Lloyd George and the partition of Ireland', *Moirae*, 6 (Trinity, 1981), pp 1–16, has cogently discussed Lloyd George's record, though without specific reference to his attitude towards the northern minority.
5. *The factory of grievances: devolved government in Northern Ireland 1921–39* (Dublin, 1979). This interesting discussion (pp 179–205) of security is slightly weakened by a relatively low utilisation of London sources and by the decision not to use Dublin sources at all. Buckland's more recent work adopts a much more sophisticated stance. In his impressive biography of *Sir James Craig* (Dublin, 1980), p. 87, he correctly points out that Solly-Flood was also capable at times of anti-catholic partisanship. Even more recently, Buckland's *A history of Northern Ireland* (Dublin, 1981), p. 42, adopts an assessment of the Solly-Flood affair which is explicitly close to that in Bew *et al*, op. cit., pp 57–62.
6. P.R.O.N.I., 7 B/201; the document is dated 23.8.1924. For these changes, see D. Pringle, 'Electoral systems and political manipulation: a case study of Northern Ireland in the 1920s' in *Economic and Social Review* 11, no. 3 (April, 1980), pp 187–205.
7. Sir Wilfrid Spender's financial diary, 24–29 May 1943 (F.D.) (P.R.O.N.I., D715). This comment may be found in one of Spender's frequent retrospective historical notes.

8. R. Skidelsky, 'The reception of Keynesianism' in M. Keynes (ed.), *Essays on John Maynard Keynes* (Cambridge, 1975), p. 101.

9. P. Shea, *Voices and the sound of drums* (Belfast, 1981), p. 138.

10. See Philip McVicker's discussion in *Books Ireland* (Feb. 1980).

11. P. Bew and C. Norton, 'The unionist state and the outdoor relief riots of 1932' in *Economic and Social Review* 10, no. 3 (April, 1979). Sir James Craig did not dismiss these events. He reacted by flouting the British treasury in setting up a substantial public works scheme. This was on top of the concessions on police pay.

12. See A. C. Hepburn (ed.), *The conflict of nationality in modern Ireland* (London, 1980), p. 164. The document here cited is P.R.O.N.I., 4/304/21.

13. Bew *et al*, op. cit., ch. 3.

14. D. W. Harkness's review of P. Buckland, *Factory of grievances* in *E.H.R.*, xcvi, no. 378 (Jan. 1981), p. 176.

15. P.R.O.N.I., D 715, F.D. (24 July 1932).

16. P. Buckland, *A history of Northern Ireland*, p. 32. It must be admitted, however, that in one unacknowledged respect Andrews lived up to this billing. In the late thirties he did display a consistent and generous interest in the wages of agricultural labourers.

17. *F.D.*, 29 March 1943. Spender tacitly assisted the rise of Sir Basil Brooke who deposed Andrews in 1943. Spender speaks of Brooke's 'outstanding qualities' and indeed in this period he was far from being the 'lazy man of limited ability' of Buckland's *A history*, p. 83. Although Bew *et al* at least campaign against uncritical acceptance of Terence O'Neill's version of Unionist affairs (see also S. McAughtry's articles in the *Irish Times*, 15, 19, 20 May 1981), by their inadequate acount of the depth of opposition to the post-1945 Labour government in Ulster, they may underestimate Brooke's subtlety. The work of Denis Norman, *Books Ireland* (Sept. 1981) is helpful here. Spender, it is clear, was a very political civil servant.

18. *Left Perspectives* i, no. 1 (Summer, 1980), pp 32–34. One general comment: Johnson argues that *The state in Northern Ireland 1921–72* dismisses the role of unionist fears, while the recent book by L. Dowd *et al., Northern Ireland: from civil rights to civil war* (London, 1980), p. 2, argues that it is too keen to accommodate the unionist point of view!

19. R. Fanning, *The Irish department of finance* (Dublin, 1978).

20. P.R.O., T 160/1138/15586.

21. Shea, *Voices*, p. 156.

22. Ibid., p. 156.

23. *Irish Times*, 19 April 1950.

24. Shea, *Voices*, p. 156.

25. Bew *et al.*, op. cit., pp 79–80.

26. *F.D.*, 30 April 1938.

27. *Belfast Newsletter*, 19 Nov. 1931.

28. Johnson, op. cit., p. 33.

29. Spender to Montgomery, 2 Nov. 1937 (P.R.O.N.I., D715).

30. Tom Garvin's review of Bew *et al.* in *Economic and Social Review*, 12, no. 1 (Oct. 1980), p. 64. Elsewhere, to give but one example, Peter Gibbon, *Origins of Ulster unionism* (Manchester, 1975), p. 145, explicitly states: 'Ulster Unionism emerged as the product neither of a conspiracy of landed notables and industrialists to dupe the people nor from the spontaneous convergence of a

set of forces without poor relations'. For expansion of this, see Paul Bew and Frank Wright, 'The agrarian opposition in Ulster 1846-87' in S. Clark and J. Donnelly (eds), *Irish peasants* (Princeton, 1982).

31. K. Boyle, T. Hadden, P. Hillyard, *Law and state: the case of Northern Ireland* (Oxford, 1975).

32. 'The state in Northern Ireland' in *Marxism Today* 24, no. 1 (Jan. 1980), pp 25-28.